WJEC
CBAC

DLE **Library**

D1628586

EDUQAS GCSE

English
Language

WITHDRAWN
FROM
STOCKPORT COLLEGE
LEARNING CENTRE

Paula Adair
Jamie Rees
Jane Sheldon

Series Editors:
Jonathan Harrington
Paula Adair

HODDER
EDUCATION
AN HACHETTE UK COMPANY

147043

This material has been endorsed by WJEC and offers high quality support for the delivery of WJEC qualifications. While this material has been through a quality assurance process, all responsibility for the contents remains with the publisher.

Every effort has been made to trace or contact all copyright holders, but if any have been inadvertently overlooked the Publishers will be pleased to make the necessary arrangements at the first opportunity.

Acknowledgements can be found on page iv.

The publisher would like to thank the following for permission to reproduce copyright material:

Photo credits:
p. 3 © Lewis Clarke; **p. 5** © erectus/Fotolia; **p. 7** © PCN Photography/Alamy; **p. 11** © Brian Rasic/REX; **p. 15** © belizar/Fotolia; **p. 20** © lilu13/Fotolia; **p. 23** © FLPA/REX; **p. 35** © Jürgen Fälchle – Fotolia; **p. 37** © SplashdownDirect/REX; **p. 40** © National Geographic/Getty Images; **p. 43** © Mark Little/Alamy; **p. 44** © industrieblick/Fotolia; **p. 45** © Ed Ironside; Elizabeth Whiting & Associates/Corbis; **p. 47** © AF archive/Alamy; **p. 48** © Stockbyte/Getty Images Ltd; **p. 51** Library of Congress Prints & Photographs Division; LC-USF33-030291-M4; **p. 52** © imagedb.com/Fotolia; **p. 53** © alswart/Fotolia; **p. 58** © Ersoy Emin/Alamy; **p. 65** © Floydine – Fotolia; **p. 68** © Billy Stock/Robert Harding/REX Features; **p. 72** © mocho/Fotolia; **p. 75** © sas/Fotolia; **p. 79** © Daily Mail/Rex/Alamy; **p. 86** © mitifoto/Fotolia; **p. 88** © mr.Markin/Fotolia; **p. 90** © olly - Fotolia; **p. 92** © Sam Spiro/Fotolia; **p. 94** top © Pictorial Press Ltd / Alamy; **p. 94** middle © nickolae – Fotolia; **p. 96** © London Stereoscopic Company/Getty Images; **p. 100** © Gina Sanders/Fotolia; **p. 108** © Samir Hussein/WireImage/Getty Images; **p. 113** © Yeko Photo Studio/Fotolia; **p. 116** © PYMCA / Alamy; **p. 126** © Mikkel Bigandt/Fotolia; **p. 132** © Grant Symon/Getty Images; **p. 137** © c.20thC.Fox/Everett/Rex Features; **p. 149** © Netfalls/Fotolia; **p. 152** © Premier / Alamy; **p. 157** © Sapsiwai/Fotolia; **p. 160** © V&P Photo Studio/Fotolia; **p. 162** © Derek R. Audette/Fotolia; **p. 180** left © Wrangler/Fotolia; **p. 180** right © Warren Goldswain/Fotolia; **p. 181** © Jeffrey Blackler / Alamy; **p. 186** left © De Visu/Fotolia; **p. 186** middle © pressmaster/Fotolia; **p. 186** right © william87/Fotolia; **p. 189** left © cjorgens/Fotolia; **p. 189** right © Ror – Fotolia; **p. 198** © puckillustrations/Fotolia; **p. 203** © Jason Merritt/Getty Images; **p. 209** © Pictorial Press Ltd/Alamy; **p. 218** © Alexmillos/Alamy; **p. 225** © Photos 12/Alamy; **p. 230** © elen_studio – Fotolia.

Although every effort has been made to ensure that website addresses are correct at time of going to press, Hodder Education cannot be held responsible for the content of any website mentioned. It is sometimes possible to find a relocated web page by typing in the address of the home page for a website in the URL window of your browser.

Orders: please contact Bookpoint Ltd, 130 Milton Park, Abingdon, Oxon OX14 4SB. Telephone: (44) 01235 827720. Fax: (44) 01235 400454. Lines are open 9.00–17.00, Monday to Saturday, with a 24-hour message answering service. Visit our website at www.hoddereducation.co.uk

© Paula Adair, Jamie Rees, Jane Sheldon 2015

First published in 2015 by

Hodder Education

An Hachette UK Company,

Carmelite House, 50 Victoria Embankment

London EC4Y 0DZ

Impression number	5	4	3
Year	2019	2018	2017

All rights reserved. Apart from any use permitted under UK copyright law, no part of this publication may be reproduced or transmitted in any form or by any means, electronic or mechanical, including photocopying and recording, or held within any information storage and retrieval system, without permission in writing from the publisher or under licence from the Copyright Licensing Agency Limited. Further details of such licences (for reprographic reproduction) may be obtained from the Copyright Licensing Agency Limited, Saffron House, 6–10 Kirby Street, London EC1N 8TS.

Cover photo (and repeated use throughout) by Ria Osborne

Illustrations by Aptara, Inc.

Typeset in chaparral light 11/14 by Aptara, Inc.

Printed in Dubai

A catalogue record for this title is available from the British Library

ISBN 9781471831850

STOCKPORT COLLEGE
LIBRARY+

I-1762742	5/6/17
13906	
147043	
4wk	426 ADA

Introduction

This student book gives you the chance to practise all the skills you will need for the new Eduqas GCSE in English Language. For the new GCSE you will need to take two exams, called Component One and Component Two.

The exams

- **Component One** is also called 20th Century Literature Reading and Creative Prose Writing. For this you will need to answer questions about an extract (of about 60–100 lines) of literature from the 20th century and also complete a creative writing task from a selection of four titles. This exam lasts for one hour and 45 minutes.

- **Component Two** is also called 19th and 21st Century Non-Fiction Reading and Transactional/Persuasive Writing. In this exam you will need to answer questions about two extracts, totalling about 900–1200 words, of high quality non-fiction writing from the 19th and 21st centuries. You will also need to complete two transactional/persuasive writing tasks. This exam lasts for two hours.

This book takes you through every one of the skills that are being assessed in this GCSE and shows you how to improve and become more confident in using them so that you can do as well as possible in the exams. There are lots of interesting and exciting texts to read and tips to follow, as well as easy to follow stages in each section so that you can become exam ready.

There are some challenges to meet as you work through the skills tested in these exams. For instance you will need to use Subject terminology when talking about language use (AO2) and this is introduced through a series of activities that focus on appropriate use of terms in helpful, developmental stages.

Please remember

None of the activities in this book are actual exam questions but they all focus on the skills assessed in the two components of the Eduqas English Language exams. None of the approaches suggested in this book, such as Point, Evidence, Explanation are recommended by Eduqas as the only way of setting about particular tasks but are offered here as various ways to help you meet the demands of the examinations.

As well as learning how to complete the various tasks in the exams you will also be encouraged to mark your own work and sample answers so that you can see what is needed for success. The Marking grids used for the activities are not meant to represent the full sets of marking criteria available in the Sample Assessment Materials from Eduqas but are there to give you the chance to assess your own work against the skills required under each AO.

Acknowledgements

p. 1 from 'Winter Sports around the UK' from *The Guardian* (The Guardian, 11th January 2014), copyright Guardian News & Media Ltd 2014, reproduced by permission of the publisher; **p. 3** Lewis Clarke: from 'British teenager breaks South Pole Record' from *Youngest-To-SouthPole* (https://youngesttosouthpole. wordpress.com, 19th January 2014); **p. 5** David Harrison: from 'Ben Fogle reveals moment he faced death ' from *The Telegraph* (The Telegraph, 24th January 2009), reproduced by permission of Telegraph Media Group; **pp. 7–8** from 'The Wonderful Games' (WJEC, date unknown); **p. 11** Joe Wade: from 'Why I pray for Glasto hell' from *Don't Panic* (Don't Panic London, 24th June 2011), reproduced by permission of the publisher, www.dontgesttosouthpole.com; **pp. 12–13** Charlotte Bronte: from a letter to Ellen , (October 29th, 1848); **pp. 13–14** Dave Boling: from *Guernica* (Picador, 2009), reproduced with permission of the publisher; **pp. 15–16** Rowenna Davis: from 'The left's opposition to badger culls ignores the plight of our farmers' from *New Statesman* (New Statesman, 19th October 2012) reproduced by permission of the publisher; **p. 20** from ''Handbag' dogs- Why you should never see your pet as a fashion accessory' (Pets4Homes, 2014), (c) Pets4Homes.co.uk. Reproduced by permission of the publisher; **p. 21** from 'The Prize Pugs of America and England' (1891); **p. 23** from 'Puppy Farming' (The Kennel Club, 2014), www.thekennelclub.org.uk; **p. 23** from Lord Erskine's speech on preventing malicious and wanton cruelty to animals (1809); **p. 27** Lord Byron: from a journal of the conversations of Lord Byron, ed. T. Medwin (1821); **p. 35** Juliette Garside: from 'Ofcom: six-year-olds understand digital technology better than adults' from *The Guardian* (The Guardian, 7th August 2014), copyright Guardian News & Media Ltd 2014; **p. 37** Rachael Misstear: from 'Watch the amazing sight of 1,000 dolphins swimming together off the Pembrokeshire coast' from *Wales Online* (Wales Online, 30th September 2014), reproduced by permission of the publisher; **p. 40** Gloria Chan: from 'Cardboard dreams: a day with an elderly Hong Kong woman who must scavenge to survive' from South *China Morning Post* (South China Morning Post, 27th October 2014), reproduced by permission of the publisher; **pp. 43–44** Alexander McCall Smith: from *Tears Of The Giraffe* (No. 1 Ladies' Detective Agency) (Abacus, 2003); **p. 44** David Lodge: from *Nice Work* (Secker, 2011), reproduced by permission of The Random House Group Ltd.; **pp. 45–46** William Trevor: 'Broken Homes' from THE COLLECTED STORIES by William Trevor (Penguin Books 2003) Copyright © William Trevor, 1992; **pp. 47–48** Nick Hornby: from *About a Boy* (Penguin, 2002) © 1998 by Nick Hornby. Used by permission of Riverhead, an imprint of Penguin Publishing Group, a division of Penguin Random House LLC; **pp. 48–49** Bill Bryson: from 'Junk Food Heaven' from *Notes from a Big Country* (Black Swan, 1999), reproduced by permission of The Random House Group Ltd.; **p. 52** George Orwell: from *The Road to Wigan Pier* (Penguin Classics, 2001), (Copyright © George Orwell, 1945) Reproduced by permission of Bill Hamilton as the Literary Executor of the Estate of the Late Sonia Brownell Orwell; **p. 53** from 'Boxing...The Facts' (British Boxing Board of Control, 2015), reproduced by permission of the publisher; **pp. 56–57** Peter Baumgartner: from 'Canada: At home with Polar bears ' from *The Independent* (The Independent, 1st December 2001); **p. 58** Anne Johnson: from 'Going the distance' from *The Guardian* (The Guardian, 6th April 2004), copyright Guardian News & Media Ltd 2004, reproduced by permission of the publisher; **p. 62** Peter Scudamore: from 'I love the Grand National - but this was agonising to watch' from *The Daily Mail* (The Daily Mail, 12th April 2011); **p. 62** Richard Girling: from 'The rise of the urban seagull' from *The Sunday Times* (The Sunday Times, 4th January 2009); **p. 63** Charles Starmer-Smith: from 'Cycling in Britain: Re-inventing the wheel' from *The Telegraph* (The Telegraph, 16th April 2010), reproduced by permission of Telegraph Media Group; **pp. 67–68** Roy Hattersley: from 'The Lasting Resort' (WJEC, date unknown); **p. 69** Lucie Morris: from 'The Sunshine Isle Where Teenage Tearaways Are Sent to Learn a Lesson' from *The Daily Mail* (The Daily Mail, 23rd October); **p. 72** from 'Do Something Amazing Today' (National Blood Service, 2015), www.blood.co.uk; **p. 73** Alan Paton: from *Tales of a Troubled Land* (Scribner, 1996); **pp. 75,132** Bill Bryson: from *Notes from a Small Island* (Black Swan, 1996), reproduced by permission of The Random House Group Ltd.; **p. 76** Arthur C. Clarke: from *The Collected Stories of Arthur C. Clarke* (Gollancz, 2001), reproduced by permission of David Higham Associates Ltd; **pp. 79–80** Petronella Wyatt: 'The fastest lady on two wheels!' from *The Daily Mail* (The Daily Mail, 8th May 2007); **p. 82** Kate Atkinson: from Behind the Scenes at the Museum (Black Swan, 1996), reproduced by permission of the publisher; **p. 86** Bill Bryson: from Neither Here, Nor There: Travels in Europe (Secker, 1998), reproduced by permission of The Random House Group Ltd.; **p. 86** from a review of the short film 'Danny MacAskill: The Ridge' (Cut Media, 2nd October 2014); **p. 88** Bill Bryson: from A Walk in the Woods (Doubleday, 1998), reproduced by permission of The Random House Group Ltd.; **p. 88** Emily Thornwell: from 'The Lady's Guide to Perfect Gentility' (1856); **p. 90** Steve Doughty: from ''Young people are sloppy and don't dress or talk properly': Ofsted boss claims teenagers are not taught the right skills for surviving in the world of work' from *The Daily Mail* (The Daily Mail, 10th September 2014);

p. 90 from 'How to combine elegance, style and economy' (1856); **p. 92** from 'Day of surgery' from Our patients gastric bypass diary (St Anthony's. The Surrey Weight Loss Surgery Centre, 2015); **p. 92** F. Burney: from 'The Paris Review: Medical Literature' (1811); **p. 94** Christopher Hart: from 'Genius or Hype?' from *The Daily Mail* (The Daily Mail, 27th June 2009); **p. 95** Christopher McDougall: from 'The painful truth about trainers: Are running shoes a waste of money?' from The Daily Mail (The Daily Mail, 15th April 2009); **p. 96** from 'Attire for the female cyclist' (New York Magazine, 1895); **pp. 98–99** William Blaikie: from *How to get strong and how to stay so* (1883); **pp. 99–100** Rebecca Armstrong: from 'Silver sprinters: defying-age athletes' from *The Independent* (The Independent, 20th November 2007), reproduced by permission of the publisher; **pp. 108–109** Fay Schlesinger and Maysa Rawi: from 'First the Great Unveiling... and then a collective gasp: With a plunging neckline and lots of lace, the gown was a timeless triumph' from *The Daily Mail* (The Daily Mail, 29th April 2011); **p. 109** from 'Our Queen: a sketch of the life and times of Victoria, Queen of Great Britain and Ireland' (1883); **p. 112** from instructions for the board game 'The Game of the District Messenger Boy' (1886); **p. 112** from a description of 'Trivial Pursuit' (Hasbro, date unknown); **p. 113** Matt Cunningham: from '10 Reasons People Start Smoking' from *How Stuff Works* (How Stuff Works, 2015); **p. 113** Rev. Benjamin Lane: from 'The Mysteries of Tobacco' (1845); **p. 115** E. Ferrero: from 'The Art of Dancing' (1859); **p. 116** Jack Spencer: from '10 rules of mosh pit etiquette' from *City Pages* (Minneapolis City Pages, 2015); **p. 117** J. Crawfurd: from 'On the History and Migration of Cultivated Plants Producing Coffee' (1869); **p. 117** Simon Brooke: from 'Costa lotta?' from *World of Coffee* (Raconteur Media, 2011); **pp. 119–120** Jane Mulkerrins: from 'Nik Wallenda: The man crossing the Grand Canyon on a tightrope' from *The Telegraph* (The Telegraph, 20th June 2013), reproduced by permission of Telegraph Media Group; **p. 120** from 'AN EXCITING SCENE. M. Blondin's Feat at Niagara Falls' from *The Buffalo Republic* (1st July 1859); **p. 124** C.J. Sansom: from *Winter in Madrid* (Pan Macmillan, 2006), reproduced by permission of the publisher; **p. 125** from 'The moment that the bus moved on...' from *WJEC SAM* (WJEC, 2014); **p. 126** Colin Shindler: from *High on a Cliff* (Hodder and Stoughton, 1999), copyright © Colin Shindler 1999, reproduced by permission of the publisher Hodder and Stoughton; Headline, 1999); **p. 127** Britt Collins: from 'South Africa's animal rescue' from *The Guardian* (The Guardian, 27th March 2010), copyright Guardian News & Media Ltd 2010, reproduced by permission of the publisher; **p. 128** Doris Lessing: from *The Grass is Singing* (Harper Perennial, 2007); **p. 130** George Borrow: from 'The Bible in Spain' (1842); **pp. 134–135** Toni Morrison: from *The Bluest Eye* (Vintage, 1999), reproduced by permission of the publisher; **pp. 137-138** Yann Martel: from *Life of Pi* (Canongate Books, 2012); **pp. 141– 142** Reverend Edward John Hardy: from 'How to be happy though married' (1849); **p. 144** Florence Hartley: from 'The Ladies' Book of Etiquette' (1860); **p. 146** from 'Another Whitechapel Murder' from *The London Times* (The London Times, 1888); **p. 147** Toni Cade Bambara: from 'The Hammer Man' from *Gorilla, My Love* (Vintage, 1992); **pp. 151–152** George Borrow: from Wild Wales (1862); **p. 157** adapted from 'Mauritius' (Thomson, 2015), www.thomson.co.uk; **p. 159** Penelope Lively: from 'Help' from *Pack of Cards: Stories 1978-1986* (Penguin, 1987), reproduced by permission of the publisher; **pp. 159–160** John Steinbeck: from *Of Mice and Men* (Penguin, 2006); **p. 177** Mark Haddon: from *The Curious Incident of the Dog in the Night-Time* (David Fickling Books, 2004), reproduced by permission of The Random House Group Ltd.; **pp. 177, 178** George Orwell: from *Nineteen Eighty-Four* (Penguin Books, 2013), (Copyright © George Orwell, 1945) Reproduced by permission of Bill Hamilton as the Literary Executor of the Estate of the Late Sonia Brownell Orwell; **p. 178** Douglas Adams: from *The Hitchhiker's Guide to the Galaxy* (Pan, 2013); **p. 178** Suzanne Collins: from *The Hunger Games* (Scholastic, 2009), reproduced by permission of the publisher; **p. 178** Michael Morpurgo: from *Private Peaceful* (HarperCollins, 2004); **p. 181** Wilfred Owen: from 'Anthem for Doomed Youth' from *Wilfred Owen: The War Poems*, Jon Stallworthy (Chatto & Windus, 1994); **p. 185** N.K. Jemisin: from *The Hundred Thousand Kingdoms* (Orbit, 2010), reproduced by permission of the publisher; **p. 186** Philip Pullman: from *Northern Lights* (Scholastic, 2011), Text copyright © Phillip Pullman, 1995. Reproduced by permission of Scholastic Ltd. All rights reserved; **p. 188** Charles Dickens: from *Bleak House* (1853); **p. 203** Alexis Petridis: from 'Take Me Home – review' from *The Guardian* (The Guardian, 8th November 2012), copyright Guardian News & Media Ltd 2012, reproduced by permission of the publisher; **p. 212** George Orwell: from *Animal Farm* (Penguin, 2000), (Copyright © George Orwell, 1945) Reproduced by permission of Bill Hamilton as the Literary Executor of the Estate of the Late Sonia Brownell Orwell; **p. 225** Mark Kermode: from 'The Hobbit: The Desolation of Smaug – review' from *The Observer* (The Observer, 15th December 2013), copyright Guardian News & Media Ltd 2013, reproduced by permission of the publisher; **p. 227** Oliver Franklin: from 'Why England should drop Wayne Rooney' from *GQ Magazine* (GQ, 6th March 2014).

Contents

Unit 1 Extracting key information   1
Get going   1
Be exam ready   7

Unit 2 Interpreting information   10
Get going   10
Be exam ready   15

Unit 3 Synthesising information   18
Get going   19
Improve your skills   22
Be exam ready   26

Unit 4 Types of information   30
Get going   30
Improve your skills   34
Be exam ready   39

Unit 5 Explaining language   43
Get going   43
Improve your skills   47
Be exam ready   51

Unit 6 Talking about language   56
Get going   56
Improve your skills   61
Be exam ready   67

Unit 7 Analysing language   71
Get going   71
Improve your skills   74
Be exam ready   79

Unit 8 Comparing writers' ideas   85
Get going   85
Improve your skills   91
Be exam ready   98

Unit 9 Comparing language   104
Get going   104
Improve your skills   111
Be exam ready   119

Unit 10 Using textual references 123

Get going 123
Improve your skills 128
Be exam ready 137

Unit 11 Evaluating critically 141

Get going 141
Improve your skills 145
Be exam ready 151

Unit 12 Communicating clearly and effectively 155

Get going 156
Improve your skills 166
Be exam ready 172

Unit 13 Communicating imaginatively 176

Get going 176
Improve your skills 183
Be exam ready 190

Unit 14 Style and register, purpose and audience 194

Get going 194
Improve your skills 205
Be exam ready 214

Unit 15 Transactional and persuasive writing 216

Get going 216
Improve your skills 224
Be exam ready 232

Unit 1
Extracting key information

OBJECTIVES

▶ To recognise questions asking for specific information
▶ To work systematically through a text, selecting relevant information
▶ To present the extracted information appropriately

How confident are you in these skills already?

I recognise questions that ask for specific information.

I use key words to guide me to the correct information.

I can quickly find and identify a key piece of information in a text.

I can write these in a clear answer.

Always ▢⇨ Usually ▢⇨ Sometimes

Get going

Step 1 Work on your skills

  ACTIVITY 1: WINTER SPORTS

Read the following extract, taken from *Winter sports around the UK* (from *The Guardian* newspaper/website).

When you are presented with unseen material in Component Two you will firstly need to read through the text and get a clear overview of what it is about. Your teacher may suggest ways to tackle unfamiliar texts and approaches you may like to take.

When you have a good understanding of the text, consider the first question. This will often ask you to extract specific key information in order to show your understanding of what you have read. There will be precise, 'correct' answers that the examiner will be looking for. These might be signified by command words such as: list, find, identify, write, name.

Winter sports around the UK

From snowboarding to snow walking, we find the best wintertime activities around the British isles.

Curling

If you're not comfortable in skates, try curling – often described as 'bowls on ice'. The ice in most arenas is too sticky for the smooth glide required in curling, so the sport requires dedicated rinks. Fenton's in Tunbridge Wells is the UK's only one. From £20 a person for 2 hours, including equipment and instruction.

In Scotland, the home of curling, the North West Castle in Stranraer is the first hotel in the world with its own indoor curling rink.

Skiing

Indoor lessons are a great way to get started and are much cheaper than flying to the Alps. Chill Factore, just a few miles outside Manchester, has the UK's longest indoor real snow slope. There is a range of courses with introductory freestyle lessons from £35 (discounts for juniors/seniors). They also provide adaptive skiing for individuals with any disability including physical, sensory and learning difficulties.

And now read the questions.

You may encounter individual questions like the ones below. They require you to find exact and specific pieces of information. It is worth noting how many marks each is worth (in brackets) as this will guide you to the number of points to make.

a. Why are most arenas not suitable for curling? [1]

b. What is special about the North West Castle in Stranraer? [1]

c. What are the benefits of indoor skiing lessons, according to the article? [2]

d. Where is the UK's longest indoor real snow slope? [1]

Top tips

Before looking for the answer, note what each question asks you to focus on. Identify what you think is a key word or phrase in each question. For example, in the first question it seems sensible to look for 'arenas' and 'curling'. You can then use your scanning skills to locate these words or phrases in the text. Read around the phrase to find the relevant answer. Remember to be precise in the information you select.

Step 2 Practise your skills

ACTIVITY 2: QUESTIONS

Now, have a go at answering questions a–d.

Self-assessment

Check your answers – award 1 mark for each answer. Look for precise information. Also consider how long this took you. By the time you sit the exam, you need to be able to find these answers in a few minutes.

a. The ice in most arenas is too sticky for the smooth glide required. [1]

b. It is the first hotel in the world with its own indoor curling rink. [1]

c. It is a great way to get started **and** it is much cheaper than flying to the Alps. [2]

d. Chill Factore. [1]

Top tips

Sometimes questions only ask you to look at a paragraph, column or page. Looking outside this section will lose you marks.

ACTIVITY 3: IN REVERSE

Now let's try this in reverse! Read the first part of the following article.

BRITISH TEENAGER BREAKS SOUTH POLE WORLD RECORD

After a 48 day, 702 mile journey from the Antarctic Coast to the South Pole, 16-year-old Lewis Clarke, from Bristol, arrived at the South Pole at 3pm local time (6pm GMT) on Saturday 18 January 2014, setting a new World Record for the youngest person ever to do it (the current world record holder is an 18 year old Canadian).

Teenager Lewis Clarke set out on his epic expedition from Hercules Inlet on the Antarctic coast on 2 December 2013, just two weeks after his 16th birthday. After 48 gruelling days travelling across one of the most inhospitable environments on earth, in temperatures as low as minus

40 and gale force winds of up to 60 mph, Lewis has become the youngest person in the world to ski the full 702 miles from coast to Pole, on the well established Hercules Inlet route.

Lewis was guided by experienced polar guide, Carl Alvey. They travelled on skis, pulling all their own supplies, but received three re-supplies during the expedition. There have been many ups and downs, from white outs and blizzards to Lewis breaking a ski. They had only one full day off (on Christmas Day) during the 48 day expedition. They usually skied around 8 or 9 hours a day, covering roughly 18 miles daily. Their last day, Saturday 18 January, was a very tough one, with the lowest temperatures of the whole trip (around −50°C including windchill).

These were a student's responses to some questions set on the article. Can you use your scanning skills to find the answers in the article and work out what the questions were?

a. Lewis began his journey at Hercules Inlet.
b. 2 December 2013
c. 702 miles
d. 18 January 2014
e. Three
f. Christmas Day
g. Lewis is 16 years old
h. −50°C.

Your teacher will provide some suggested questions that you can compare with your own.

 Top tips

Remember:

- Get a clear understanding of the text by reading through first.
- Highlight the key information you are asked to locate in the question.
- Use the question's key information to scan and highlight the answers in the text.
- Be precise: check that you answer the question.
- Remember to look at the number of marks each question is worth to guide you as to the number of points you need to make.

Step 3 Challenge yourself

As an alternative to questions that require you to extract single pieces of specific information, you may be asked one longer question that requires you to 'list'.

 Top tips

If asked to 'list', think of a shopping list and just put your answers down, one underneath the other. You may use bullet points in a 'list' question.

ACTIVITY 4: ANTARCTIC ADVENTURE

Read the first part of the newspaper article 'Antarctic Adventure' opposite.
List **five** of the problems the men faced on their expedition.   [5]

 Top tips

Remember to track through and highlight your answers.
Take approximately 8 minutes to write your highlighted points into a list.

Antarctic Adventure

Ben Fogle tells David Harrison of a terrifying journey

It was the moment when Ben Fogle thought he was going to die. The television presenter and his fellow adventurers, James Cracknell and Ed Coats, were deep into their gruelling expedition to the South Pole when they realised they had strayed on to a giant crevasse. This was a huge crack in the ice, hidden from view by a thin cover of snow and ice.

'We were walking,' Fogle said, 'when suddenly I heard a loud boom, then another one. I realised it was the sound of snow falling into a crevasse.'

'We had been told that there were no crevasses on our route but I could feel the snow shifting beneath me. Crevasses can be a mile deep and I was terrified that I would be dragged down. I thought, "I could die here". My mouth went dry and I started to panic.'

Fortunately, Fogle, 35, and his colleagues managed to calm themselves enough to navigate out of danger.

The team was one of a number competing in a race to the South Pole. They eventually finished second behind two Norwegians. 'I'm just delighted to have finished,' he said. 'I knew it would be tough but I had no idea it would take such a toll on our bodies.'

He added: 'It's the hardest thing I've ever done. It started with frostbite, then I burnt my lips, got blisters on my feet and had a bit of hypothermia. It all just starts to get on top of you. There were many days when I thought we were not going to finish the race.'

Fogle has frostbite on his nose. 'I was worried I might lose my nose,' he said. 'For the last 43 miles I put a hand-warmer on it and wrapped it in a bandage to try and keep it warm.' Doctors at the Antarctic base have told him the frostbite will clear up in a couple of months.

The British team all suffered from blisters. Cracknell, 36, the former Olympic rowing champion, had frostbite on his fingers and pneumonia, and both he and Coats, 28, a Bristol doctor, suffered chest infections. Bitterly cold winds pushed the temperature as low as −50 °C at times and whipped the snow up to create a 'white-out'. Some days brought bright blue skies and lifted the temperatures to −15 °C. Throughout their expedition across the vast, hostile landscape they saw no sign of wildlife.

'Not even a single bird,' said Fogle. 'That tells you how hostile the landscape was.' The trio skied for around 16 hours a day, slept for just four hours, and spent the rest of the day eating and preparing for the next stage of the race.

ACTIVITY 5: KEY POINTS

If the word 'list' is not used in the question, you should write a paragraph picking out the key points that would answer the question. Think of it in the same way, but write your answer as a paragraph.

The following words/phrases might help you structure your answer:

▶ Also …

▶ In addition …

▶ Another way they got through was …

▶ The text also states …

▶ Finally …

Try rewriting your last list answer as a paragraph using some of these connectives.

? Assess your progress. Did you:

- find at least five separate points by working through the extract, highlighting answers?
- methodically list the evidence in the same order it appears in the text?
- complete it in the time allowed?

⇨ Next steps...

1 Using a range of texts such as extracts from novels, leaflets, advertisements and brochures, practise this type of question. Use 19th century non-fiction texts too.

2 Practise answering questions under timed conditions so you will be able to work under pressurised conditions when you finally sit your exam.

3 Make sure you work through the whole of the extract. Be methodical. Use the number of marks a question is worth as a guide to the number of points to make.

BE EXAM READY

OBJECTIVES

▶ To practise answering a question
▶ To mark my own response using a mark scheme
▶ To assess sample answers to the question

How confident are you in these skills already?

I can use a mark scheme to assess my own work.

I can use a mark scheme to assess other students' work and suggest improvements.

Always   ▯⇨   Usually   ▯⇨   Sometimes

We have now looked at questions that require you to look for:
● one specific piece of information
● several pieces of information (and list or write them into a paragraph).
Now you will have the chance to look at sample answers and mark your own responses.

 QUESTION 1

Read the newspaper article, 'The Wonderful Games'.

List ten events in which British competitors won gold medals in the London Olympics, according to the newspaper article.

THE WONDERFUL GAMES

The London Olympics of 2012 have been described as the most spectacular sporting occasion that Britain has ever staged. Who will ever forget that amazing Saturday night when, with an estimated television audience of seventeen million, Britain won three gold medals? Jessica Ennis won the heptathlon and Mo Farah won the 10,000 metres, the first of his two gold medals. Then, most unexpected of all, Greg Rutherford won the long jump.

7

The real excitement for British spectators started on 1st August when Helen Glover and Heather Stanning won a gold medal in the female rowing pairs. On the same day Bradley Wiggins, who a week earlier had won the Tour de France, won the individual time trial for cycling, the first of seven cycling events in which Britons won gold medals. Sir Chris Hoy thrilled spectators in the Velodrome, and those watching on television, as he won gold medals for the cycling team sprint and individual cycling sprint. Two days later came one of the most popular victories of all as Kath Grainger, along with her partner Anna Watkins, won gold in another rowing event, the double sculls. Kath had three silver medals already but at thirty-six this was almost certainly her last chance to win that all important gold. Sir Steve Redgrave, proud winner of five rowing gold medals in previous Olympics, called it his single favourite moment of the whole games.

Almost every day there was another gold medal to celebrate. There were five British medals for boxing, three of them gold, including one for Nicola Adams, the girl from Leeds who fought so hard to win the first ever gold medal for women's boxing. Of course there was more to admire than just British success. The Jamaican athlete, Usain Bolt, thrilled the sporting world with his sprint double in the 100 metres and the 200 metres, and Kirani James in the 400 metres won Grenada's first ever gold medal.

The most demanding of all the athletic events, the triathlon, had a gripping ending as two brothers from England battled for first place. In the end it was older brother Alistair Brownlee who triumphed with the gold medal and younger brother Jonathan who took the bronze medal. Another unforgettable moment was when Jade Jones, the teenager from Wales, took off her helmet and treated us all to her golden smile of sheer delight as she realised she was the first Briton to win an Olympic taekwondo gold medal.

Did you highlight the question to focus on exactly what you were looking for?

Did you track through the extract chronologically and methodically, highlighting the answers?

Did you write 10 answers, one under the other in a list?

 Self-assessment

Check your answers below (1 mark per answer):

- heptathlon
- 10,000 metres
- long jump
- female rowing pairs
- cycling individual time trial
- cycling team sprint
- individual cycling sprint
- double sculls
- women's boxing
- triathlon
- taekwondo

You must precisely select the correct phrase.

There may be more possible answers than marks, as in this case.

Comparing sample answers

What feedback would you give to the following students?

Think about:

- the amount of information given
- the accuracy of the points
- whether the points are in the same order as you find them in the text.

Answer A

100 metres
400 metres
Mo Farrah won two medals.

Answer B

Sports were:
- taekwondo
- boxing
- sprinting
- the triathlon
- cycling

Answer C

Ten events in which British competitors won gold medals were:
- heptathlon
- 10,000 metres
- long jump
- female rowing pairs
- cycling (individual time trial, team and individual sprint)
- double sculls
- boxing
- triathlon
- taekwondo

Now you have completed the section, do you think your confidence has increased?

I am confident in my ability to recognise a question that asks me to extract key information.

I can confidently use a question's key words to guide me to the correct information.

I understand how to track and highlight key pieces of information in a text.

I can use various strategies to enable me to plan my answer.

Always ⬛⇨ Usually ⬛⇨ Sometimes

Unit 2
Interpreting information

OBJECTIVES

▶ To gain an understanding of what it means to 'interpret' information
▶ To be able to recognise questions that ask you to interpret information
▶ To practise working systematically through a text, selecting relevant information and applying an interpretation in order to answer the question

How confident are you in these skills already?

I understand what it means to 'interpret' information.

I recognise questions that ask me to interpret information.

I can find and comment on key pieces of information in order to answer the question.

I can write up my interpretations quickly and in a clear, precise answer.

Always ⇨ Usually ⇨ Sometimes

In the last unit (Extracting key information) you were able to find precise and specific pieces of information quickly and methodically. The next step is not only to **find** but also to **interpret** the information – in other words, give the meaning.

Get going

Step 1 — Work on your skills

ACTIVITY 1: INTERPRETING PHRASES

In the same way as the example to the right, interpret the following phrases:

▶ add insult to injury
▶ a blessing in disguise
▶ read between the lines
▶ add fuel to the fire
▶ feather your own nest

Can you think of five of your own? Test them out on a learning partner.

Some questions may ask you to interpret phrases (idioms), for example:

● What does the writer mean by 'Time is money'?

These will expect you to interpret the meaning behind the phrase. In this case, an answer might read:

The phrase means that time is precious and shouldn't be wasted – we need to use our time to earn money (or at least do something profitable).

As well as these basic kinds of interpretation questions, you may be required to find information, just as we covered in the previous unit. The difference here is that you must also **interpret** which bits of information answer the given question.

ACTIVITY 2: INTERPRETING THE EVIDENCE

Consider the following question:

Look at Joe Wade's blog, 'Why I pray for Glastonbury hell', below. Explain why Joe Wade hates Glastonbury Festival. **[10]**

You must use the text to support your answer.

The text related to this question has been highlighted by a student looking to interpret the information that answers **why** Joe Wade hates Glastonbury festival.

WHY I PRAY FOR GLASTONBURY HELL

What we needed this week was a nice dry spell from Monday to Friday so rain wouldn't stop play at Wimbledon and then a biblical downpour during the weekend to ensure maximum misery for all those up to their necks in mud in inadequate, cheap tents at Glastonbury Festival.

My delight in the misery of Glastonbury is partly caused by resentment of success. In 2007, for example, the festival sold 137,500 tickets at £185 in one hour and forty five minutes. It is also partly that when I attended the event it was like the Wild West with large numbers of people arriving with no provisions. 'How on earth will those poor chaps survive?' I wondered, before they tore through the site like a plague of locusts, stealing tents and their contents. I've also experienced the sort of delays you usually get at airports when trying to get out of the car park.

However, none of that completely explains why I pray for Glastonbury hell. I'm infuriated by Glastonbury, not because of the people who organise it, but by the people who go there. The reason I hate them is because they're actually having a terrible time but just can't admit it to themselves, let alone anyone else. In fact, I reckon they are all going there just so they can talk about it afterwards and get some good images of themselves acting happy for Facebook.

I mean, what is there to enjoy? All you do is wander from one place to the next all day long, thinking 'It's boring here, let's go over there. We're here now and (surprise, surprise) we can barely hear the band, let alone see them.' For that matter what are you meant to do when you're standing watching live music? A bit of swaying is sometimes possible in the crush but usually the neck-stretch, straining to see, is the only move that makes sense. Burn all those flags too. I don't care that you're from Wales or what football team you support. No-one does.

The misery is so great that getting drunk is the only way to ease the tedium of the incessant milling around in the mud. But that is not as easy as you might hope as there are massive queues for all the bars and when you finally get served you have to pay over the odds for a watery pint of beer in a flimsy plastic glass. All of this pain and suffering is at the cost of a week's holiday from which you could have returned to work well-rested and tanned and not looking as if you've been on a city-break to a war zone.

The truth is I want Glastonbury hell so everyone will admit they hate it too.

Can you interpret each piece of evidence to explain why this adds to Joe Wade's hatred of the festival? Present the information as a table like the one below:

EVIDENCE	INTERPRETATION
'resentment of success'	Hates that it makes so much money and is so popular
'like the Wild West'	
'like a plague of locusts'	

ACTIVITY 3: INTERPRETING INFORMATION

Having worked through this activity, work with a learning partner and say in your own words, what interpreting information means. When you have a concise explanation, write it down and compare to others in your class.

Step 2 Practise your skills

ACTIVITY 4: FINDING EVIDENCE

Read the following letter which was written by Charlotte Brontë in October 1848. Charlotte's brother, Branwell, died in September 1848, and a month later Charlotte wrote this letter with a heart full of misgivings. A short time afterwards, the illness that killed her brother came to her sister Emily and she died the same year.

Dear Ellen   October 29th, 1848.

I am sorry you should have been uneasy at my not writing to you ere this, but you must remember it is scarcely a week since I received your last, and my life is not so varied that in the interim much should have occurred worthy of mention. You insist that I should write about myself; this puts me in straits, for I really have nothing interesting to say about myself. I think I have now nearly got over the effects of my late illness, and am almost restored to my normal condition of health. I sometimes wish that it was a little higher, but we ought to be content with such blessings as we have, and not pine after those that are out of our reach.

I feel much more uneasy about my sisters than myself just now. Emily's cold and cough are very obstinate. I fear she has pain in the chest, and I sometimes catch a shortness in her breathing, when she has moved at all quickly. She looks very, very thin and pale. Her reserved nature occasions me great uneasiness of mind. It is useless to question her—you get no answers. It is still more useless to recommend remedies—they are never adopted. Nor can I shut my eyes to the fact of Anne's great delicacy of constitution. The late sad event has, I feel, made me more apprehensive than common. I cannot help feeling much depressed sometimes. I try to leave all in God's hands; to trust in His goodness; but faith and resignation are difficult to practise under some circumstances.

The weather has been most unfavourable for invalids of late: sudden changes of temperature, and cold penetrating winds have been frequent here. Should the atmosphere become settled, perhaps a favourable effect might be produced on the general health, and those harassing coughs and colds be removed. Papa has not quite escaped, but he has, so far, stood it out better than any of us. You must not mention my going to Brookroyd this winter. I could not, and would not, leave home on any account. I am truly sorry to hear of Miss Heald's serious illness, it seems to me she has been for some years out of health now. These things make one feel as well as know, that this world is not our abiding-place. We should not knit human ties too close, or clasp human affections too fondly. They must leave us, or we must leave them, one day. Good-bye for the present. God restore health and strength to you and to all who need it.

Yours faithfully,

C. Brontë.

Read, but do not answer, the following exam question:

Read Charlotte Brontë's letter, above.

Explain why Charlotte is unhappy at the time she writes the letter. [10]

You must use details selected from the text to support your answer.

Find evidence in the letter to support the following interpretations:

▶ Nothing much has happened to her in the past week.

▶ She has not been well lately.

▶ She is worried about her sisters, especially given Emily's appearance and physical health.

▶ Her sister will not speak about her illness or take advice/medicine.

▶ The death of her brother has unsettled her.

▶ She feels depressed.

▶ Her faith in God is being tested.

▶ The weather has been bad.

▶ She is unable/unwilling to leave home.

▶ She is too aware of how brief life can be.

Step 3 | Challenge yourself

ACTIVITY 5: JUSTO ANSOTEGUI

Now that you have completed these activities, use the skills you have practised to read the passage below and answer the question that follows it:

Justo Ansotegui's reputation rose uphill to the village of Lumo. There Maria Onati heard that he was a defender of causes and a wit, although some suggested he was too eager to create his own mythology. Most often she'd heard that he was the one to watch during the strength events on feast days. One friend claimed that he had carried an ox into town across his shoulder and celebrated the feat by throwing the beast across the river.

'Yes,' said Justo when asked about the story. 'But it was only a small ox and downhill most of the way into town. And the wind was with me when I threw it.'

Maria came to dance at one of the festivals with her sisters. She also decided to watch the men's competitions, which she usually avoided. Justo, the largest man standing beside a log at the start of the wood-chopping event, joked with the crowd as he removed his boots and grey socks. Going barefoot seemed foolhardy to Maria for one who would be flailing an axe so near his feet.

'After all these years of competitions I still have nine toes,' he said, proudly wiggling the four remaining toes on one of his bare feet. 'But this is my only pair of boots and I can't afford to damage them.' He bent at the waist and tore into the pine log between his feet. The log split beneath him well before any others in the competition. Justo was seated, nine toes intact, and replacing his boots before the runner-up broke through his log.

In the wine-drinking event, Justo was less impressive but in the 'farmer's walk' contest he was unmatched. This event tested strength and endurance as the competitors carried 50 kg weights in each hand along a measured course until they dropped. For most competitors the collapse followed a familiar pattern. On the second lap, the knees began to bend dramatically. On the third, the shoulders pulled the spine into a dangerous curve and finally gravity yanked the weights and the man to the turf.

Maria stood near the starting point when Justo was called. He grasped the weights, his face straining as if he'd never get them off the ground. It was false drama for the benefit of the audience because he easily hoisted them and marched without a struggle, his back rigid. Past the marks where others had fallen in exhaustion, Justo nodded to the little ones who would praise him to future generations. 'Doesn't it hurt?' a young boy asked.

'Of course, how do you think my arms got so long?' Justo answered and at that moment he straightened his arms against his sides, a move that caused the sleeves of his shirt to ride up, making his arms appear to grow in length.

What do you learn about Justo in these lines?

Write about:

► **facts and details about him**

► **the kind of person he is.**   **[10]**

You must use details selected from the text to support your answer.

Write up your response and then use the mark scheme provided by your teacher to self assess your work.

Top tips

Note the two bullet points in the question. The first is more reminiscent of Unit 1 (Extracting key information). The second asks you to draw on your interpretation of information skills.

For the second bullet point, you **may** want to complete a table like the ones we have used previously using the headings Evidence and Interpretation in order to help formulate your thoughts.

? Assess your progress. Did you:

- understand the two parts of the question and know exactly what you were looking for to answer it?
- track methodically through the text, highlighting the answers?
- support each comment with a detail from the text?
- interpret five different pieces of information for each bullet point (ten in all)?
- make sure you were precise in explaining why they answered the question?

 Next steps...

1 Using a range of texts, practise questions that require you to interpret information.
2 Practise answering questions under timed conditions.
3 Assess your own and others' work in this area.

OBJECTIVES

▶ To put into practice everything learned so far on interpreting information
▶ To practise these skills under timed pressure

How confident are you in these skills already?

I can answer this type of exam question in 12 minutes or less.

I can use a mark scheme to assess my own work.

I can use a mark scheme to assess other students' work and suggest improvements.

Always ⇨ Usually ⇨ Sometimes

QUESTION 1

Read the internet article, 'We must not ignore the plight of our farmers', which is about the spread of tuberculosis, a serious disease, in cattle.

WE MUST NOT IGNORE THE PLIGHT OF OUR FARMERS

ROWENNA DAVIS REPORTS ON ONE FARMER'S STRUGGLE TO COPE.

'Dave' is not his real name. He's too scared to tell me that in case his family farm becomes a target for animal rights activists, just because he agrees with the government's plan to cull badgers as a way of stopping the spread of tuberculosis (TB), a serious disease, in cattle.

He's been a farmer in Devon for over fifty years. His family works an exhausting fourteen hours a day, seven days a week, to look after their dairy herd of 1,000 cows, nursing them through birth and hand feeding them when they're sick. When Dave started farming fifty years ago, he used to shoot badgers, and none of his cows suffered from TB. When badgers became a protected species he stopped shooting them.

Now there are badgers on his land and regular cases of TB in his herd. This picture has been repeated at a national level. TB is now devastating herds of cattle across the countryside.

In 1998, fewer than 6,000 cows were killed because they had TB. In 2011, the figure rose to 34,000. To deal with the huge number of cattle being infected with TB, the government is planning to allow farmers to shoot badgers. It believes that badgers are responsible for spreading this devastating infection that is killing cattle and driving farmers out of business.

Science is very much on the side of culling badgers, because TB was under control in the 1970s and 1980s and has only become a problem since 1992 when it was made illegal to kill badgers. Since then the badger population has grown considerably and TB in cows has increased dramatically.

'Farmers don't want to kill all badgers, just those that have TB,' says Dave. 'It's only when their numbers get out of control that they start causing infections. Because they have no natural predators, it's up to us to keep the numbers down or they take over.'

Working so closely with infected animals meant that Dave's son-in-law came down with TB himself. His family stood by as he lay in bed rapidly losing weight and coughing, but they still want to keep going. 'My family want to carry on farming,' says Dave, 'They love it and their children love it. It's in our blood.'

Animal rights groups and charities say that the answer is vaccines. But there is no suitable vaccine for cows. The National Farmers Union says vaccinating badgers is incredibly difficult because to be effective each badger has to be caught in a cage and needs to be vaccinated once every year for four years. This makes it a very expensive operation.

It's difficult to explain how difficult life in the countryside already is. Back in Devon, one of Dave's neighbours has recently gone out of business. The price of milk paid to farmers has been slashed by 4p a litre this year, and supermarkets now sell milk at barely the cost of production. It's been too wet to graze the cows outside, so feed supplies have been used up and the increased price of grain is hitting farmers hard. Britain has lost 40 per cent of its dairy farms over the last ten years and TB is increasing that percentage every year. Something has to be done.

Explain the difficulties Dave faces as a result of farming. [10]

You must use the text to support your answer.

Write your answer and use the marking checklist (provided by your teacher) to assess your answer.

Sample answer

Look at the model answer below. What is good about it and why would it get full marks?

Answer

'It is clear that 'Dave' faces difficulties as a farmer. To begin with, he can't use his real name for fear of being 'targeted' by animal rights activists. He has cows in his herd affected by TB ('regular' shows that this happens often) and this has even spread to a member of his own family, showing the impact farming problems have had on his life. In 1998 fewer than 6,000 cows were killed because of TB, but this had risen in 2011 to 34,000 showing just how quickly and widespread the disease has become.

A number of dairy farms have gone out of business (a 'decrease' in the number) and farmers are now not allowed to shoot badgers to protect their cows, as new laws mean that badgers are a protected species. As a result, badgers' numbers have 'got out of control' showing there is no end to the problem in sight.

In addition to the TB problem, farmers work very long hours every day of the week, so there is no let up in the work and it is 'intensive' work meaning it is very demanding ('nursing' and 'hand feeding' the animals). Also, the money they receive from milk has been 'slashed' whilst the price of grain has increased so costs have increased and shows that the hard work brings less benefits. Finally, the recent bad weather can make things worse for farmers. Overall, the situation for farmers seems very bleak.

Now you have completed the section, do you think your confidence has increased?

I am confident with what it means to 'interpret' information.

I am confident that I can recognise questions that ask me to interpret information.

I can confidently select details from the text in order to answer the question.

I can interpret these details quickly and precisely in order to answer the question.

I can write these up in a clear answer, using appropriate vocabulary.

Always ⇨ Usually ⇨ Sometimes

Unit 3
Synthesising information

OBJECTIVES

▶ To understand what is meant by synthesising information
▶ To select information from different parts of a text or texts
▶ To combine different pieces of information in your answer

How confident are you in these skills already?

I understand what it means to synthesise information.

I can recognise questions that ask me to synthesise information.

I can select the information I need from different parts of a text or different texts.

I can combine and connect information.

Always ⇨ Usually ⇨ Sometimes

(!) Top tips

You may know the correct term for words that give you a command, as exam questions do. When you are asked to explain, examine, explore, compare or compare, an imperative is being used.

What does synthesis mean?

If you synthesise information, you don't just find it in the text. This is just the first step and is a skill you learned in Unit 1.

The *Oxford English Dictionary* defines synthesis as 'combining elements to form a whole'.

In an English Language exam, this means that you gather ideas from two texts and put them together to form a conclusion about them. You will also be able to use your Unit 2 skills where you learned how to interpret information. You are still doing that but now it is for two texts. You will find questions like these in the Component Two examination – 19th and 21st century non-fiction reading.

To synthesise information in this exam, you need to follow these steps.
1 Identify the demands of the question.
2 Locate the information you need in the first text.
3 Locate the information you need in the second text.
4 Combine this information to form your answer.

Synthesising information is processing your findings into an answer.

(!) Top tips

Even high ability students can score poorly on the search and find questions because they don't believe that the question is as straightforward as it seems. Detailed analysis of language in a search and find question does not earn you extra marks and, most crucially, wastes valuable time. Read the question carefully!

Get going

Step 1 Work on your skills

 ACTIVITY 1: INSTRUCTIONS

The steps on page 18 form a plan for approaching this type of question.

The first step asked you to identify the demands of the question.

You will have to gather information from more than one text but, of course, you will not know before the exam, exactly what question you will get.

Read the table below and discuss with a learning partner what each instruction would be asking you to do in the exam. The first is done for you.

TERM	WHAT IT'S ASKING YOU TO DO
Find	Locate information
List	
Explain	
Examine	
Explore	
Compare	
Contrast	

 Top tips

'Explain', 'examine' and 'explore' are not asking you to do widely different things. Don't struggle to come up with completely different definitions.

 ACTIVITY 2: COMPLEXITY OF QUESTIONS

The English Language exam questions often follow a pattern where they become progressively more difficult. A guide to judging the complexity of your question is often to look at the number of marks that it is worth.

▶ Unit 1 showed you how to do search and find questions, which are often at the beginning of the exam. They often ask you to find or list some points.

▶ Unit 2 showed you how to tackle the more difficult interpret questions, where you find the information first, then explain it.

▶ The synthesis question is usually the last one. It draws on all the skills you have displayed in the exam so far – searching, finding and explaining – and now asks you to do this across two texts. It will

not have the word 'synthesise' in the question but it will be asking you to connect two texts to find your answer. This question may also ask you how the writers create a certain impression in their work.

Rank these questions in ascending order from what you think is the easiest to the hardest question.

Explain	Examine	List	Compare how the writers …	Find

With a learning partner, now discuss how you could tell. Remember, a good guide for assessing the difficulty level is to look at how many marks are awarded for each question.

Step 2   Practise your skills

ACTIVITY 3: DOGS

Remember that the four steps formed a plan for approaching this type of question.

Step 2 asked you to locate the information you need in the first text.

Step 3 asked you to locate the information you need in the second text.

Read the two text extracts below, then answer the questions that follow.

'Handbag' dogs – why you should never see your pet as a fashion accessory

Tiny Chihuahuas, teacup Yorkies, Pomeranians and more … The popularity of toy dogs has been on the rise for some years now, leading to a modern phenomenon known as the 'handbag' dog – literally, a toy dog small enough to be carried in an oversized handbag.

This trend for 'handbag' dogs may have begun with celebrity dog lovers such as Paris Hilton and Nicole Richie, but it didn't take long to filter down into the land of us mere mortals too.

The image of someone carrying a small dog about in a handbag while they go about their business, something that would once have raised eyebrows, has become incredibly mainstream over the last few years, even within the UK.

Having a toy dog that is the height of fashion and can be carried in a suitably trendy underarm carrier should always be a secondary consideration to actively wanting to own a dog and committing to caring for it for the duration of its life. If you are considering getting a toy dog just because you think they are fashionable or 'cool' or can be ported around in your bag – think again! While undeniably small and cute, toy dogs are still dogs. They require a significant commitment of both time and money to their care and wellbeing, and live for well over a decade in most cases. If you see owning a toy dog as a short-term option, something to be discarded when fashions change – walk away now. Battersea Dogs' Home has reported an increase of over 40% during 2012 in the number of toy dogs coming into the shelter for rehoming, with Chihuahuas and Yorkshire Terriers topping the list. Owning a dog of any size is a lifetime commitment. Don't be tempted to buy a toy dog for yourself or your child on a whim.

The Prize Pugs of America and England (1891)

The question is often asked in a critical manner, of what utility is the pug? It has lately become the fashion for some people to buy a pug as they would a diamond pin, a silk hat or fine clothes. Yet, the pug is not just a 'fancy' dog but a good, intelligent watch dog, ever on the alert for an intruder. It is a faithful companion, affectionate in disposition, and, having a fine smooth coat, is easily kept clean in the house. With a little attention given to its teeth, its breath is as free from odour as that of any other dog. Pugs are easily trained, and are, as a rule, good with children, though they should not have to endure having the curl taken out of their tail by a teasing two-year-old. It has been said that pugs are stupid, but such is not the case, and, like any other dog, their intelligence depends upon the attention given them by intelligent people. Bring them up among ignorant, careless people or keep them away from the family, and it follows that they will not display that intelligence which is seen in dogs that are properly trained. Of course to the sportsman or farmer, a pug would be useless, but as a family pet, he is all that can be desired.

1 Look at the article 'Handbag dogs'.
  a Give three breeds of toy dogs that the article mentions. [3]
  b Give two reasons why people want to own a toy dog. [2]
  c By what percentage has Battersea Dogs' Home seen an increase in the number of toy dogs coming to its shelter? [1]

2 Look at the extract from *The Prize Pugs of America and England*.
  a Why is a pug dog easy to keep clean? [1]
  b What two groups of people would not see a use for a pug dog? [2]

✔ Self-assessment

Check your answers.

1 'Handbag dogs'
  a Any three of: (Tiny) Chihuahuas, teacup Yorkies/Yorkshire Terriers, Pomeranians. [3]
  b Any two of: to copy celebrities like Paris Hilton and Nicole Ritchie, to be fashionable/'trendy'/'cool', they can be carried in a bag, they're small and cute. [2]
  c 40% [1]

2 From *The Prize Pugs of America and England*
  a It has a fine, smooth coat. [1]
  b Sportsmen and farmers. [2]

When locating the information you needed, you probably took care to make sure that you were looking at the correct text. If you did not do this, you would have been unable to find the answers. You must now take the same amount of care when you move on to synthesise your information in the more difficult questions that follow.

Step 3 Challenge yourself

ACTIVITY 4: POINTS TO CONSIDER

Refer to the texts 'Handbag dogs' and from *The Prize Pugs of America and England* again.

According to these two writers, what points should an owner consider before buying a dog? [8]

Self-assessment

Check your answers and reward a mark for any of the following:

- Consider whether you actually want to own a dog.
- Consider whether you are committed to caring for it for its whole life./It is a lifetime decision./They live for well over a decade.
- You should not buy one just to be fashionable/'trendy'/'cool'.
- They cannot be discarded when fashions change.

- It requires a significant commitment in both time and money.
- It is not simply another item like a diamond pin, silk hat or fine clothes.
- It is not just a 'fancy' dog.
- Children should not be allowed to tease them.
- Dogs must not be brought up by ignorant, careless people or kept away from the family.
- They should be properly trained.

Congratulations! You have now synthesised information from two texts.

Now you have completed the section, do you think your confidence has increased?

I can identify the demands of the question.

I can locate the information needed in the first text.

I can locate the information needed in the second text.

I combine this information to form an answer.

Always ➪ Usually ➪ Sometimes

Improve your skills

OBJECTIVES

▶ To recognise questions that ask me to synthesise information
▶ To find the information needed to answer the question
▶ To group this information
▶ To synthesise this information
▶ To interpret the synthesised information and form a conclusion about it

---

How confident are you in these skills already?

I can recognise questions that ask me to synthesise information.

I can select the information I need from different texts.

I can combine, connect or group this information.

I can interpret the synthesised information and come to a conclusion about it.

Always ➪ Usually ➪ Sometimes

 Top tips

This is an English Language exam so it is worth getting your grammar right. When you compare *two* texts, you may wish to say which is the *more* effective, or the one that you would consider to be *better*. The superlatives 'most' and 'best' are only used for more than two things.

Comparing two texts:
- I think the first one is most effective. ✗
- I think the second text is the best text. ✗
- I think the first one is more effective. ✔
- I think the second one is the better text. ✔

In this unit, you have already practised how to identify what a question is asking you to do, to find the information required and to combine it in an answer.

Some questions ask that your answer is presented under separate headings and this requires you to group your information.

More difficult synthesis questions will also ask you to form a judgement on the information that you have found and come to a conclusion about it. This is often done by asking you *how* the writers convey their information and what their attitudes might be.

The questions will present opportunities for you to identify and interpret information, analyse the writers' ideas and techniques, compare them and form judgements on their effect.

Read each question's requirements carefully as more than one skill may be assessed in a question.

Step 1   Work on your skills

ACTIVITY 1: MISTREATED ANIMALS

Read the two brief extracts below, then answer the question that follows.

PUPPY FARMING

A puppy farmer is defined as a high volume breeder who breeds puppies with little or no concern for the health and welfare of the puppies or their mothers. Some farmers have up to 200 breeding dogs on their farms! A puppy farmer breeds only for selfish profit. As a result, the puppies bred by puppy farmers are more likely to suffer from genetic diseases, painful abnormalities, behavioural problems and short life spans. If you are thinking of buying a puppy, go to a reputable breeder, not a puppy farm.
The Kennel Club, online

Lord Erskine's speech

Public cruelty to animals is an offence. One hears of horses sinking and dying under crushing loads, left without sustenance, and literally starved to death so that they are forced to gnaw their own coats in the agonies of hunger.
Lord Erskine's speech on Preventing Malicious and Wanton Cruelty to Animals, 1809

What problems do animals suffer if they are mistreated?   **[8]**

Organise your answer under two headings:

▶ The problems puppies suffer

▶ The problems horses suffer

This is not a particularly difficult question in itself. However, it teaches you an important lesson. You need to group your information under the given headings. If you do not do this, it shows the examiner that you have not read the question properly. In a short extract, like the one given, you will probably not find the task particularly difficult but in a longer examination passage you will need to be particularly careful to group the information under the correct headings.

Step 2 | Practise your skills

ACTIVITY 2: SPEECH AND ARTICLE

You have just worked on organising an answer correctly.

A grouping question may also refer you to the different text types. Look again at the two short extracts on previous page and answer a similar question to the one you just did to help you practise your new skills.

What problems do animals suffer if they are mistreated? [8]

Organise your answer under two headings:

▶ The problems given in the speech

▶ The problems given in the article

✔ Self-assessment

Now check your answers.

- The problems given in the speech – horses sinking and dying under loads, left without sustenance, starved to death, forced to gnaw their own coats
- The problems given in the article – puppies suffer from genetic diseases, painful abnormalities, behavioural problems, short life spans

Are your answers under the correct headings or have you confused the article with the speech? You may have noticed that the first question asked you to list the puppies' problems first, then the horses. The second question asked you to list the horses' problems first, then the puppies. Always make sure that you read the question very carefully and group the answer as you are asked to do.

Step 3 | Challenge yourself

The final objective in this section of the unit, is to interpret synthesised information and come to a conclusion about it. This usually requires you to look at *how* the writer conveys their information and form a judgement on its effectiveness.

ACTIVITY 3: TECHNIQUES

The writer of a non-fiction text will use a variety of techniques in order that the text has an effect on the reader. Of course, this depends on the purpose of the text. The writer of an advertisement wants to persuade you to make a purchase, the author of a charity leaflet wants to persuade you to donate money, the writer of a road safety leaflet wants to warn you of dangers. These writers will employ different language but they will use similar techniques:

▶ Strong, emotive language

▶ Facts

▶ Expert advice

▶ Personal pronouns

▶ Dramatic punctuation

▶ Pictures related to the text

Look again at the puppy farming article and Lord Eskine's speech on page 23. In a copy of the table opposite, give an example of each technique you find. Note that not every technique will be in each extract. This is not a checklist.

	EXAMPLE FROM PUPPY FARMING ARTICLE	EXAMPLE FROM LORD ERSKINE'S SPEECH
Strong, emotive language		
Facts		
Expert advice		
Personal pronouns		
Dramatic punctuation		
Pictures related to the text		

 ## ACTIVITY 4: EFFECT OF TECHNIQUES

You now need to consider the effect these techniques have on the reader. As stated, the writer's aim depends on the purpose on the text. In an advertisement, strong language and striking adjectives may persuade you to buy a great, new product, facts might impress you and expert advice might recommend the product to you. In a charity leaflet, however, strong language may encourage your sympathy for those the charity is trying to help, facts might shock you and expert advice might advise that you act quickly by sending money.

Look at your completed table and now add a third column. In this column, you should suggest the effect that each of your selected techniques has on the reader. By doing this, you are interpreting the information and coming to a conclusion about it.

	EXAMPLE FROM PUPPY FARMING ARTICLE	EXAMPLE FROM LORD ERSKINE'S SPEECH	EFFECT THE TECHNIQUES HAVE ON THE READER
Strong, emotive language			
Facts			
Expert advice			
Personal pronouns			
Dramatic punctuation			
Pictures related to the text			

Now you have completed the section, do you think your confidence has increased?

I can recognise questions that ask me to synthesise information.

I can select the information I need from different texts.

I can combine, connect or group this information.

I can interpret the synthesised information and come to a conclusion about it.

Always ⇨ Usually ⇨ Sometimes

BE EXAM READY

▶ To put all your synthesis skills into practice
▶ To practise these skills under timed pressure

How confident are you in these skills already?

I can put my synthesis skills into practice – understanding the question, locating information and combining it.

I can practise these skills under timed pressure.

Always ⫸ Usually ⫸ Sometimes

In this unit, you have practised identifying the demands of an examination question, locating the information needed to answer it, synthesising the information and forming a judgement on its effect.

QUESTION 1

Read the two extracts below and answer the questions that follow.

You are advised to spend your time as follows:
- about 5 minutes reading
- about 40 minutes answering the questions.

Note: your actual GCSE examination timings will be a little longer to reflect the longer extracts.

RIDICULOUS CELEBRITY DEMANDS

It seems that there are no limits to the excessive demands of the rich and famous. In Beyoncé's deal with Pepsi, she can only be seen drinking their products and even the heat and smell of her dressing-room is controlled as she insists on a constant temperature of 78 degrees and the aroma of rose-scented candles. Rihanna favours 'Black Forest' candles, an animal-print rug and blue chiffon curtains, whilst Kanye West requests all white décor and a special $8000 bed for his daughter, North. Mere mortals like us would be glad if anyone bought us flowers, but in the pampered world of celebrity, there's stringent requirements, with white lilies and roses for Jennifer Lopez and white hydrangeas for Katy Perry, but, take care – she doesn't like carnations! Katy also has very specific menu demands. Inexplicably listed in her food requirements are freeze-dried strawberries. As a strict supporter of animal rights, Sir Paul McCartney bans any leather, fur and meat backstage. Yet the most bizarre demands come from Will Ferrell. For his 'Semi-Pro' promotional tour, he asked for a three wheel mobility scooter and a rainbow with wheels!

Conversations of Lord Byron – Medwin's journal

I went to Italy late in the autumn of 1821, for the benefit of my health. Lord Byron, had passed there a few days before me, and was already at Pisa when I arrived. His travelling equipage was rather a singular one, and afforded a strange catalogue. He insisted on seven servants, five carriages, nine horses, a monkey, a bull-dog and a mastiff, two cats, three pea-owls and some hens! These, and all his books, consisting of a very large library of modern works, (for he insisted on buying all the best that came out), were brought together with a vast quantity of furniture. I had long formed a wish to see and be acquainted with Lord Byron; but his known refusal at that time to receive the visits of strangers, even of some who had brought him letters of introduction from the best friends he had, and a prejudice excited against his own countrymen by a late insult, would have deterred me from seeking an interview with him, had not the proposal come from himself, in consequence of his hearing his friend, Mr Shelley, recommend me.

Journal of the Conversations of Lord Byron: noted during a residence with his Lordship at Pisa in the years 1821 and 1822, by T. Medwin.

Read the online article, 'Ridiculous Celebrity Demands'.

A1
(a) What requests does Beyoncé have for her dressing room? [3]
(b) What flowers does Katy Perry refuse to have backstage? [1]
(c) Why does Sir Paul McCartney ban, leather, fur and meat backstage? [1]

A2

The writer conveys an impression that celebrities' dressing room demands are excessive. How does he try to do this? [10]

You should comment on:
- what he says to influence readers
- his use of language and tone
- the way he presents his argument.

To answer the following, read Medwin's journal, 'Conversations of Lord Byron'.

A3
(a) Why did the writer travel to Italy? [1]
(b) What did Lord Byron insist on travelling with, apart from a variety of animals? [4]

A4

How does the writer convey the impression that Lord Byron was very difficult to please? [10]

You should comment on:
- what is said
- how it is said.

You must refer to the text to support your comments.

To answer the following question you will need to use both texts.

A5

What are the writers' attitudes to celebrities? [10]

You should consider:
- the writers' attitudes to celebrities' demands
- how the writers convey their opinions.

You must use the text to support your comments and make it clear which text you are referring to.

Self-assessment

A1

(a)

- can only be seen drinking Pepsi
- heat of dressing-room is controlled at 78 degrees
- rose-scented candles [3]

(b) carnations [1]

(c) he is a strict supporter of animal rights. [1]

A2

This is not a checklist. You may identify:

- strong, negative language: 'ridiculous,' 'excessive, 'pampered', 'stringent', 'specific', 'bizarre'. (You may note that these are adjectives.) Strong, negative verbs: 'insists', 'bans'
- frequent use of adjectives and specific detail, such as use of colours to convey a sense of fussiness
- a negative tone in phrases like, 'can only be seen,' 'but take care' 'inexplicably listed in her food requirements' and 'a rainbow on wheels!' (exclamatory tone/dramatic punctuation implies mockery)
- use of fact, such as '78 degrees' and '$8000 bed'
- use of tripling to convey a sense of multiple demands
- quite a lot of celebrities are referenced, which suggests that most of them are demanding
- the structure of the article, which finishes with 'yet the most bizarre requests' for maximum impact.

Note: a response could be balanced by the fact that only McCartney's requirements have an understandable reason behind them.

A3

(a) for the benefit of his health [1]

(b) seven servants, five carriages, all his books (a very large library) and furniture [4]

A4

This is not a checklist. You may identify:

- negative language to suggest that Byron's behaviour is odd, in 'singular', 'strange'. (You may note that these are adjectives.) Strong verbs are associated with him in 'insisted' and 'excited' and there is a suggestion that he 'deterred' visitors.
- The animals he selected to travel with him is a rather strange mix.
- Numbers are given to suggest he has odd, very specific predilections.
- Excessive quantities of items are suggested in 'very large library', and 'vast quantity'.
- The exclamatory mood is used when the animals are listed, suggesting that he needs to be pandered to.
- The list of animals (using commas instead of conjunctions) suggests that he demands a lot.
- He likes to indulge whims and 'insisted on buying all the best (books) that came out'.
- Judgemental behaviour is suggested in 'prejudice'.
- The writer had 'long formed' a wish to meet him but knew of his 'refusal' to 'receive the visits of strangers'.
- He seems to be rankled by a 'late insult' suggesting that he takes things personally and bears grudges.
- He ignores the advice and recommendations of his best friends.
- The last sentence is very long and full of subordinate clauses. Through this, the writer conveys a sense of Byron's continuous, awkward behaviour.

A5 This question combines your answers to **A2** and **A4**. You do not need to deal with each text equally but you must refer to both texts.

Comparing sample answers

Read the sample answers and discuss which is better and why.

What are the writers' attitudes to celebrities?

You should consider:
- the writers' attitudes to celebrities' demands
- how the writers convey their opinions.

[10]

Sample answer 1

A5 The writers' attitudes to celebrities are that they don't like them. The first writer tells us that celebrities like Beyoncé, Kanye West, Rihanna, Katy Perry, Paul McCartney and Will Ferrell ask for weird things when they go on tour. Celebrities want strange foods and flowers. They tell us that Will Ferrell asks for the strangest things of all and they say that he even wanted a scooter! Byron sounds really fussy.

Sample answer 2

A5 The writers seem to have a negative attitude to celebrities. They show this through the information they choose to tell us, which conveys celebrities as shallow and demanding. The heading 'Ridiculous celebrity demands' already suggests that celebrities' behaviour is over the top. The writer gives examples of Beyoncé's requirements when on tour, which include her room being a certain temperature and the fact that she can only drink Pepsi. Both Beyoncé and Rihanna insist on a particular type of candle in their room, which makes them sound fussy. The writer is telling us this to suggest that the celebrities mentioned have got too many demands. Words like 'excessive', 'demands' and 'controlled' make us think that celebrities are bossy and unpleasant.

Medwin conveys a sense of Byron's eccentric character through listing a range of unusual things that he travels with, like 'three pea-owls'. Byron seems to need a lot of unnecessary things with him. Byron sounds like he doesn't like anyone.

Now you have completed the section, do you think your confidence has increased?

I understand what it means to synthesise information.

I can put my synthesis skills into practice – understanding the question, locating information and combining it.

I can follow logical steps in order to approach a synthesis question.

I can interpret synthesised information and form a judgement on it.

Always Usually Sometimes

Unit 4
Types of information

OBJECTIVES

▶ To identify different types of information – fact, opinion and bias
▶ To understand what a writer is trying to convey by using a certain type of information
▶ To understand why a writer uses a certain type of information.

How confident are you in these skills already?

I can identify different types of information.

I can tell if information is fact, opinion or bias.

I can understand why a writer uses different types of information.

| Always | ⇨ | Usually | ⇨ | Sometimes |

Information is the knowledge you receive from being told about something. In the English Language GCSE you will read texts to gather the information you need to answer the questions. This information will be presented in different ways. Different text types present their information differently – such as letters, articles, reports, blogs, factsheets – but the *type* of information you receive will also differ. Some information that you read will be factual and true, other points will be opinion.

Get going

Step 1 Work on your skills

  ### ACTIVITY 1: FACT OR OPINION

Do you know the difference between a **fact** and an **opinion**?

Decide whether the following statements are fact or opinion.

STATEMENT	FACT OR OPINION?
Andy Murray is a Scottish tennis player.	
Lionel Messi is the best football player of all time.	

> A **fact** is something that we all agree is true and that can be confirmed.
> The most obvious or indisputable facts are mathematical ($2 + 2 = 4$) or scientific (the Earth is the third planet from the Sun).
> An **opinion** involves belief. It is something that we or someone else believes to be true. Opinions can be held with confidence or conviction but cannot be backed up with absolute proof.

Young people should do more exercise.	
Star Wars is the best film ever made.	
There are one hundred pence in a pound (£).	
England won the World Cup in 1966.	
Obesity is a growing problem in the United Kingdom.	
Metallica are the best band of all time.	
Politicians should smile a bit more.	
Chickenpox is most common in children under ten.	

Superlatives

The grid told us that Lionel Messi is the *best*, *Star Wars* is the *best* and Metallica are the *best*. The word 'best' is a superlative. Superlatives are used to convince us that something or someone is at the most extreme point that can be achieved. Charity leaflets use negative superlatives, such as 'worst', 'most dreadful', 'poorest' to incite our sympathy.

Step 2 Practise your skills

In our competitive world, many people try to convince us that their opinions are facts. Saying opinions loudly or repeatedly or calling on the shared belief of other people does not make an opinion a fact. Most football supporters sing at home games that their team is the greatest and a biscuit maker may advertise their biscuits as the best but there are others who would dispute this claim so it cannot be a fact. Similarly, at election times, politicians will promote their opinions (dressed as facts usually) to convince voters that they, alone, have the best plan for our future.

 Top tips

Your response to information also depends how you interpret it. If you hold a similar opinion to that being presented to you, you are likely to agree with it. If not, you may object strongly to that opinion. Remember, if you agree with an opinion, however strongly, this does not make it a fact. A fact needs to be a point that is proven and undisputed.

 ACTIVITY 2: FACTS AND OPINIONS

Read the following extract from an article about Rocawear clothing.

Copy and complete the table with three facts and three opinions from the extract.

Rap star, Jay-Z, has made millions from his clothing line, Rocawear, which was founded in 1999. At its peak, the company had an annual turnover of $700 million. Fans of Jay-Z's music love Rocawear's urban style. Jay-Z, real name, Shawn Carter, has certainly profited from the lifestyle clothing line. At the height of their popularity, the casual clothes appealed to everyone because their styling was so unique.

FACTS	OPINIONS

The extract is a mixture of facts and opinions, with opinions promoted as if they are facts. The writer is not trying to outright lie to you by doing this, but to convey the popularity of the clothing line in a lively piece of writing. The writer is using information to interest you in the article.

The extract is not an advertisement, yet it still comes across as in favour of the clothing line.

▶ How can you tell this?

▶ What is the effect of the techniques used?

TECHNIQUE USED	EVIDENCE FROM THE TEXT	EFFECT ON THE READER
Positive facts	'annual turnover of $700 million'	Makes the company sound extremely successful
Language that makes the brand sound successful		
Language that makes the brand sound popular		
Vocabulary that might appeal to teenagers (the market for these clothes)		
A confident tone		

Rocawear did not continue making $700 million a year. The writer hints at this.

▶ Find three examples that hint at falling success for the company.

▶ Why doesn't the writer give us a detailed explanation of Rocawear's decline in fortunes?

The writer want us to feel positively toward Jay-Z and his company so gives us positive information and filters out negative information. This is cleverly done. The fact that Rocawear went on to make less money is not ignored, however, it is only hinted at. The writer's **bias** presents Rocawear favourably.

You should now be able to review the extract and tell that:

▶ there is fact, opinion and bias

▶ the writer is trying to convey a positive image

▶ this is done to try to make the reader regard the clothing line positively.

> **Bias** is a concentration on one particular area or subject. In a written text, it is a writer's tendency to hold an opinion that only considers part of an outlook. A biased text only presents a particular angle.

 Top tips

Note the spelling of 'bias' and 'biased'. It is commonly misspelt with a 't' at the end. Make sure that you know how to spell it correctly.

Step 3 Challenge yourself

> Now you should be able to identify fact, opinion and bias and understand why it is used.

 ACTIVITY 3: CREDIT CARD

Read this advertisement for taking out a credit card and answer the question that follows.

The Compare Credit Card is more friendly than other credit cards because it has the quickest application process. Simply fill in your details online and your Compare Credit Card application will be processed in the next 24 hours. With a credit limit up to £1500, Compare Credit Card helps you enjoy your money more. You will never have to worry about money again because your card is accepted in all major retailers. Compare Credit Card is the best in the UK!

How does the writer try to persuade us to take out a Compare Credit Card?

 Top tips

Remember to structure your answer:

● Technique used
● Evidence from the text
● Effect on the reader

Self-assessment

- Facts are used: 'processed in ... 24 hours', 'credit limit up to £1500' – sounds good.
- Four opinions presented as facts: It is 'more friendly than other credit cards,' it 'helps you enjoy your money more.' 'You will never have to worry about money again' and the card is 'the best in the UK.' These are presented as facts, or 'truths' to promote the card.
- A comparative is used: 'more friendly' – sounds better than other cards.
- Superlatives are used: 'the quickest application process,' 'the best in the UK.' – sounds great.
- Direct address: 'your details', 'helps you enjoy' – personal pronouns appeal to you directly.
- Exclamatory tone: 'the best in the UK!' – encourages excitement/a desire to own it.
- Short sentences help us to absorb the information.

The advertisement appears, on the surface, to simply inform us what the Compare Credit Card does. However, the text is trying to persuade you to take out this card, so presents opinions as persuasive facts in the hope that you will be convinced. If you can separate the facts from the opinions, then you can answer comprehension questions thoughtfully in exams and also make considered judgements in the real world.

The examples we have looked at demonstrate that a mixture of fact and opinion can be used to interest us in a piece of writing or attempt to persuade and convince us.

Now you have completed the section, do you think your confidence has increased?

I can identify different types of information.

I can tell if information is fact, opinion or bias.

I can understand why a writer uses different types of information.

Always ⇨ Usually ⇨ Sometimes

! Top tips

Remember that advertisers and promoters are not always trying to trick you. You may well want a certain product and it may be a very good one. You just need to be aware that advertisers are paid to tell you that a certain product is the best, so you need to assess how far this is true and if you want their product or a different one.

! Top tips

When you are analysing an advertisement or persuasive text, you may wish to say that the techniques have a certain *effect*, or that they *affect* the reader in a certain way.

affect = verb   effect = usually a noun

- I was so *affected* by the sad music that it made me cry.
- The *effect* of this technique is striking.
- This piece of writing was very *effective*.

There are some exceptions. 'Effect' can be used as a verb, meaning to bring about a certain situation, for example:

- By adding a chemical to the liquid, we *effected* a dramatic change, as it turned blue.

Improve your skills

OBJECTIVES

▶ To identify main ideas and supporting ideas in a text
▶ To understand the difference between explicit and implicit meaning
▶ To understand how different types of information affect our understanding of a text
▶ To interpret this information and draw inferences from it

How confident are you in these skills already?

I can identify the main point from a piece of information.

I can identify supporting points from a piece of information.

I know what explicit and implicit meanings are.

I can 'read between the lines' of the information I am being given and work out if there is a 'hidden' second meaning.

Always ⇨ Usually ⇨ Sometimes

The main idea in a text is usually presented early on but a piece of writing may also draw you in with examples and present its main idea later when you are already 'hooked'. Charity leaflets do this so that your sympathy is engaged before a donation is asked for. In newspapers the main idea is presented first. The further on you read the more detailed it will become. Newspaper articles are written so that wherever you stop reading, you have the main story but the number of supporting ideas will vary.

> **! Top tips**
>
> You probably know what the word 'impact' means. However, students commonly use it incorrectly. When we use the word 'impact' to describe a writer's style, we need to use it as a noun and say that it has an impact on the reader. 'Impact' can be used as a verb but it means 'to bring about a high force or shock'. If you use 'impact' as a verb when describing a writer's style, you are actually implying that the techniques used physically hit you.
>
> 'This impacted me' or 'It impacts the reader' is incorrect. In these examples, you are better off using the verb 'affect'.
>
> If you can put an article such as 'an' or 'the' in front of 'impact', you are using it in the most correct way for English GCSE.

Step 1   Work on your skills

Main ideas and supporting ideas are usually used together to create a convincing argument or fact sheet. They are often signalled by a system of headings and subheadings. Size of text and colour can also be used to clarify the difference.

> **! Top tips**
>
> When you highlight a text you usually pick out the main ideas. If you go on and highlight too much of a text, then the difference between key information and supporting information is lost, so use it sparingly.

ACTIVITY 1: MAIN AND SUPPORTING POINTS

Read the following article from *The Guardian* online newspaper.
▶ **Identify the main points.**
▶ **Identify the supporting points.**

Six-year-olds understand digital technology better than adults

They may not know who Steve Jobs was or even how to tie their own shoelaces, but the average six-year-old child understands more about digital technology than a 45-year-old adult, according to an authoritative new report published on Thursday.

Children learn how to use smartphones before they are able to talk

The advent of broadband in the year 2000 has created a generation of digital natives, the communication watchdog Ofcom says in its annual study of British consumers. Born in the new millennium, these children have never known the dark ages of dial up internet, and the youngest are learning how to operate smartphones or tablets before they are able to talk.

Changing communication trends

"These younger people are shaping communications," said Jane Rumble, Ofcom's media research head. "As a result of growing up in the digital age, they are developing fundamentally different communication habits from older generations, even compared to what we call the early adopters, the 16-to-24 age group."

For those aged 12 to 15, phone calls account for just 3% of time spent communicating through any device. For all adults, this rises to 20%, and for young adults it is still three times as high at 9%. Today's children do the majority of their remote socialising by sending written messages or through shared photographs and videos. "The millennium generation is losing its voice," Ofcom claims.

From *The Guardian* online

 Top tips

The writing section of the exam often does ask you for your opinions about a topic but the reading section requires you to answer the question given. This may well be about the writer's opinion but don't be tempted to fill your answer with personal opinions about the topic of the comprehension.

✔ Self-assessment

In this text, the main points can be identified by the main heading and subheadings. These are that:

- Six-year-olds understand digital technology better than adults.
- Children learn how to use smartphones before they are able to talk.
- Communication trends are changing.

The supporting points can be identified when you read the rest of the article and are given more facts and detail, such as young children being unaware of 'the dark ages of dial up internet' and that phone use varies widely between different age groups.

You would not know that 'the millennium generation is losing its voice' unless you read to the very end of the extract, which illustrates how the main points are usually introduced early on and then developed with supporting points.

📄 ACTIVITY 2: IMPLICIT MEANING

The article's aim is to inform us about children's confidence with technology and that the way the younger generation communicates is different from that of the older generation. This is the clear, explicit meaning of the text. The explicit meaning is usually quite obvious and stated directly.

Implicit meaning needs to be worked at. It is 'reading between the lines' and inferring (working out) what might be another meaning behind the text. Implicit meaning is hinted at or suggested by the writer. The meaning is understood (usually) but it lies behind the words.

Imagine that the article continued with the section below.

▶ **What do you think is the explicit meaning of the text?**

▶ **What is the implicit meaning of the text?**

❗ Top tips

To separate main ideas from supporting ideas in a clearly presented, non-fiction text, try holding it at arm's length. If the text has a heading and subheadings, these will stand out to you. These can be your starting point for identifying main and supporting ideas. Note that this is just an entry point for your understanding of the text. If these larger headings are all you base your answer on, you will have no detail in your response.

No need for words

Accustomed to recording video messages, swapping pictures and sending abbreviated texts that rely on shortened versions of words, today's youngsters seemingly have no need for a wide-ranging vocabulary in order to share information with friends. 'Instant' communication has gone so far that a text or Facebook update can even rely on an impersonal emoticon to convey feelings.

What the future holds

With more screen time than face-to-face time, the art of reading real human emotions may be in decline. Teenagers don't need to tell their friend that they enjoyed hearing about an event or smiled at a photo they saw – just press 'like' on Facebook. No need to explain your reaction to an amusing event with well chosen words about how it made you feel – not when LOL will do. Give it another five years and maybe we won't need to connect emotionally with other human beings at all. Just plug in and shut up.

Self-assessment

The explicit meaning is that young people communicate in a quicker, more economical way than older people.

The implicit meaning is that important skills are being lost.

The article does not state explicitly (obviously) that young people are losing important communication skills and that this is a shame, but this idea is implied.

The final statement 'Plug in and shut up' is our strongest hint of this as it is such a negative indictment of humanity.

Step 2 Practise your skills

ACTIVITY 3: SUPPORTING EVIDENCE

Read through this Visit Wales piece. Look at the different types of information, draw inferences and identify bias.

Dolphin superpod spotted in Welsh waters

A superpod of over 1,000 dolphins was spotted off the coast of Pembrokeshire by the marine wildlife conservation charity Sea Trust during a routine survey.

A spokesperson from the conservation group who witnessed a 'mile long wall of dolphins' said it was the 'most spectacular' sighting in 10 years of surveying the Welsh waters

'On three occasions we have encountered superpods of common dolphins in Pembrokeshire waters but this was the most spectacular with wall-to-wall dolphins.'

The dolphins were seen on a 30-mile stretch between Milford Haven and Lundy. Cardigan Bay is a fantastic area to spot dolphins, with the UK's biggest pod of dolphins calling it home.

Visit Wales website

The writer reinforces the article's main ideas with supporting evidence that backs it up.

Put these pieces of supporting evidence in order of importance (in your opinion). Be prepared to justify your list.

1 Quotes from a conservation group spokesperson
2 Photographs
3 Superpods have been seen before on three occasions.

4 The numbers of dolphins were estimated.
5 The report was able to say where the dolphins were seen.

ACTIVITY 4: EXPLICIT AND IMPLICIT MEANING

Read the statements below. Identify which are explicit and which are implicit.

1 Over 1,000 dolphins were seen off the Pembrokeshire coast.
2 We like dolphins.
3 Dolphins are a sign of healthy seas.
4 The dolphins were seen somewhere between Milford Haven and Lundy.

5 Such a large number of dolphins have never been seen before in this area.
6 This is a good place to spot dolphins.
7 It's a privilege to see them.
8 A conservation charity conducts surveys of dolphins quite often.

ACTIVITY 5: DRAWING INFERENCE

Drawing an inference means using knowledge and information to come to conclusions, as you did in the earlier article on children's confidence with technology. From the article we can infer that:

▶ dolphins are quite rare in British waters

▶ large numbers of dolphins are not often seen together

▶ the waters off the Pembrokeshire coast are reasonably clean and healthy.

The piece is also biased as it is very pro-dolphin. We can see that from words like 'spectacular' and the 'super' in superpod. The fact that Cardigan Bay is a 'fantastic' area to spot dolphins suggests that they are a sight people are keen to see. A similar piece about sharks or dogfish is unlikely, as we tend to fear sharks and have little knowledge about dogfish.

> **Now you have completed the section, do you think your confidence has increased?**
>
> I can identify the main point from a piece of information.
>
> I can identify supporting points from a piece of information.
>
> I know what explicit and implicit meanings are.
>
> I can 'read between the lines' of the information I have been given and infer the hidden meaning or subtext.
>
> Always ⇨ Usually ⇨ Sometimes

! Top tips

'Quote' can be used as a noun, 'The quote tells us…', or as a verb, 'He quoted Shakespeare perfectly.' In the English GCSE, you will need to find quotes from the given text and use them in your answer. You can say: 'The quote tells us …' or 'Another quote to illustrate this is …'. However, the writer or the characters in the passage are likely to be using their own words, not taking them from someone else, so to say 'The writer quotes that …' is incorrect.

BE EXAM READY

▶ To identify and interpret fact, opinion, bias, inference, subtext, main ideas and supporting ideas in a text
▶ To understand the effect of these types of information
▶ To explain why a writer uses these types of information

How confident are you in these skills already?

I can identify fact, opinion, bias, inference, subtext, main ideas and supporting ideas in a text.

I can understand the effect of these types of information.

I can explain why a writer uses these types of information.

Always ▯⇨ Usually ▯⇨ Sometimes

In this unit, you have built up your skills from identifying fact and opinion, understanding the difference between main and supporting points, explicit and implicit meaning and learning how to infer 'hidden' meaning. You will now combine these skills in analysis of the text on page 40.

 Top tips

When you are answering a comprehension question, never say what is *not* in the text. You may feel anxious if you cannot find the techniques you were taught to look for by your teacher. Not all techniques are in every text. There is no point saying 'there are no facts in this text' or 'no opinions are given here'. Concentrate on analysing the techniques that *are* used.

 QUESTION 1

Read the following extract on page 40 about life in Hong Kong.
What impression does the writer convey of Dai Mui's life?
Look for:
• fact and opinion
• main and supporting points
• evidence of bias
• explicit and implicit meaning. [10]

 Top tips

Don't concentrate your answer on the text's presentation. Comments on heading size, font and general layout should be *extremely* brief. In an English exam, your examiner wants to award most marks for your response to language and meaning. Talking at length on how the text *looks* is a superficial interpretation and will not earn you many marks.

CARDBOARD DREAMS

In one of the most amazing cities on earth, dawn has yet to break. 79-year-old Dai Mui begins her daily routine: collecting cardboard boxes from a 24-hour convenience store near her home.

At 5am, Dai has already filled her metal pushcart with boxes, cans, plastic bottles, and satchels of expired bread.

"The shopkeepers are very kind. They give me food that expired the day before, which cannot be sold anymore," Dai smiles as she pushes her little four-wheeler up a short slope in Ho Man Tin.

MONEY FROM WASTE

A streetlamp shines on the drops of sweat on Dai's wrinkled face, accentuating the lines that mark the passing of almost eight decades.

She unloads her cardboard boxes at a street corner where they will be collected by a recycling truck in return for money. She will earn 70 Hong Kong cents (50p) for every 1kg of waste she collects.

"I work every morning, every day of the week. I can earn HK$40 to HK$60 (£3.50–£5) a day and I save it up to pay for my rent," she says as she walks around in search of more cardboard. Dai seems upbeat about her housing costs, in a city where the average apartment in central Hong Kong has just 40 metres square of floor space and costs around £450,000 to buy.

As the sky turns into a sleepy shade of morning blue, Dai glances at her watch and hurries to a nearby bus stop.

NEXT STOP

Dai is on her way to her next checkpoint: the Hung Hom cross-harbour bus station where she collects newspapers from stock market traders and millionaires, bustling on their way to the glittering office blocks of Hong Kong's Central District.

Life in Hong Kong is not always easy for older people who don't have a family to support them

In Hung Hom, Dai quickly checks each rubbish bin for newspapers. She then hovers to and fro between bus stops where passengers have just got off double-deckers.

"Thank you, sir! Thank you, miss!" she calls out as people hand her newspapers and magazines.

As the clock ticks to 9.30am, Dai sits on the roadside and bundles up the fruits of her labour with pieces of white nylon string. When evening turns to night and the rich will sweep back to the mansions of Victoria Peak, Dai will shuffle back to her cramped, dilapidated flat in the working class West Kowloon area of the city, ready to begin it all again tomorrow.

South China Morning Post, 16 November 2014

Self-assessment

- Explicit meaning. The text is about someone who is desperately poor. Dai Mui's life seems very hard: she 'collect(s) cardboard boxes', relies on food donations and gathers recycling from 'each rubbish bin'. They are desperate actions.
- Opinion in the opening line: 'one of the most amazing cities on earth'. Strikes a contrast with her lowly life.
- Facts: she is 79, working by 5am, earns a meagre wage in contrast to high housing costs. These statistics shock us.
- Main and supporting points: main points in heading and subheadings; supporting points in the smaller details of her life.
- Structure also follows main and supporting point pattern: follows a day in her life, with main events and small details of each of her stopping points.
- Bias/implicit meaning: the writer never offers outright sympathy for Dai Mui but it is implied throughout. Her age, 'wrinkled face', 'drops of sweat' and her 'smiles', 'upbeat' nature and grateful thanks to commuters, portray her as vulnerable and likeable.
- The stark contrast presented between rich and poor not only further highlights her difficult life but is an implicit criticism of those who live in luxury. 'Bustling on their way' and 'sweep back' suggest self-absorption. Mansions are contrasted with her 'cramped, dilapidated' flat, in a 'working-class' area.
- Verbs which suggest Dai Mui's hard work and constant movement and which further our sympathy include 'collecting', 'filled', 'pushes', 'unloads', 'walks', 'glances', 'hurries', 'hovers', 'calls' and 'bundles' and contrast with 'shuffles' at her day's end when she is clearly exhausted.
- Adverbs further the idea of her hard work, as she works 'quickly'.

Comparing sample answers

Tick every point you think deserves credit.

Can you think of any advice to give the first candidate?

What is good about the second answer and why would it get full marks?

Sample answer 1

Dai Mui's life seems very hard. She is old and very poor and is working at five o'clock in the morning so that she can earn a bit of money. She eats out of date food and collects rubbish so that she can survive. The facts about her life are very shocking. It tells us that she is 79 years old and will only earn about £3.50–£5 a day which makes us feel very sorry for her. She seems grateful for the little things in life. We feel even sorrier for her when we read about 'the stock market traders and millionaires' who live in mansions when she lives in a 'cramped, dilapidated' flat. The writer wants us to feel sympathy for her when we read this and to dislike the rich people who don't seem to care that much about her.

Sample answer 2

The writer conveys a striking impression of Dai Mui's life. In the first line, we are given the writer's opinion of Hong Kong as 'one of the most amazing cities on earth' and then immediately move to the contrast of this poor and elderly woman's harsh life. She pushes a cart of recycling, practically begs for food and is trapped in this 'daily routine'.

The main points of her life are presented clearly and then the details add even more sympathy.

Her age is emphasised. Her 'wrinkled face' with its 'lines' of 'nearly eight decades' highlights the fact that she is too old to be working at all. This builds our sympathy for her.

Shocking facts are used. She earns £3.50–£5 a day, which is clearly never going to be enough for the £450,000 apartments which the writer tells us are an 'average' price for Hong Kong. We are told that she consequently lives in a 'cramped, dilapidated' flat. The writer is clearly biased towards this lady and wants us to feel sorry for her and we can understand why. Her situation is desperate and seems even worse when the writer tells us about the 'stock market traders and millionaires' who seemed locked in their own, perfect world. The rich aren't criticised explicitly but we receive the impression that the writer believes they should do more to help people like Dai Mui, instead of 'bustling on their way' to work to make more money. This seems even more unfair when we read how busy Dai Mui is herself, 'collecting' rubbish, as she 'pushes' her cart, 'unloads' it and 'hurries' around, all for £3.50.

At the end of the passage, she 'shuffle(s)' back home. The verb reminds us of how old she is, and conveys an impression of hopelessness.

Now that you have completed the section on explaining about language, do you think your confidence has increased?

I can identify and interpret fact, opinion, bias, inference, subtext, main ideas and supporting ideas in a text.

I can understand the effect of these types of information.

I can explain why a writer uses these types of information.

Always ⇨ Usually ⇨ Sometimes

Unit 5
Explaining language

OBJECTIVES

▶ To be able to understand why a writer has chosen certain words
▶ To be able to explain the effect of the words chosen

How confident are you in these skills already?

I understand what the question is asking me to do.
I can find and identify the key words in a piece of writing.
I can understand why a writer has chosen to use certain words.
I can explain the effect of the words clearly and effectively.

Always   ▯⇨   Usually   ▯⇨   Sometimes

When you read a passage, article, leaflet or report, you will often be expected to explain what impressions the writer wanted to create.

Get going

Step 1   Work on your skills

ACTIVITY 1: IMPRESSIONS OF THE JEWELLER

Read the following extract from *Tears of the Giraffe* by Alexander McCall Smith, set in Botswana. Mma Ramotswe and Mr Matekoni are a middle-aged couple who have just become engaged.

Think about what impressions you have of the jeweller.

The premises of Judgement-day Jewellers were tucked away at the end of a dusty street. Inside the shop, standing behind the counter, was the jeweller. He smiled at them. 'I saw you outside,' he said. 'You parked your car under that tree.'
Mr Matekoni introduced himself, as was polite, and then he turned to Mma Ramotswe. 'This lady is now engaged to me', he said. 'She is Mma Ramotswe, and I wish to buy her a ring for this engagement.' He paused. 'A diamond ring.'
The jeweller looked at him through his shifty eyes, and then glanced sideways at Mma Ramotswe. She looked back at him, and thought: There is intelligence here. This is a clever man who cannot be trusted.

'You are a fortunate man,' said the jeweller. 'Not every man can find such a cheerful, fat woman to marry. There are many thin, complaining women around today. This one will make you very happy.'

Mr Matekoni acknowledged the compliment. 'Yes,' he said. 'I am a lucky man.'

'And now you must buy her a very big ring,' went on the jeweller. 'A fat woman cannot wear a tiny ring.'

Mr Matekoni looked down at his shoes. 'I was thinking of a medium-sized ring,' he said. 'I am not a rich man.'

'I know who you are,' said the jeweller. 'You can afford a good ring.'

Mma Ramotswe decided to intervene. 'I do not want a big ring,' she said firmly. 'I am not a lady to wear a big ring. I was hoping for a small ring.'

The jeweller threw her a glance. He seemed almost annoyed by her presence – as if this were a transaction between men and she was interfering.

'I'll show you some rings,' he said, bending down to slide a drawer out of the counter below him. 'Here are some good diamond rings.' He placed the drawer on top of the counter and pointed to a row of rings nestling in velvet slots. Mr Matekoni caught his breath. The diamonds were set in the rings in clusters: a large stone in the middle surrounded by smaller ones.

'Don't pay any attention to what the label says,' said the jeweller, lowering his voice. 'I can offer very big discounts.'

Find a quotation or piece of evidence from the extract to support each of these impressions of the jeweller:
▶ He is a good salesman.
▶ He is observant/nosy.
▶ He may be untrustworthy.
▶ He uses flattery.
▶ He is sneaky.
▶ He is prepared to embarrass Mr Matekoni.
▶ He is sexist.
▶ He knows the townspeople and all about them.
▶ He is a persistent salesman.

Step 2 Practise your skills

ACTIVITY 2: IMPRESSIONS OF THE FOUNDRY

Read the following extract taken from *Nice Work* by David Lodge.

Jane Penrose is an English teacher who is being shown around a factory.

Think about what impressions you have of the foundry and identify the key words used by the writer to create these impressions.

Even this warning did not prepare Jane for the shock of the foundry. They entered a large building with a high roof hidden in gloom. The place rang with the most barbaric noise Jane had ever experienced. The floor was covered with a black substance that looked like soot, but grated under her shoes like sand. The air reeked with a sulphurous smell and a fine drizzle of black dust fell on their heads from the roof. It was a place of extreme temperatures: one moment you were shivering in an icy draught from some gap in the wall, the next you felt the frightening heat of a furnace on your face. Everywhere there was indescribable mess and disorder. It was impossible to believe that anything new and clean and mechanically efficient could come out of this place.

Now copy and complete the table.

POINT	EVIDENCE	EXPLANATION
The **foundry** was not what Jane was expecting.		
The building was dark.		
It was noisy.		
Everything was unpleasant.		
The smell was unpleasant.		
There were extremes of heat and cold.		
The mess was indescribable.		

 Top tips

Remember to use phrases such as:

- This suggests . . .
- This implies . . .
- The word . . . creates the impression that . . .
- The writer makes us think . . . by using the words . . .

Foundry – a factory specialising in producing things made from metal moulds, such as wheels

Step 3 Challenge yourself

 ACTIVITY 3: IMPRESSIONS OF THE TEACHER

Read this passage from *Broken Homes* by William Trevor. A teacher from a local school has visited Mrs Malby because he wants some of his pupils to paint her kitchen.

What impressions does the writer create of the teacher and how are they created?

'It's just that I wondered,' she said, 'if you could possibly have come to the wrong house?'

'Wrong? *Wrong?* You're Mrs Malby, aren't you?' He raised his voice. 'You're Mrs Malby, love?'

'Oh, yes, it's just that my kitchen isn't really in need of decoration.'

He said quite softly, what she'd dreaded he might say: that she hadn't understood.

'I'm thinking of the community, Mrs Malby. I'm thinking of you here on your own. Put it like this, Mrs Malby: it's an experiment in community relations.'

'It's just that my kitchen is really quite nice.'

'Let's have a little look, shall we?'

She led the way. The man glanced at the kitchen's pink walls and the white paintwork and then, to her horror, he began all over again as if she hadn't heard a thing he'd been saying. He repeated he was a teacher from the local school. He repeated what he had said before about these children: that some of them came from broken homes. The ones he wished to send her on Tuesday came from broken homes, which was no joke for them. He felt, he repeated, that we all had a special duty where such children were concerned.

Mrs Malby nodded. It was just, she explained, that she was thinking of the cost of decorating a kitchen which didn't need decorating. 'Freshen it over for you,' the man said, raising his voice. 'First thing Tuesday, Mrs Malby.'

He went away and she realised that he hadn't told her his name. The visit from this man had bewildered her from the start. As well as the oddity of not giving his name, he had not said where he'd heard about her. Added to which, and most of all, her kitchen wasn't in the least in need of decoration. However, she went over in her mind what the man said about community relations. There was also the fact that the man was trying to do good, helping children from broken homes.

Top tips

- Identify the key words/ phrases in the passage.
- Track through the passage methodically from beginning to end.
- Try to include an overview of your impression at the beginning of you answer.
- Remember to use the P-E-E technique (point, evidence, explanation).

ACTIVITY 4: MODEL ANSWER

Here is a model answer to show you how to write your own response:

From the beginning the teacher doesn't seem to be a very pleasant man (overview) because he seems quite rude in the way he treats Mrs Malby. When Mrs Malby thinks he might have the wrong house, he seems to snap at her, repeating 'Wrong? *Wrong?*' twice as if he can't believe what she has said. The writer has used italics the second time so he might be almost shouting at her. He asks her twice if she is Mrs Malby which seems quite aggressive and unpleasant to an old woman and he raises his voice so he seems a bit of a bully . . .

Top tips

Remember:

- Every sentence should earn you a tick.
- Use textual evidence to support your points.
- Look at what is said and the words used by the writer to create this impression.

Finish writing this answer yourself.

Now that you have completed the section on explaining about language, do you think your confidence has increased?

I understand what the question is asking me to do.

I can find and identify the key words in a piece of writing.

I can understand why a writer has chosen to use certain words.

I can explain the effect of the words clearly and effectively.

Always ⟹ Usually ⟹ Sometimes

Improve your skills

OBJECTIVES

▶ To practise explaining a writer's ideas and viewpoints
▶ To develop a secure approach to explaining the effect of the words chosen

How confident are you in these skills already?

I understand which questions are asking me to give my impressions of a text.

I can use a variety of reading strategies to understand the impressions created in a text.

I can select relevant details and key words to prove how an impression is created.

I can structure and organise my answer chronologically, methodically and effectively.

Always   ▢⇨   Usually   ▢⇨   Sometimes

You have already learned that impressions are the views you might have of a person, place or organisation and that these impressions are created by the way details and words are chosen by the writer.

Step 1   Work on your skills

 ## ACTIVITY 1: P-E-E PARAGRAPH

Read the following extract from the novel *About a Boy* by Nick Hornby.

What impression does the writer create of Marcus's mum? Write a P-E-E paragraph (point, evidence, explanation) to explain your decision.

Marcus knew he was weird and knew that partly it was because his mum was weird. She just didn't get this, any of it. She was always telling him that only shallow people made judgements on the basis of clothes or hair. She didn't want him to watch rubbish television or listen to rubbish music or play rubbish computer games. She could explain why it was better to listen to Joni Mitchell or Bob Marley (who happened to be her two favourite singers) than Snoop Doggy Dogg, and why it was better to read books than to play on the Gameboy. But he couldn't pass any of this on to the kids at school. Lee Hartley – the biggest, loudest and nastiest of the kids he'd met yesterday – would thump him if he tried to explain that he didn't approve of Snoop Doggy Dogg because he had a bad attitude to women.

It wasn't all his mum's fault. Sometimes he was weird just because of who he was, rather than what she did.

You could begin with the following overview or write your own.

> Marcus's mum tries hard and seems to mean well but her influence is not very helpful and not necessarily good . . .

! Top tips

- Remember to pull out words and phrases that help create this impression.
- Aim to write at least three quarters of a page.
- Take approximately 12 minutes to write your answer.
- Remember to begin by including an overview.

Step 2   Practise your skills

ACTIVITY 2: JUNK FOOD HEAVEN

Read the extract 'Junk Food Heaven' from Bill Bryson's *Notes from a Big Country*. Bill Bryson is an American who lived for many years in Britain.

Some weeks ago I announced to my wife that I was going to the supermarket with her next time she went because the stuff she kept bringing home was not fully in the spirit of American eating. Here we were living in a paradise of junk food – the country that gave the world cheese in a spray can – and she kept bringing home healthy stuff like fresh broccoli. It was because she was British, of course. She didn't really understand the rich, unrivalled possibilities for greasiness and goo that the American diet offers. I longed for artificial bacon bits, cheese in a shade of yellow unknown to nature and creamy chocolate fillings, sometimes all in the same product. I wanted food that squirts when you bite into it or plops onto your shirt in gross quantities. So I accompanied her to the supermarket and while she was off squeezing melons and pricing mushrooms I made for the junk food section – which was essentially all the rest of the store. Well, it was heaven. The breakfast cereals alone could have occupied me for most of the afternoon. There must have been 200 types, and I am not exaggerating. The most immediately arresting was called Cookie Crisp, which tried to pretend it was a nutritious breakfast but was really just chocolate chip cookies that you put in a bowl and ate with milk. Brilliant. I grabbed a box of the cereals and sprinted back to the trolley.

'What's that?' my wife asked in the special tone of voice with which she often addresses me in retail establishments.

'Breakfast,' I panted as I dashed past, 'and don't even *think* about putting it back and getting muesli.'

I had no idea how the market for junk food had grown. Everywhere I turned I was confronted with foods guaranteed to make you waddle, including a whipped marshmallow sandwich spread called Fluff, which came in a tub large enough to bath a baby in. Aisle 7 ('Food for the Seriously Obese') was especially productive. It had a whole section devoted exclusively to Toaster Pastries. And what exactly is a toaster

pastry? Who cares? It was coated in sugar. I grabbed an armful.

I admit I got a little carried away – but there was so much and I had been away so long. It was the breakfast pizza that finally made my wife snap. She looked at the box and said, 'No.'

'I beg your pardon, my sweet?'

'You are not bringing home something called breakfast pizza. I will let you have' – she reached into the trolley for some samples – 'Cookie crisp and Toaster Pastries and . . .' She lifted out a packet she hadn't noticed before. 'What's this?'

I looked over her shoulder. 'Microwave pancakes,' I said.

'Microwave pancakes,' she repeated, but with less enthusiasm.

'Isn't science wonderful?' I said.

'You're going to eat it all,' she said. 'Every bit of everything that you don't put back on the shelves now. You do understand that?'

'Of course,' I said in my sincerest voice.

And do you know she actually made me eat it. I spent weeks working my way through a symphony of American junk food, and it was awful. Every bit of it.

 What impressions do you get of Bill Bryson, his wife and the relationship between them?

You must refer closely to the text in your answer.

Practise your exam timing by writing your answer in approximately 12 minutes.

! **Top tips**

- Make sure every sentence you write will gain a tick. Every sentence should be making a point.
- Work through the passage in a chronological, methodical way from the beginning to the end.
- Remember to include at least six points with evidence from the extract in support.
- Begin your sentences with 'I think . . .' or 'I feel . . .' to keep your answer focused.

Step 3   Challenge yourself

ACTIVITY 3: ASSESS YOURSELF

Write down one thing you think you did well and one thing you need to improve in order to boost your mark.

? Assess your progress. Did you:

- give a range of points?
- work through the extract methodically and chronologically?
- use plenty of evidence from the text to support your points?

Now you have completed the section, do you think your confidence has increased?

I understand which questions are asking me to give my impressions of a text.

I can use a variety of reading strategies to understand the impressions created in a text.

I can select relevant details and key words to prove how an impression is created.

I can structure and organise my answer chronologically, methodically and effectively.

Always ⬜⇨ Usually ⬜⇨ Sometimes

⬜⇨ Next steps...

1 Using a range of texts such as extracts from novels, leaflets, advertisements and brochures, practise this type of question.
2 Practise answering questions under timed conditions so you will be able to work under pressurised conditions when you finally sit your exam.
3 Always use words/phrases from the text to support your answer.
4 Make sure you work through the whole of the extract. Don't give up! The more points and evidence you provide, the higher the mark you will score.

OBJECTIVES

▶ To adopt a confident approach to answering exam questions
▶ To feel confident about writing under timed conditions

How confident are you in these skills already?

I am confident about what the question is asking me to do.

I feel confident about explaining the effect of key words in a piece of writing.

I am confident about answering exam questions.

I feel confident about explaining my points under timed conditions.

Always   ⇨   Usually   ⇨   Sometimes

You have already practised explaining the impressions a passage might give and how these impressions are created by the way details and words are chosen by the writer. Now you will have the chance to look at sample answers to exam questions, mark your own responses and write under timed conditions.

 QUESTION 1

Read this extract from *The Road to Wigan Pier* by George Orwell which was first published in 1937 after he had visited the industrial north of England.

What impressions does Orwell create of the working conditions in a coal mine? How does he create these impressions?

When you go down a coal mine it is important to try to get to the coal face when the 'fillers' are at work. The machines are roaring and the air is black with coal dust and you can actually see what the miners have to do. At those times the place is like hell, or at any rate like my own mental picture of hell. Most of the things one imagines in hell are there, except the fire, for there is no fire down there except the feeble beams of lamps and electric torches which scarcely penetrate the clouds of coal dust.

When you have finally got there – and getting there is a job in itself – you crawl through the last line of pit props and see opposite you a shiny black wall three to four feet high. This is the coal face. Overhead is the smooth ceiling made by the rock from which the coal has been cut; underneath is the rock again, so that the space you are in is only as high as the ledge of coal itself, probably not much more than three feet. Most shocking of all is the frightful, deafening din from the conveyor belt which carries the coal away. The air is foul, the heat is unbearable and you cannot see very far, because the fog of coal dust throws back the beam of your lamp, but you can see the line of kneeling men driving their shovels under the fallen coal and flinging it swiftly over their left shoulders. They are feeding it on to the conveyor belt, a moving rubber belt a couple of feet wide which runs behind them. Down this belt a glittering river of coal races constantly. In a big mine it is carrying away several tons of coal every minute. The coal is shot into tubs and then dragged to the cages and hoisted to the outer air.

✔ Self-assessment

Here are some points you may have included in your answer.

Some impressions:

- the heat
- the noise
- the darkness
- the dust
- the cramped space
- the lack of fresh air
- the difficulty of movement
- it is like hell

How the impressions are created:

- The heat is 'unbearable'.

- The machines are 'roaring'/the 'din' is 'frightful' and 'deafening'.
- Lamps and torches scarcely penetrate the dust/ the beam is thrown back.
- The dust is a 'fog'/the air is 'black'.
- Men have to crawl/they work kneeling/only three to four feet of space.
- The air is 'foul'.
- 'getting there is a job in itself'
- The simile of hell is used except for the fire.

Did you find a quote to support each point you made?

Did you score a tick/credit for every sentence you wrote?

Did you find at least six impressions?

Did you track through the extract chronologically and methodically?

⏱ QUESTION 2

Read this factsheet adapted from material provided by the British Boxing Board of Control. What impression do you have of the British Boxing Board of Control in this extract?

BOXING. . .THE FACTS

There is considerable ignorance about the way in which professional boxing is administered in Britain today and this is something we, the British Boxing Board of Control, wish to put right.

IN DEFENCE OF BOXING

The belief that it is wrong for young men to be paid, sometimes handsomely, to hit each other and for an audience to pay to witness such a performance is a belief that all Board representatives respect, although we do not agree with it.

We would make a number of points in defence of boxing:

No one is forced either to box, or to pay to watch boxing. Boxing audiences are not motivated by any bloodlust, but in the main are knowledgeable and compassionate.

Boxing gives young men a chance to achieve something and be somebody; it teaches the need for law and order, and encourages the learning of self-discipline and respect.

Boxing promotes qualities such as sportsmanship, courage and dignity. It appeals to many young people on the fringes of society, offering them a chance of avoiding delinquency and of growing into responsible citizens. It is therefore an acceptable activity both morally and socially. Boxing is highly regulated and safer than most other physical-contact sports.

The banning of boxing would merely send it underground and the era of the illegal prize fight would return with all its horrific implications.

THE SAFEGUARDS

Of course, boxing is not to everyone's taste and the British Medical Association has campaigned against it. However, the facts, both medical and statistical, support boxing. The main danger is the risk of brain damage, but we recognise that it is there and we have taken a series of steps to counteract it.

These include:
- Compulsory brain scans for every boxer on an annual basis
- Two medical officers at the ringside for every contest
- Compulsory medical checks after every contest
- Clearly identifiable doctors and paramedics at the ringside, seated where they can see clearly and gain immediate access to the ring should a boxer require treatment.

CONCLUSION

We believe that the good the sport can do for young people far outweighs the fact that they take punches under strictly controlled conditions. They do so of their own free will and it must remain their right to make that decision. We exercise our authority in a totally unbiased way. It is worth stressing that the Board is a non-profit making organisation and that none of our members can have a financial interest in the sport. Peter Corrigan wrote in *The Independent on Sunday*: 'The British Boxing Board of Control is without doubt the most responsible body in world boxing.' Statements of this kind show that we have a great deal to live up to, and we fully recognise that we have to continue our mission to make boxing even safer.

Self-assessment

Here are some points you may have included in your answer.

Some impressions of the British Boxing Board of Control:
- They are lovers of boxing as a sport.
- They are experts/knowledgeable/official/authoritative.
- They are responsible.
- They sound unbiased/balanced view/fair-minded/reasonable.
- They are not involved for personal gain.
- They are concerned about the health and safety of the boxers/compassionate/caring.
- They think it is good for society.

- They are not complacent.
- They are defenders of individual freedom.

How the impressions are created:
- 'we understand'/'we recognise'/'we respect'
- 'the right balance'
- Stress on 'non profit making'
- List of personal and social benefits
- Recognise dangers but show what they have done (list of safeguards)/medical checks
- Quotation from journalist
- Sense of 'mission' to make boxing safe/dedicated to the sport
- Looking for improvements
- Unemotional, factual approach

Did you find a quote to support each point you made?

Did you score a tick/credit for every sentence you wrote?

Did you find at least six impressions?

Did you track through the extract chronologically and methodically?

Comparing sample answers

Tick every point you think deserves credit.

Could you find evidence to support each point?

What two things would you do to improve each response?

Answer 1

Boxing is shown as a very safe sport with lots of safety controls such as compulsory brain scans and two medical officers at every ringside. No one is forced to box and it's the boxer's right to choose. The factsheet shows all the good side of boxing.

Answer 2

The impressions we have of the British Boxing Board of Control is that they are a caring, responsible organisation as they emphasise how much they've done to make it safer with lots of medical supervision, etc. The quote from the newspaper at the end shows that they are well thought of. They are also not greedy because they are a non-profit making organisation. They only use facts not opinion which makes them seem really honest.

Answer 3

The impression we have of the British Boxing Board of Control is that it is a caring organisation because they have taken 'a series of steps' to ensure that the boxers are as safe as possible. To emphasise how much they've done they list these safeguards with bullet points under a separate heading and imply that there are even more they haven't mentioned. They also appear to be fair and reasonable because they don't pretend that theirs is the only viewpoint. In fact, they 'respect' the opposition's opinion and 'recognise' that there is some danger, which makes them seem very unbiased and balanced. The whole factsheet is calm and quite unemotional, as if the 'facts' speak for themselves and they don't have to use a lot of dramatic, emotive language or manipulative devices to put their case. The quotation from the journalist prominently placed at the end is obviously very influential and presents the Board in a positive and glowing light. A superlative is used in 'the most responsible body in the world of boxing' and presumably Peter Corrigan is not biased or connected to the British Boxing Board of Control so we can trust his view, especially as 'The Independent' is a well-respected newspaper. They cleverly emphasise the freedom of the boxers so that they appear to be defenders of free choice. They also stress that they are a non-profit making organisation so they are only interested in the sport, not in cashing in on the boxers who are risking their health. Finally, the word 'mission' right at the end makes them seem almost like religious crusaders with a sacred duty to protect boxing!

Now you have completed the section, do you think your confidence has increased?

I am confident about what the question is asking me to do.

I feel confident about explaining the effect of key words in a piece of writing.

I am confident about answering exam questions.

I feel confident about explaining my points under timed conditions.

Always ⇨ Usually ⇨ Sometimes

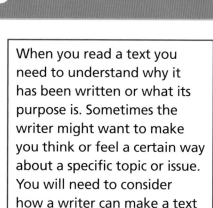

Unit 6
Talking about language

OBJECTIVES

▶ To understand how a writer makes a text interesting
▶ To be able to explain how writers use language and structure to make a text interesting

How confident are you in these skills already?

I can understand what makes an interesting text.

I can understand how writers communicate meaning.

I can comment on how effective meaning is conveyed.

Always ⇨ Usually ⇨ Sometimes

When you read a text you need to understand why it has been written or what its purpose is. Sometimes the writer might want to make you think or feel a certain way about a specific topic or issue. You will need to consider how a writer can make a text interesting for a reader.

Get going

Step 1 Work on your skills

 ACTIVITY 1: POLAR BEARS

Study this article from the *Telegraph* magazine by Peter Baumgartner about an adventure holiday he took to the town of Churchill in Canada – polar bear capital of the world.

HELP! IT'S THE SCARE BEAR BUNCH

Churchill is the polar bear capital of the world; every year the town's 1000 inhabitants have to share their living space with 200 of them. The bears invade Churchill while waiting for Hudson Bay to freeze over so they can hunt on the ice for seals. Just before the onset of winter, Churchill has a six week 'season' and adventure tourists arrive to watch them. However, as amusing and clumsy as they look, polar bears are among the most dangerous predators on earth. Fast,

strong and unpredictable, they weigh up to 600kg and attack without warning.

Denise, our tour guide, cautions me at once when I try to photograph a warning sign that reads, 'Polar bear alert. Stop. Don't walk in this area.' The notice is at the edge of town in front of a few rocks. 'That is not a good idea,' she snaps, pulling me back. She has twice seen a bear appear suddenly from behind the rocks. 'What do you do in such cases?' I ask.

'Take your clothes off and slowly walk backward.'
She laughs. 'Bears are naturally curious. They stop at each garment and sniff it. You must never run away. The best thing is gradually to make for the nearest house.'

In Churchill, house doors are supposed to be unlocked all the time for just such emergencies. If someone sees a bear in town, they call the polar bear police and the rangers come and knock it out with an anaesthetic gun. The sleeping white giant is placed in the 'polar bear jail'. At the jail we find just two bears under lock and key. There is space for 32. Last year the rangers caught and freed 108 bears. When the jail is full, the bears are flown out 30 miles to the north and released.

How does the writer try to make this article interesting for the reader?
You might find it useful to complete this grid to help you organise your ideas.

EVIDENCE	WHY IT IS INTERESTING
Use of 'Help!'	
Use of 'scare bear'	(rhyme) to suggest danger/excitement
Invasion of a large number of bears	
Tone is informal and humorous	
Use of 'polar bear capital'	
First person viewpoint	
Writer unaware of dangers	
Tour guide snaps at him	
Use of dialogue	
Advice from the guide	
Use of 'polar bear jail'	
Use of statistics	
Emotive words/phrases	
Contrast between the look of the animals and their deadly potential	

Using the P-E-E technique (point, evidence, explanation) that you have already learned and practised, write ten sentences making use of the information you have collated in the grid.

Step 2 — Practise your skills

ACTIVITY 2: MAKING IT INTERESTING

Read the article *Going the Distance* by Anne Johnson.

Going the Distance

At this year's London marathon, Fauja Singh aims to beat his best time of six hours. It seems a modest ambition – but then, he is 93. Anne Johnson finds out what drives him on.

He trains in a calm, measured way, maintaining a steady pace like a man entirely in control of himself and his destiny. He likes routine and he runs 9 or 10 miles a day, every day, clocking up 70 miles a week. There is nothing particularly unusual about that, you think – there are plenty of people who take their training seriously – until you discover that this man is 93 years old. He ran in the London marathon for the first time at the age of 89 with no course preparation. He looks the picture of health. He keeps his weight to just eight stone, which for his height of six feet, is almost nothing. Surprisingly, Fauja Singh hasn't been running for very long. He took it up when his wife died 11 years ago and since then it has been the focus of his life. Initially he thought of running as therapy. Then it became his passion. It wasn't long before he was introduced to Harmander

Singh who took on the role of being Fauja's trainer, although training does not involve a proper track: Fauja simply trains by running on his local streets. In all, he has done six marathons – four in London and one each in Toronto and New York. When he runs in London, he is hoping to come in below the six hour mark – having crossed the line last year in his best time of 6 hours and 43 seconds.

Fauja is intensely competitive and loves the fact he has beaten the London Marathon record for his age group – runners in their 90s – every year. So his pace may be steady, but it's obviously not quite as slow as it looks. 'He loves being a star,' Harmander says. 'He values being recognised and he sees it as raising the profile of Sikhs.' He also believes that his running can help others. Currently he runs for Bliss, a charity that helps premature babies; he sometimes also runs under the banner of the British Heart Foundation in honour of some of his jogging friends.

Now answer the following question.

How does the writer, Anne Johnson, try to make this article interesting?

You should think about:

▶ the use of headline, introduction and photograph

▶ what she tells us about Fauja Singh that is interesting.

Try to make at least seven points and select details/evidence from the article to support each point.

Remember that every sentence you write in your answer should earn you a tick/credit otherwise there is no point in writing it.

When you have completed your response, look at this list of possible points you could have made in your answer. How many did you include?

Use of headline, introduction and photograph

▶ Headline suggests pushing on to the very end (pun connected with finishing the rounds in a boxing contest) but also literally the 26 miles.

▶ Introduction highlights contrast between 'modest ambition' of completing marathon in 6 hours but then set against his astonishing age.

▶ Picture shows an old – but determined – man/he's training on pavement.

What she tells us about Fauja Singh that is interesting

▶ He's 93!

▶ His training/routine/he has a trainer

▶ He's not been running very long

▶ Why he ran–wife died/therapy

▶ He's done six marathons in four years

▶ Runs it in around six hours

▶ Despite his age he's intensely competitive

▶ Holds records for his age group

▶ Raises money for charity

Do you think that every sentence you wrote was relevant to answering the question?

Do you think that every sentence would earn you a tick/credit?

Did you remember to support each point with evidence or details from the article? If you didn't, go back and find the evidence you could have used.

Step 3 Challenge yourself

 ACTIVITY 3: IMPROVING THE RESPONSE

Read these sample student responses to the question you have just completed.

Sample answer 1

Anne Johnson tries to make it interesting by giving facts about him. 'This man is 93 years old.' She tells us the targets he sets himself – to beat the six-hour mark. Anne Johnson puts a picture of him training, which enables us to imagine him actually running the London Marathon. She says that he only started running when his wife died 11 years ago.

What advice would you give this student in order to improve the response?

For example, do you think the student has done the following things successfully:

▶ written enough?

▶ selected details from the article?

▶ selected enough details from the article?

▶ explained his/her points?

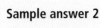

Sample answer 2

The title 'Going the Distance' suggests that the article has something to do with long distances. It is short but yet makes you want to read on. The subtitle is like a small summary about what the article is about. In it, it says 'finds out what drives him on'. This shows that even a quite serious article is quite jokey and makes you want to read more. Anne Johnson tells us he is 93. This is interesting because you don't see many elderly people compete in events like this. Also when you look at the photo you can tell he's old but not as old as he is. He travels to New York to compete and this shows great ambition. She tries to make the article interesting by not making it too long with too many facts as that just puts people off reading because there isn't a real story to it. Here she's added things to make it interesting like 'he loves being a star'.

Do you that this answer is better than Sample answer 1?

Explain why/why not.

For example, do you think the student has written enough?

Has the student selected enough details from the article?

Has the student selected details from the beginning, middle and end of the article?

This answer can still be improved.

What advice would you give this student in order to improve the response?

Sample answer 3

At first you don't become interested in the title as it just seems to be an average man who wants to run the marathon. What catches your eye is the fact that he is 93. You are shocked and want to read on to see if it is really true. His age has been put at the end of the sentence so that it comes as a surprise after what you've read. She makes it interesting as well to reveal his training programme which is very basic to run a marathon. 'He likes routine and he runs 9 or 10 miles a day.' This grabs the reader's attention as you are amazed at how a man of 93 can run 9 to 10 miles a day and you want to read on. 'He ran in the London event for the first time at the age of 89.' It is shocking to think that he could have taken it up at such an old age. When you look at his picture you can see that he is actually real because of the photo. It inspires everyone in a way. She then goes on to talk about his background and how he took up running because his wife died. So this is where you realise what is actually driving him on. What also makes it interesting is that he's doing it for charity and also for himself, 'he initially thought of running as therapy. Then it became his passion.'

Is this response better than the previous two sample answers?

Explain why/why not. Decide what this student does that the previous two students don't.

Can you think of anything this student needs to do in order to improve the response?

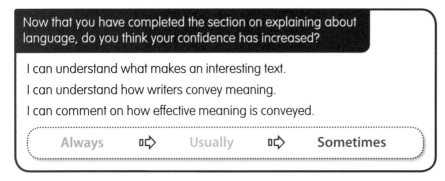

Now that you have completed the section on explaining about language, do you think your confidence has increased?

I can understand what makes an interesting text.

I can understand how writers convey meaning.

I can comment on how effective meaning is conveyed.

Always ➡ Usually ➡ Sometimes

Improve your skills

OBJECTIVES

▶ To understand how a text presents the viewpoint and attitude of the writer
▶ To identify and write about **bias**

How confident are you in these skills already?

I can work out what a writer thinks or believes.

I can work through the text line by line so I can recognise any change in the thoughts and feelings of the writer.

I can link each different thought or feeling of the writer to evidence from the text.

I can use the words in the question as a way into my answer.

Always   Usually   Sometimes

! Top tips

Here are a few techniques writers sometimes use to communicate their opinion. You may come across these features in some of the texts that you read.

- Sarcasm – saying the exact opposite of what they really mean with the intention to mock or insult
- Humour
- Opinion
- Facts and statistics
- Italics – can be used as a form of emphasis and to suggest emotion and surprise or disbelief
- Repetition

It is not always easy or straightforward to work out a writer's **point of view** about a person, place or issue because writers do not always say exactly what they mean. As a result of this, the reader often has to play the role of detective and read between the lines of what is actually stated in order to decide what a writer's words and language are really telling us. This is often known as '**implied meaning**' or '**implicit meaning**'.

> **bias** – when the writer only gives his/her point of view so the text is one sided
> **point of view** – the writer's opinion
> **implicit/implied meaning** – what is suggested, not explicitly stated, by the writer's use of language

Step 1 Work on your skills

ACTIVITY 1: EMOTIVE LANGUAGE

a You have already learned that emotive language causes people to feel emotional about people, places or issues. Rank this list of adjectives in order from least emotive to most emotive.

- ▶ good
- ▶ superb
- ▶ wonderful
- ▶ OK
- ▶ nice
- ▶ dreadful
- ▶ appalling
- ▶ bad
- ▶ frustrating
- ▶ disappointing

Writers will often use emotive words and language when they are communicating their thoughts and feelings. Remember to look out for this and be prepared to explain what the words tell us about their point of view.

b Using this knowledge, read the following paragraph from an article by Peter Scudamore, a champion jockey, in which he writes about The Grand National.

> I love the Grand National – it's the toughest horse race in the world, demanding the very most from both horse and rider – and I'll defend it to my last breath. But even I can see that this year's race was agonising to watch for many, and not the greatest advertisement for the sport. Two horses were killed on live television and the winning horse seemed close to collapse as it passed the winning post.

What does Peter Scudamore think about the Grand National horse race?

Pick out some emotive words and phrases to prove your points.

Write a paragraph to answer this question, remembering to refer closely to the text.

Remember to use the P-E-E chain (point, evidence, explanation).

c Now study this article by Richard Girling from *The Sunday Times* about the problem of seagulls in Britain's cities.

> Seagulls are thriving in cities – attacking people, deafening residents, damaging buildings, spreading urban panic and disease. By 2014 there could be as many as 6 million of them, a new urban menace. Herring gulls are huge birds, each one a kilo in weight, with a wingspan of $4\frac{1}{2}$ ft. A thousand of them in the air together are a tonne of hardened muscle, and they possess vicious beaks and claws. The way things are heading, Britain's town centres are going to be overrun by an army of greedy and aggressive birds that will defend the rooftops against all-comers. They have already made headlines with their attacks on humans, whose heads they slash with their claws at 40 mph. They are notorious for the way their cries keep people awake, and their droppings also cause damage to buildings and cars.

What are the writer's thoughts and feelings about seagulls?

Copy and complete the grid to help you organise and formulate your ideas.

EVIDENCE	WRITER'S OPINION
Seagulls are thriving.	
A list of damaging verbs, 'attacking', 'deafening', 'damaging', 'spreading'	
They are 'huge' birds.	
'hardened muscle'	
'vicious beaks and claws'	
'an army of greedy and aggressive birds'	
They have attacked humans.	

Can you add any more details to the grid?

Step 2 Practise your skills

(!) Top tips

- Always work through your answer line by line so you can recognise and track any changes in the writer's thoughts and feelings.
- Think about how you begin your sentences. It is helpful to begin your sentences with 'The writer thinks …' or 'The writer feels …' because this will make sure you have the correct focus on the question.
- Avoid beginning sentences with 'I think …' or 'I feel …' because you are not asked for your thoughts and feelings and this approach could easily lead you away from the question.
- Remember to use evidence to support every thought and feeling expressed by the writer.

📄 ACTIVITY 2: REINVENTING THE WHEEL

Read the article 'Reinventing the Wheel' in which Charles Starmer-Smith rediscovers his lost love of cycling.

My own conversion to cycling has come late. I remember childhood holidays in France where I would pedal among the villages in search of bread and adventure, revelling in the freedom of pedal power as I sped past vineyards, forests and fields, imagining I was one of the Tour de France greats. Then came adolescence and girls and guitars and cars. Cycling was no longer cool and the limitations of a bike, rather than its freedoms, became all too apparent. It couldn't play Pearl Jam on the stereo, with the roof down and a pretty girl in the passenger seat, like my battered silver Mini. However, there is nothing like purchasing new gear to give you an inflated sense of your sporting prowess. Only a week ago, tackling the gentle contours of Richmond Park, I was puffing like a man on an epic ascent of some legendary alpine peak. Now, dressed in the outfit I spent a small fortune on this morning. I stride down the stairs with new purpose, ready to join the British Lycra Brotherhood. I feel streamlined and ready for anything the Alps of Surrey can throw at me.

'I want a divorce.' My wife's words stop me in my tracks. She looks both amused and horrified as I put on my helmet and fluorescent bib. 'You look like a Village People tribute act.' Deflated, I hurry past the mirror and wheel my bike out into the winter drizzle for the short journey to the North Downs.

A wave of smugness washes over me as I weave easily through the noisy commuters and choking traffic which stall everyone else's progress. One right turn towards Box Hill and suddenly … silence.

✏️ **What thoughts and feelings has Charles Starmer-Smith had about cycling at different stages of his life? You should write about his thoughts and feelings as:**

▶ **a boy**

▶ **an adolescent**

▶ **a man.**

You must select detail from the text in your answer.

Practise your exam timing by writing your answer in approximately 12 minutes.

When you have finished your answer, have a look to see how many of these possible points you have included.

As a boy he loved it.

- ▶ It was a source of 'adventure'.
- ▶ He revelled in the 'freedom'/excitement.
- ▶ He could go fast, imagining he was in the Tour de France.

As an adolescent he lost interest.

- ▶ He was distracted by girls, guitars and cars.
- ▶ He no longer thought cycling was 'cool'.
- ▶ He thought the bike had 'limitations'.
- ▶ A bike couldn't play music or have a pretty girl in the passenger seat.
- ▶ He thought his car was better.

As a man he rediscovered cycling.

- ▶ He found it exhausting/daunting ('puffing like a man on … an alpine peak').
- ▶ The purchase of new gear makes him feel 'purposeful' and 'ready for anything'.
- ▶ He feels an 'inflated sense' of his 'sporting prowess'.
- ▶ He feels 'deflated' when his wife mocks his appearance/feels ridiculous or embarrassed.
- ▶ He feels smug as he negotiates the busy traffic.
- ▶ He feels happy/content as he experiences 'silence'/release.

Did you include enough detail in your answers?

How many of these points did you make in your answer?

Did you include points to answer each of the three bullet points?

Did you begin your sentences with 'The writer thinks …' or 'The writer feels …' ?

Step 3   Challenge yourself

ACTIVITY 3: HOW FAIR IS FAIRTRADE?

Study the following internet essay 'is Fairtrade really fair?'

IS FAIRTRADE REALLY FAIR?

Fairtrade products and labels are all around us and while we appear to be willing to pay that little bit extra for Fairtrade goods, I am beginning to wonder whether it is really beneficial to farmers in developing countries.

We are surrounded by Fairtrade products. No longer do we have to trek to a shop in the back of beyond to purchase that chocolate bar or woolly jumper. Now you can find it all on the High Street. Retailers like Top Shop sell Fairtrade tunics, bubble tops and racer back vests. Marks and Spencer work with more than 600 Fairtrade cotton farmers in developing countries, using their products in the making of chinos, jeans and a variety of fashion items. You can find Fairtrade coffee and chocolate at Sainsbury's and they have just made it known that in future they will only sell bananas from Fairtrade producers.

At the moment there are more than 2,500 products and lines carrying the Fairtrade mark in the UK. Last year we spent £290 million on Fairtrade food, furniture and clothing. The aim of Fairtrade is obvious – to help producers in developing countries get a fair deal. In order to earn the Fairtrade label, companies have to pay more than the market price for their product. As a result the producers have more money to spend on educating their children and other things needed in their community.

However I'm not completely convinced that Fairtrade is a good idea. By concentrating on just getting a fair price, the Fairtrade movement doesn't develop mechanisation so workers are still forced to do back breaking, strenuous work and don't escape from their poverty trap.

So, is Fairtrade really fair? Is it simply about helping workers in developing countries to accept their position by giving them, at best, just a little bit more? I fear that workers in developing countries could become trapped by Fairtrade, making them rely on charity minded shoppers in the West. I fear that these workers will become prisoners of our shopping patterns as they depend on us paying higher prices for their goods.

We all want to show charity to those who are less fortunate than ourselves but I also wonder how we can view a few extra pennies a day from Fairtrade as an amazing achievement for poor workers. I have just read about Fairtrade farmers in Peru who were paid about £2 a day from working from 6am to 4.30pm. This would be more than they would normally earn but not significantly more. Surely we are right to be anxious that the Fairtrade movement is concentrating on raising wages by fairly small amounts instead of really changing poor countries through development and modernisation. Maybe Fairtrade is more about making Western shoppers feel good about themselves instead of changing the lives and futures of people in developing countries. It feeds our vanity and flatters ourselves but at the end of the day does little to improve the lives of the poor.

In my opinion, Fairtrade is not the best way out of poverty for everyone.

What does the author think and feel about Fairtrade?

Write your answer to this question.

Now look at this list of possible points.

How many did you include in your answer?

- ► He feels that Fairtrade is 'increasingly common'.
- ► He thinks its aims are clear and admirable.
- ► He is not convinced it is a really good idea.
- ► He thinks it doesn't address mechanisation.
- ► It allows poverty and back-breaking work to continue.
- ► It can be a trap for workers.
- ► They can become dependent on charity shoppers/prisoners of the well intentioned.
- ► He thinks a few pennies extra is not a great success or achievement.
- ► He thinks Fairtrade just gets small amounts of extra money for the poor.
- ► It doesn't change anything.
- ► It is more about 'flattering' Western shoppers.
- ► It makes us feel good about ourselves.
- ► It doesn't really improve the lives of the poor.

Use the guide below to award a mark for your answer.

Give 1 mark if you …	made simple comments and occasionally selected detail from the text, or if you copied out parts of the text which are irrelevant to the question. You haven't really answered the question.
Give 2–4 marks if you …	made simple comments based on surface features of the text or showed awareness of more straightforward implicit meaning. Your answer may have been thin, brief or the details you selected from the text were not relevant to the question.
Give 5–7 marks if you …	selected appropriate detail from the text to show clear understanding of the writer's viewpoint/ideas.
Give 8–10 marks if you …	selected appropriate detail to sustain a valid interpretation. Your answer may have been be detailed, thorough, perceptive and covering a range of points accurately and coherently.

Now that you have completed this section, do you think your confidence has increased?

I can work out what a writer thinks or believes.

I can work through the text line by line so I can recognise any change in the thoughts and feelings of the writer.

I can link each different thought or feeling of the writer to evidence from the text.

I can use the words in the question as a way into my answer.

Always   ▯⇨   Usually   ▯⇨   Sometimes

BE EXAM READY

OBJECTIVES

▶ To adopt a confident approach to answering exam questions
▶ To feel confident about writing in timed conditions

How confident are you in these skills already?

I am confident about what the question is asking me to do.

I feel confident about explaining a writer's viewpoint in a text.

I feel confident about answering exam questions.

I feel confident about writing under timed conditions.

Always ⇨ Usually ⇨ Sometimes

QUESTION 1

Read this piece of travel writing by Roy Hattersley.

The Lasting Resort

Blackpool is the seaside resort of regular return. The more you see of it, the more you want to see. Blackpool is part of Britain's gloriously unsophisticated past. That is its charm and its attraction. The tourist office is anxious to emphasise that the typical Blackpool holiday maker gets younger by the year. The elderly gent with the exposed braces, knotted handkerchief on his head, rolled up trousers and wife who spills over the side of her deckchair, is rare enough to become a protected species.

   Whatever the weather, people still go to Blackpool for fresh air and fun. It competes successfully with package tours to Spain because it exudes a respectable sort of vulgarity. This is what makes Blackpool a continuing delight. Along the front – where the souvenir shops seem dedicated shrines for the hunter of kiss-me quick hats – they argue that Blackpool, with its mammoth coach park within walking distance of the sea, space invader games in the amusement arcades and the brightest stars of television in the Winter Gardens, is as up to date as any of its competitors. However, it is different. It is this difference that creates its sometimes bewildering popularity. On a wet summer morning the rain sweeps in from the sea … and the visitors show every sign of enjoying themselves. Blackpool must be the cold-weather bathing capital of the world. Even in the holiday season, the seafront is sometimes prohibited to tourists to safeguard them against being swept into the Irish Sea. But everybody seems happy. Couples walk arm in arm, leaning backwards against the wind at 45 degrees to the pavement. And they find it fun.

The magic is at its strongest after the illuminations have been switched on. Blackpool undoubtedly possesses the best collection of flickering electric light bulbs in western Europe. It is difficult to describe the special delight of sitting, bumper to bonnet, in a stream of traffic which moves forward at less than five miles an hour whilst the drivers stare at flashing shapes and colours between the lampposts. Passengers on the illuminated tramcar – proud to become part of the glory they had only aspired to observe – describe their evening's pleasure in basic terms. Asked why they spend the time and money, they reply, 'To come to Blackpool.' Being in Blackpool is enough.

Blackpool offers a special sort of summer pleasure. It is quite cheap, heroically cheerful and perfectly matched to the needs of its visitors. Blackpool is the idea of happiness. Nobody can ask for more than that.

What does the writer think and feel about Blackpool?

Practise writing your answer in approximately 12 minutes.

Remember to refer to the details from the text in your answer.

✔ Self-assessment

Here are some points you may have included in your answer.

Overview/an indication or summing up of what the whole article told us about the writer's thoughts and feelings.

- It is an affectionate picture of Blackpool
- but also aware of its shortcomings.
- It praises its attractions and charms
- but also uses humour and irony.
- Blackpool is tacky but he loves it.

In more specific detail

- Gloriously unsophisticated
- Respectable vulgarity

- The elderly gent and his wife
- A continuing delight
- Commercialism of souvenir shops
- Modern attractions
- Bewildering popularity
- Description of weather
- Cold-water bathing capital
- Best collection of flickering light bulbs
- The glory
- Cheap and heroically cheerful
- Blackpool is the idea of happiness.

Did you include an overview or a general impression of what the whole article told us?

How many of the possible points did you include?

Did you write any sentences that were irrelevant to your answer and so wouldn't earn you credit?

Did you score a tick/credit for every sentence you wrote?

Did you track the writer's thoughts and feelings chronologically through the passage?

Did you include enough points in your answer?

Now read this article by Lucie Morris in the *Daily Mail*.

THE SUNSHINE ISLE WHERE TEENAGE TEARAWAYS ARE SENT TO LEARN A LESSON

With its cooling palms and spectacular views of the nearby mountains, it is an idyllic holiday destination. This Caribbean paradise is also the playground of a group of notorious teenage tearaways. While their hard-working classmates shiver in the cold and rain back home, the seven are spending two weeks in the sun, enjoying swimming, tennis and trips to the sights of Jamaica, as part of a scheme organised by the Divert Trust. The students are considered to be the most disruptive in their school, failing to do their homework or showing any commitment to school work and school activities. The youngsters are staying at a former hotel built in 1888 in a suburb of the capital Kingston ... just a few miles away are soft white beaches lapped by the bluest of oceans.

The Divert Trust, a charity which offers support to children at risk from school exclusion, has footed the full £5,000 bill for the trip and claims it will be 'highly beneficial'. The pupils have a full programme of events for their stay, which included visits to schools and cultural institutions. The tearaways will also enjoy days out at the Dunn's River Falls tourist attraction and a museum dedicated to reggae legend Bob Marley.

Outraged parents and governors at the school condemned the venture as an insult to better-behaved classmates. A governor at the school said the school was 'very annoyed' at the decision to take them away.

The trip was originally aimed at 19 pupils who were set individual targets for improvement but only 7 performed well enough to secure a place.

What is the writer's attitude to the Divert Trust scheme?

Remember to refer to details from the text in your answer.

Time yourself and write your answer in 12 minutes.

 Self-assessment

Here are some points you may have included in your answer.

Overview/an indication or summing up of what the whole article told us about the writer's attitude
- Not exactly encouraging enthusiastic support
- Tends to dwell on the 'holidays for hooligans' angle
- Encourages reader to view this as expensive, misguided and outrageous
- Emotive language
- Sarcasm and mockery

In more specific detail
- Stress on how idyllic the location is
- They are there to be taught a lesson (sarcasm?).

- The idea of a holiday is mentioned (early in article).
- A playground
- School governor's comment
- Contrast between 'tearaways' enjoying a Caribbean paradise and 'hard-working' classmates shivering in the cold and rain of Britain
- Special treat
- A former hotel
- High cost is mentioned
- Mentions visits and lots of trips
- Highlights outrage of parents and governors

Comparing sample answers

Look at these sample answers and put them in rank order from best to worst.

Sample answer 1

The writer is trying to make us disrespect the Divert Trust by making the teenagers sound as disrespectful of the education they are offered as possible and making the holiday sound very relaxing. The writer thinks the scheme is a bad thing by creating a negative picture of the Trust by explaining how close they are to the beaches and about their trips to Dunns River Falls. The writer describes the Caribbean as the 'idyllic holiday destination' and attacks the Divert Trust by saying the seven teenagers will spend their two weeks in the sun, enjoying swimming, tennis and trips to sights in Jamaica.

Sample answer 2

I think the writer is encouraging people to be bad at school and then they will get a holiday which would be a wonderful experience. She says that the Trust is really good and the teenagers would benefit from it. She says what they are going to do while they are out there.

Sample answer 3

The writer feels disgusted by the scheme. Firstly, she compares the 'disruptive' tearaways on the scheme to the 'hardworking' pupils who have to 'shiver in the cold back home'. She clearly feels anger about the Trust's policies. We see her disgust when she describes the setting with its 'cooling palms and spectacular views'. We see her negative feelings when she describes the teenagers' itinerary such as visiting 'tourist attractions' and other trips. The use of travel brochure language shows she feels angry at the scheme for rewarding troublemakers.

What would you do to improve each answer?

For example, has the student:
- written enough?
- selected details from the article?
- selected enough details from the article?
- explained his/her points?
- selected details from the beginning, middle and the end of the article?

Now that you have completed the section, do think your confidence has increased?

I am confident about what the question is asking me to do.

I feel confident about explaining a writer's viewpoint in a text.

I feel confident about answering exam questions.

I feel confident about writing under timed conditions.

Always ⇨ Usually ⇨ Sometimes

Unit 7
Analysing language

OBJECTIVES

▶ To recognise a range of techniques and their effect
▶ To write effectively about what is said (content) and how it is said (the techniques used by the writer)

How confident are you in these skills already?

I can identify techniques used for creating effects in a text.

I can use evidence from the text to support my points.

I can organise and write my answers clearly and effectively.

Always ➪ Usually ➪ Sometimes

Don't be worried by the word 'analyse'! It simply means that you need to read the text or section of writing in detail and think about how a reader would respond to it. You will need to look closely at the language used and be able to write about the effects created.

It is easy to recognise this type of question as it usually begins with the word 'how'. For example, **How does the writer make this section of the text tense and dramatic?** or **How does the leaflet persuade us to support a particular cause?**

Get going

Step 1 Work on your skills

ACTIVITY 1: CLEAR AND PRECISE

Read the following statements and decide whether they provide a clear and precise explanation, or whether they are too vague and generalised and could be applied to any text.

▶ The headline is big and bold and stands out.

▶ The words grab the reader's attention.

▶ The rhetorical question in the heading immediately draws the reader in by making him/her think about his own behaviour.

▶ The writer makes the reader want to read on.

▶ The writer uses interesting words to make us think.

▶ The writer uses emotive language such as 'agony' to make us feel sympathy for the animals.

▶ The subheading emphasises the worrying consequences and dangers caused by the hurricane.

▶ The use of alarming statistics highlights the scale of the problem of childhood obesity.

! Top tips

● Avoid making general or vague comments that don't focus on the language used or link back to the text in any way.
● If your comment could refer to any piece of text, then it is not worth making.
● Be specific.

ACTIVITY 2: HEADLINES AND HEADINGS

When you read a text containing headlines, headings and/or subheadings, you need to look closely at their specific effects.

Consider the following headlines. Identify the words and techniques that you think would affect the reader in some way. Try to explain the effects of the language/techniques you have chosen.

We can only stop the slaughter of innocent dolphins with your help.

Braving The Seas For Daring Rescue

A once-in-a-career rescue saw Brixham lifeboat men haul eight sailors from a cargo ship that was dangerously listing in a heaving sea in the middle of the English Channel.

Cabin Boy Conqueror of the World

After nine months, teenager Mike Perham is set to become the youngest person to sail solo around the globe when he returns to Britain next week.

> **! Top tips**
>
> Don't always use the phrase 'The writer says . . .' to show what the writer is trying to do.
>
> Instead use some of the following verbs, which indicate how the writer is trying to influence the reader:
> - suggests
> - implies
> - emphasises
> - shows
> - illustrates
> - gives an example

Step 2   Practise your skills

ACTIVITY 3: GIVE BLOOD

Look at the following heading and opening section from a leaflet encouraging readers to give blood.

Do something amazing today . . . practically anyone can . . .

Becoming a blood donor is really very simple. As a rule as long as you're in good health and aged between 17 and 60 you can become a regular blood donor. The National Blood Service which covers all of England and North Wales needs nearly two and a half million blood donations in each year to help the NHS save lives.

But only 6% of the UK population who are currently eligible, do so . . .

Consider this student response which is explaining the effects of the headline and language.

The words in the headline are in bold so they stand out. The headlines are coloured red so this makes it bright so the reader will think. There are interesting words in the headline such as 'amazing', 'today' and 'anyone' and this makes the reader want to read on.

How would you improve this student response?

▸ Has the student selected evidence from the headline?

▸ Has the student explained the effects of the words?

▸ Are the student's comments detailed and specific to this text?

 Write your new improved version.

Then continue your answer by focusing on the paragraph of text.

Step 3   Challenge yourself

 ACTIVITY 4: P-E-E TECHNIQUE

You can apply the same techniques to any piece of text.

Study this extract from *Tales of a Troubled Land* by Alan Paton and consider how the writer shows that Mike is frightened in these lines.

Then suddenly Mike was free. He saw the bus returning, and in its headlights he could see the shape of a man close to him. He was facing death and for a moment he was filled with the injustice of life: why should he have to die like this when he had always been hardworking and honest? He lifted the heavy stick and brought it down on the head of his pursuer, so that the man crumpled to the ground, moaning and groaning as the life drained out of him.

Mike turned and began to run wildly again, but in the darkness ran into the side of an old lorry which sent him reeling. He lay there for a moment expecting the blow that would kill him, but even then his wits came back to him, and he turned over twice and rolled under the lorry. His stomach seemed to be coming into his mouth, and his lips could taste sweat and blood. His heart thumped wildly in his chest, and seemed to lift his whole body each time that it beat. He tried to calm it down, thinking it might be heard, and tried to control the noise of his gasping breath, but he could not do either of these things.

 You should think about:

▸ what happens to make Mike frightened

▸ the writer's use of language to show he is frightened

▸ the effect on the reader.

To help you organise your ideas, copy and complete this grid.

EVIDENCE	COMMENT
'He was facing death'	
	He thinks about the unfairness of life.
	His fear made him act with unusual ferocity.
In a panic he runs 'wildly'.	
'ran into the side of an old lorry which sent him reeling'	
He expects the blow that will kill him.	
	His instinct for self-preservation makes him act.
	He is almost sick with fear.
	He struggles to keep quiet and still.
	He thinks he will give himself away or they will discover him because of the noise he makes

Now write your answer to the question. Make sure to use the P-E-E technique (point, evidence, explanation) you have learned in earlier units.

Assess your answer.

- ▶ Would every sentence gain a tick/credit?
- ▶ Have you used evidence from the passage to prove your points?
- ▶ Tick every point you have made, highlight your evidence and underline every explanation you have given. By doing this you will easily be able to check whether you have given evidence and an explanation for each of your points.

Now that you have completed this section, do you feel your confidence has increased?

I can identify techniques used for creating effects in a text.

I can use evidence from the text to support my ideas.

I can organise and write my answers clearly and effectively.

Always ⇨ Usually ⇨ Sometimes

Improve your skills ⬇

OBJECTIVES

- ▶ To practise writing about how effects are created
- ▶ To develop a secure approach to analysing language

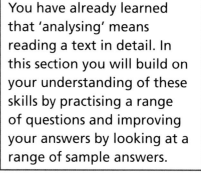

How confident are you in these skills already?

I understand which questions are asking me to analyse effects.

I can write about the effects of language in a coherent and analytical way.

I can use the P-E-E technique with some confidence.

Always ⇨ Usually ⇨ Sometimes

You have already learned that 'analysing' means reading a text in detail. In this section you will build on your understanding of these skills by practising a range of questions and improving your answers by looking at a range of sample answers.

Step 1 Work on your skills

ACTIVITY 1: LLANDUDNO

Here is a description of a guesthouse in Llandudno written by Bill Bryson and from his book *Notes from a Small Island*.

Further along the front there stood a clutch of guesthouses and a few of them had vacancy signs perched in their windows. I selected a place that looked reasonable enough from the outside – it promised colour TV and coffee-making facilities, about all I require these days for a lively Saturday night – but from the moment I set foot in the door and drew in the mildew smell of damp plaster and peeling wallpaper, I knew it was a bad choice.

I was about to flee when the proprietor appeared and revealed that a single room with breakfast could be had for £19.50 – little short of a swindle. It was entirely out of the question that I would stay the night in such a dismal place at such an extortionate price, so I said, 'That sounds fine,' and signed in. Well, it's so hard to say no.

My room was everything I expected it to be – cold and cheerless, with ugly furniture, grubbily matted carpet and those mysterious ceiling stains that bring to mind a neglected corpse in the room above. Fingers of icy wind slipped through the single, ill-fitting window. The curtains had to be yanked violently before they would budge and came nowhere near meeting in the middle. There was a tray of coffee things but the cups were disgusting and the spoon was stuck to the tray. The bathroom, faintly illuminated by a distant light activated by a length of string, had curling floor tiles and years of accumulated muck packed into every corner and crevice. A bath was out of the question so I threw some cold water on my face, dried it with a towel that had the texture of a Weetabix and gladly went out.

Bill Bryson clearly hates the guesthouse. How does he communicate these feelings to you?

First, identify the details from the passage that you want to include in your answer.

Compare your results with this list of details from the passage. How many did you identify?

▶ the mildew smell
▶ a swindle at £19.50
▶ 'cold and cheerless'
▶ ugly furniture
▶ grubby, matted carpet
▶ mysterious stains
▶ wants to flee
▶ icy wind
▶ curtains do not fit and will not move
▶ filthy bath
▶ dark, dingy bathroom
▶ towel like a Weetabix
▶ He went out 'gladly'.

As you have learned in earlier units, it is always a good idea to begin your answer with an overview.

Look at the list below. Which of these statements could you select as a possible overview statement to begin your answer?

- ► It is tacky and dreadful.
- ► It is high class and in perfect condition.
- ► It is expensive for what it is.

- ► It is warm, welcoming and pleasant.
- ► It seems dirty, neglected and uncomfortable.

Read this answer written by a student in response to this question.

Bill Bryson conveys his feelings about the guesthouse by mixing facts with his own opinions of the place. His opinions include 'cold and cheerless', 'ugly furniture' and 'the cups were disgusting' which work well with facts like 'mysterious ceiling stains', 'years of accumulated muck' and 'the spoon was stuck to the tray'. The mixture of fact and opinion work well together to make the place sound absolutely horrendous.

He uses language in words and phrases that sound disgusting. For example 'grubbily matted carpet' and 'neglected corpse in the room above'. He also describes the 'mildewy smell' of the room and 'fingers of icy wind' which give impressions of the smells and feelings in the room, also 'texture of a Weetabix'.

He creates the atmosphere mostly using language. 'I knew it was a bad choice' tells us that something bad is coming and 'cold and cheerless' tells us how the room makes him feel.

Pick out two things that the student does well.

What two pieces of advice would you give to improve this response?

Choose two sentences and rewrite them.

Step 2 Practise your skills

 ACTIVITY 2: THE RETURN OF AN ICE AGE

Now try practising your skills on this passage.

This extract is from *The Forgotten Enemy* by Arthur C. Clarke, which is about the return of an ice age to Britain.

That momentary pause almost cost him his life. Out of a side street something huge and white moved suddenly into his field of vision. For a moment his mind refused to accept the reality of what he saw. Then the paralysis left him and he fumbled desperately for his futile revolver. Padding towards him, swinging its head from side to side, was a huge polar bear. He dropped his belongings and ran, floundering over the snow towards the nearest building. The entrance to an Underground station was only a few feet away. The temptation to look back was intolerable, for he could hear nothing to tell him how near his pursuer was. For one frightful moment the steel gates resisted his numbed fingers. Then they yielded reluctantly and he forced his way through a narrow gap. The monstrous shape reared in baffled fury against the gates but the metal did not yield. Then the bear dropped to the ground, grunted softly and padded away. It slashed once or twice at the fallen rucksack, scattering a few tins of food into the snow, and vanished as silently as it had come.

How does the writer make these lines tense and dramatic? You should write about:

> ▶ **what happens to build tension and drama**
> ▶ **the writer's use of language to create tension and drama**
> ▶ **the effect on the reader.**

You must refer to the text to support your answer.

Copy and complete this grid to help you answer the question.

EVIDENCE	COMMENT
The momentary pause 'almost cost him his life'.	
Something huge and white appears suddenly.	
His mind refuses to accept the reality of what he sees.	
He fumbles desperately for his futile revolver.	
The polar bear is 'huge'.	
He drops his belongings and runs.	
The station is only a few feet away.	
He cannot hear his pursuer.	
The temptation to look back is 'intolerable'.	
The gates resist and this is a 'frightful moment'.	
They open 'reluctantly' and he 'forces his way in'.	
The bear is described as 'monstrous'.	
It attacks the gates in 'baffled fury'.	
It 'slashes' at the rucksack as it retreats.	

! Top tips

Bullet points may sometimes appear on a 'how' question, but this may not always be the case. If bullet points are present, they are there to help you organise your answer and give you some idea about what to cover in your answer. However, it doesn't necessarily mean that you should give equal attention to each bullet point and write the same amount to cover each one.

Step 3 Challenge yourself

ACTIVITY 3: CONSIDERING RESPONSES

Here are some sample answers in response to this question. Read them carefully.

Example A

The phrase 'almost cost him his life' immediately describes how serious the situation is and displays it as a life or death matter. As we do not know anything about the danger except that it is 'huge and white', it increases the suspense and mystery. The adverb 'desperately' portrays the drama and the verb 'floundering' shows his difficulty in getting away, increasing the tension as you are not sure if he will make it. The 'temptation' to look back is described as 'intolerable' increasing the sense of desperation and drama. The sense that he is not going to make it is increased by the fact that the 'gates resisted his numbed fingers'. The moment is described by the adjective 'frightful' and this adds to the tension. The fact that it does not mention whether the gates are locked or not, again increases tension because when the bear 'reared in baffled fury' against the gate you are not sure whether they will give or not.

Example B

This section is dramatic and the pace picks up, 'almost cost him his life'. Panic, excitement and rage all contribute to the tense atmosphere. The writer makes these lines both tense and dramatic because it is sudden and unexpected. The language is strong and words like 'suddenly' and 'frightful' are used. The writer uses a lot of full stops and commas to create short and medium length, dramatic sentences to build up suspense and tension.

Which is the more successful response?

What comment would you make on each response?

Think about the things the answers do well and the areas for improvement.

Now write your own response to this question.

When you have finished, go back and reflect on your performance. Did you:

▶ use a quote to support each point you made?

▶ score a tick/credit for every sentence you wrote?

▶ make at least six points?

▶ track through the extract in order (chronologically) and without missing out chunks/important parts (methodically)?

Now that you have completed this section, do you think your confidence has increased?

I understand which questions are asking me to analyse effects.

I can write about the effects of language in a coherent and analytical way.

I can use the P-E-E technique with some confidence.

Always   ⇨   Usually   ⇨   Sometimes

BE EXAM READY

OBJECTIVES

▶ To adopt a confident approach to analysing language and effects
▶ To feel confident about structuring an answer under timed conditions

How confident are you in these skills already?

I am confident about what a 'how' question is asking me to do.

I feel confident about analysing the effect of language and techniques in a text.

I can use the P-E-E technique with some confidence.

I can write about the effects of language in an organised and thoughtful way

Always ⇨ Usually ⇨ Sometimes

You have already practised answering 'how' questions by developing your skills of analysis. In this section you will have the opportunity to write under timed conditions and improve your technique.

QUESTION 1

Read this article by Petronella Wyatt who describes her experiences with Milky Quayle, a previous champion, at the Isle of Man's infamous TT course, the most dangerous circuit in the world.

Milky is having none of it and I am dragged over to a gargantuan Suzuki. I notice that the starting line is opposite a graveyard. This rather does for my composure, but Milky is on the bike raring to go. I put on my crash helmet and clamber onto the pillion seat. Milky is wearing straps around his waist, which I am supposed to hold onto. I am instructed to punch him if I become nervous. He has evidently never taken a course in logic. In order to punch him I would have to let go of the straps. If I let go of the straps I will fall off and break open my head. It is, as the youth of today would say, a no brainer. Unfortunately, that seems to be exactly what Milky is as well.

We head towards a village on the coast. Before us is a series of evil looking bends. Suddenly Milky drops his elbow and opens the throttle. I am nearly thrown over the front of the bike. Ahead of us is Ballaugh Bridge. It has seen eight fatalities in three years. 'Stop going so fast,' I scream at Milky. He accelerates. Then he decides to brake. My head flies forward as if it has been severed by an axe.

'I just thought I'd stop to point out the areas of interest,' Milky explains. 'We are approaching Ballagarey Corner. It's one of the most dangerous on the circuit.' He continues cheerfully, 'Once I lost a mate there.'

'Lost him? You mean he took a wrong turning?'

'No, he crashed and went home in a coffin.'

We round the corner at 120mph. Sweat is trickling down my arms. Another graveyard flashes by. Does this island consist only of graveyards? Finally, we leave for the Snaefell Mountain Course. Milky tells me we will get up to such speed that to any bystanders I will be a blur. I say I do not want to be a blur. I can see the obituary in the papers: 'A blur died yesterday while attempting the Isle of Man TT course.' As Milky opens the throttle again, we hurtle past another discouraging sign: 'Be very careful. 164 casualties in 3 years.'

We are on dangerous ground. In fact, we are no longer on the ground at all. We are going so fast we are flying three feet above it. 'Where's the bloody ground gone?' I croak. Scenery seems to be zooming towards me. All at once we are back on the ground but I don't like it any better for my left ear is nearly scraping it. A passing lorry almost hits us. I think I am going to black out.

When Milky slows down and finally brakes. 'How fast did we go?' I gasp. He looks at me oddly. He tells me we have hit 166mph and have broken the course's pillion speed record. I shriek with ecstasy and insist we do a lap of triumph. I punch the air and shout out, 'Look at me. I'm on top of the world.'

How does Petronella Wyatt get across to you what it is like to ride the TT course?
You should think about:
- what happens
- the writer's use of language to communicate her feelings
- the effects on the reader.

You must refer to details from the text in your answer.

Now write your answer to the question. Time yourself and write your answer in 12 minutes.

✔ Self-assessment

Here are some points you may have included in your answer.

Techniques (how the writer says it)
- First-hand account stresses pure fear/extreme speeds/danger
- Irony and 'graveyard' humour
- Exaggeration
- Present tense for immediacy
- The language shows her range of emotions, including the thrill of speed.

Content (what the writer says)

Here are some points you may have explored.
- She has to be 'dragged' to a 'gargantuan' bike (nervous and reluctant).
- She notices the graveyard and her composure is 'gone' (images of death).
- She is convinced she will 'break open her head' if she lets go of the straps.
- She calls the situation a 'no brainer' and suggests Milky is the same (crazy).

- The bends are 'evil looking'.
- She is nearly thrown off the bike when Milky accelerates (raw power).
- She is aware of the fatalities at Ballaugh Bridge and 'screams' at Milky to slow down/unnerved.
- When he brakes, her head flies forward as if 'severed by an axe'.
- Milky's cheerful anecdote about his 'lost mate' and her reaction to it
- Sweat is trickling down her arms as they take a corner at 120 mph.
- She notices another graveyard as their speed increases.
- She doesn't want to be a 'blur' and imagines her obituary.
- The 'discouraging sign' emphasises the scale of the casualties.
- They leave the ground and she 'croaks' her question.

- Scenery 'zooms' towards her and her left ear almost scrapes the ground.
- A lorry almost hits them and she thinks she will 'black out' with fear.
- She feels a surge of adrenaline and wants it to last forever.

- She shrieks with ecstasy and wants a 'lap of triumph'.
- She punches the air and feels 'on top of the world'.

Did you find a quote to support each point you made?

Did you score a tick/credit for every sentence you wrote?

Did you track through the extract in order (chronologically) and without missing out chunks/ important sections (methodically)?

Did you include details from the beginning, middle and end of the extract?

Now use this guide to award your answer a mark out of 10.

Give 1–2 marks if …	you have found and started to write about some examples of what it is like to ride the TT circuit.
Give 3–4 marks if …	you have found and written straightforward points about some examples of what it is like to ride the TT circuit. You will have found and used some linguistic terminology simply.
Give 5–6 marks if …	you have explained how a number of different examples show what it is like to ride the TT circuit and shown some understanding of how language and the organisation of events are used to achieve effects and influence the reader, such as the short sentences to emphasise the speed and terror. You will have begun to use relevant linguistic terminology accurately to support what you say.
Give 7–8 marks if …	you have written in detail about how a range of different examples show what it is like to ride the TT circuit and begun to analyse how language and the organisation of events are used to achieve effects and influence the reader. You will have used linguistic terminology accurately to support what you say effectively.
Give 9–10 marks if …	you have made accurate and perceptive comments about how a wide range of different examples show what it is like to ride the TT circuit and provided detailed analysis of how language and the organisation of events are used to achieve effects and influence the reader. You will have explored the subtleties of the writer's technique in relation to how the reader is influenced. You will have used linguistic terminology in a well-considered and accurate way to support your comments effectively.

Now that you have awarded yourself a mark, what do you think you need to do to improve your performance next time?

QUESTION 2

Use these skills to help you tackle this next question.

This passage is taken from *Behind the Scenes at the Museum* by Kate Atkinson. It is set during the First World War. Frank and Jack, two friends from York, have enlisted and are taking part in an attack on the enemy.

Frank was determined not to lose sight of Jack but within seconds he had disappeared and Frank found himself advancing alone through a wall of fog which was actually smoke from the big guns which had started again. Frank kept on walking even though he didn't come across Jack or anyone else for that matter.

It was only after quite a long time that he thought he knew what had happened. He thought he had died, probably a sniper's bullet, and now he was walking through Hell. Just as he was trying to adjust to this new idea he slipped and he was falling down the side of a muddy crater, screaming because he was convinced this was one of the pits of hell and it was going to be bottomless. But then he stopped falling and realised that he was about two-thirds of the way down the side of a huge crater. Below him was thick, muddy-brown water. A rat was swimming around and he was suddenly reminded of a sweltering hot day when he and Jack had taught themselves to swim. Frank closed his eyes and pushed himself into the soft mud and decided that the safest place to be was in the past.

He stayed in the crater for several hours. He thought he might have fallen asleep because he looked up suddenly and the gunsmoke fog had cleared and the sky was blue. Standing above him on the edge of the crater he thought he saw Jack, laughing and smiling and looking like an angel dressed in khaki. There was a thin line of blood along his cheek and his eyes were as blue as the sky. Frank tried to say something but he couldn't get any words to come out. Being dead was like being trapped in a dream. Then Jack put his hand up as if he was waving goodbye and he disappeared over the horizon of the crater. Frank felt a terrible sense of despair and began to shiver with cold. He decided he should try and find Jack so he dragged himself out of the crater and set off in the direction of Jack's disappearance. When, some time later, he staggered into a dressing station and announced to the nurse that he was dead, the nurse merely said, 'Go and sit in the corner with the lieutenant then.' Frank walked over to where the lieutenant, covered in blood from head to foot, was leaning against the wall, staring at nothing. Frank offered him a cigarette and the two 'dead' men stood in silence, inhaling their cigarettes with dizzy pleasure as daylight faded over the first day of the Battle of the Somme.

How does the writer convey the horror of Frank's experience in this extract?
You should write about:
- what happens in the extract
- the language used by the writer to communicate Frank's horror
- the effect on the reader.

You must refer to details from the text in your answer.

Comparing sample answers

Find every point you think deserves a tick/credit.

Can you find evidence to explain each point?

What advice would you give to improve each response?

Now put these sample responses in rank order from best to least successful.

Sample A

The writer makes Frank seem hopeless as 'within seconds' he had lost Jack although he was 'determined' not to. This makes his position seem helpless as he has lost the most important thing to him. The word 'alone' is used which creates a feeling of complete loneliness and how there is no one to help Frank. The metaphor 'a wall of fog' is used to show how Frank cannot see what will happen and shows that it was like a barrier to him. The writer used the repetition of the word 'thought' to show how Frank does not really know what is happening to him. The writer also shows horror with a reference to 'Hell' which makes me think of eternal terror. The verb 'screaming' shows Frank's reactions and portrays a feeling of complete fear. The writer also uses Frank's past to show that he does not really know where he is. When Frank thinks he has seen Jack, the writer uses 'laughing and smiling and looking like an angel' to exaggerate how Jack looks, which makes Frank's situation seem unbelievable as they are in a battle.

Sample B

The writer effectively conveys Frank's horror in his experiences now, remarking on him 'advancing alone through a wall of fog.' There is no one to help him or back him up anymore. Jack has 'disappeared' and it seems as if Frank has lost a lifeline and thus a grip on reality. The feeling of death is a calm certainty that dawns on Frank; 'he thought he had died', and even 'Hell' seems real, as if he only had to 'adjust to the idea.' The trenches were not far removed from his picture of Hell and this only intensifies the horror of the scene. His movement is in slow motion – a 'scream' as he thinks the crater is 'a pit of hell' and 'bottomless'. Death is dragged out and endless in the 'muddy brown water'. Little touches like the 'rat swimming around' make it all seem unreal and not of this world. This is strengthened by Frank's gradual madness – he 'closes his eyes' and lets himself be transported back to the past of swimming with Jack. He concluded it was safer to stay in the past. Jack appears as an 'angel dressed in khaki' and we realise this has finally pushed Frank over the edge. Frank feels that being 'dead was like being trapped in a dream' – he is helpless and is again abandoned by the phantom Jack, succumbing to a terrible sense of 'despair'. The writer uses sardonic humour to underline the plight of the soldiers. When he 'announced to the nurse that he was dead', the nurse is businesslike adding the element of calm in a crazy, surreal environment. Two 'dead men' inhaled their cigarettes with a 'dizzy pleasure'. Frank's horror is put into perspective here and there is a sense of hysteria and turbulent emotions.

Sample C

The writer uses a selection of techniques to convey the horror of Frank's experience in these lines. There is a lot of description and imagery along these lines to describe what Frank is experiencing, 'Thick muddy brown' are words to describe the crater. They allow the reader to imagine the place that Frank has entered. The writer has also used comparisons throughout this section. At first Frank believes he is 'walking through Hell'; hell being the place of our worst fears clearly defines the horror Frank is experiencing. When Frank is in the crater full of mud he recalls a time where he was in similar water. The writer compares a time that was better with what is happening now, a time that was good in comparison with the evil that is now taking place. The sentences are long, increasing the time spent reading and shortening the pace. This extends Frank's experiences. Frank considers himself dead, at first physically 'he thought he had died' and then mentally, he 'announced to the nurse that he was dead'. The horror is portrayed here as being so terrific it has caused him to die inside. The nurse is dismissive of this and shows no consideration and his experience is brushed aside. This adds hopelessness to Frank's experience.

Now, using the skills you have learned, write your own answer to this question.

Now that you have completed this section, do you think your confidence has increased?

I am confident about what a 'how' question is asking me to do.

I feel confident about analysing the effect of language and techniques in a text.

I can use the P-E-E technique with some confidence.

I can write about the effects of language in an organised and thoughtful way.

Always ⇨ Usually ⇨ Sometimes

Unit 8
Comparing writers' ideas

OBJECTIVES

▶ To identify the main themes and ideas in a text
▶ To interpret these ideas through critical reading
▶ To compare and evaluate these ideas across more than one text

How confident are you in these skills already?

I can identify the main themes and ideas in a text.

I can read critically, drawing inferences and conclusions from a text.

I can prove my understanding through supporting my points with textual evidence.

I can compare and evaluate writers' ideas from more than one text.

Always ⇨ *Usually* ⇨ **Sometimes**

When you read a text, you work to make sense of it by understanding its content – what it is about – and engaging with the ideas that it presents. You will interpret these ideas by reading critically. Critically does not necessarily mean that you *criticise* it, it means that you make reasoned, well thought out judgements about what you are reading. In an English exam, you will be expected to justify your interpretations by finding textual evidence to explain your response.

Get going

Step 1 Work on your skills

Different writers have particular viewpoints and perspectives on issues. As we do not all hold the same opinion on subjects and themes, these different ideas will obviously vary from writer to writer. Preparation for your English GCSE requires you to read a range of texts so that you can develop your understanding of different writers' ideas and the ways these are presented. By reading texts from different periods and genres, you will gain an even better understanding of how writers' views and ideas might differ over time. This section will test, through structured questions, the reading of two high quality unseen non-fiction texts (about 900–1200 words in total), one from the 19th century, the other from the 21st century.

 ## ACTIVITY 1: SHORT EXTRACTS

Read each short extract. Identify its main idea and think critically about it, by judging and forming an opinion. If you can explain what elements of the text encouraged you to form this opinion, you are beginning to read critically.

Text A

Motor neurone disease is a debilitating condition in which parts of the nervous system become irrevocably damaged. This leads to an increased difficulty with major motor skills, such as walking, speaking and swallowing which can worsen over the years. It is a cruel condition with symptoms that typically become more marked, leading to the eventual impossibility of carrying out day to day tasks.

Text B

On my first trip to Paris, I kept wondering: "Why does everyone hate me so much?"

Fresh off the train, I went to the tourist booth at the Gare du Nord, where a severe young woman in a blue uniform looked at me as if I were infectious.

"What do you want?" she said, or at least seemed to say.

"I'd like a room please," I replied, instantly meek.

"Fill this out." She pushed a long form at me.

"Not here. Over there." She indicated with a flick of her head a counter for filling out forms, then turned to the next person in line and said: "What do YOU want?"

Bill Bryson, *Neither Here Nor There*

Text C

For the first time in one of his films, professional street trials rider, Danny MacAskill, climbs aboard his mountain bike and returns to his native home of the Isle of Skye to take on a death-defying ride along the notorious Cuillin Ridgeline. Watching this, it is no surprise that Danny has been nominated for 'Actions Sportsperson of the Year'.

You can infer the writers' ideas about their chosen subjects by looking for clues in the extracts. Copy and complete the table below:

TOPIC	WHAT DOES THE WRITER APPEAR TO THINK ABOUT THE TOPIC?	QUOTE FROM THE EXTRACT THAT LED ME TO FORM THIS OPINION
Motor neurone disease	It is a harsh condition.	
Paris		
Biker, Danny MacAskill		

We all bring our own ideas and experiences to what we read. If you know someone with motor neurone disease, you might react more emotionally to Text A than someone who knows nothing about the condition. If you have ever been to Paris, you might engage more readily with Text B. If you have an interest in mountain biking, Text C might particularly appeal to you.

Unless authors are just presenting cold, hard facts, they will write their texts with the same motivations. They bring their own experiences, opinions and even prejudices and bias to what they are writing. What you need to do in an English exam is interpret these ideas. The ideas will often come through in the vocabulary choices the writer has made. You can then evaluate (assess) how effective the writer is at conveying their ideas.

ACTIVITY 2: ANALYSIS

Now add a fourth column to your table, adding a brief analysis of the quote you chose for column 3. You are now assessing *how* the writer conveys their ideas. You are reading critically.

TOPIC	WHAT DOES THE WRITER APPEAR TO THINK ABOUT THE TOPIC?	QUOTE FROM THE EXTRACT THAT LED ME TO FORM THIS OPINION	ANALYSIS
Motor neurone disease	It is a harsh condition.	'cruel'	The disease is personified, as if it actually wants to cause harm.
Paris			
Biker, Danny Macaskill			

 Top tips

Remember that the examiner is checking that you can:

- identify the writer's ideas about a subject
- find the textual evidence that gave you this impression
- assess this evidence by analysing the techniques the writer has used.

Within this, you could also consider the reader's likely response to the topic, by saying, for example, that the ideas are refreshing, shocking or upsetting. However, do not be tempted to add personal opinions that are not linked directly to the text. The question is asking you to analyse the writer's ideas, not include your own personal musings about what you would do in a situation like this.

Step 2 Practise your skills

ACTIVITY 3: SYNTHESISING YOUR FINDINGS

You now know how to identify a writer's main ideas and assess how these are conveyed. To connect texts, you will now need to identify and assess ideas in a second text, synthesising (combining) your findings and interpretations to produce a thorough answer.

Read the extract on the next page.

▶ What are Bill Bryson's ideas about walking in this extract?

▶ Find three points of evidence that give you this impression.

▶ Comment on the evidence you chose, explaining *how* the writer conveys his ideas.

I know a man who drives 600 yards to work. I know a woman who gets in her car to go a quarter of a mile to a college gymnasium to walk on a treadmill, then complains passionately about the difficulty of finding a parking space. When I asked her once why she didn't walk to the gym and do five minutes less on the treadmill, she looked at me as if I were being willfully provocative. 'Because I have a program for the treadmill,' she explained. 'It records my distance and speed, and I can adjust it for degree of difficulty.' Before this, it hadn't occurred to me how thoughtlessly deficient nature is in this regard.

Bill Bryson, *A Walk in the Woods:* Rediscovering America on the Appalachian Trail

Now read the extract below.

▶ What are the writer's ideas about walking in this extract?

▶ Find three points of evidence that give you this impression.

▶ Comment on the evidence you chose, explaining *how* the writer conveys her ideas.

To those of our readers who have long indulged in habits of indolent repose, a walk of from two to four miles would, no doubt, appear to be an effort far too violent to be encountered, and to be suited only to those as are compelled by necessity to bodily labour for their daily subsistence; and yet it is precisely such an amount of exercise as they stand most in need of. By the more opulent of both sexes, bodily exertion of almost every species is viewed too much in the light of a punishment, or, at least, of degradation from their assumed importance; and hence, one of the reasons why it is so little resorted to either as a recreation or a duty.

Emily Thornwell, *The Lady's Guide to Perfect Gentility*, 1856

 Now synthesise your findings by copying and completing the table below.

IDEAS ABOUT WALKING	EVIDENCE FROM *A WALK IN THE WOODS*	EVIDENCE FROM *THE LADY'S GUIDE TO PERFECT GENTILITY*
People will not walk outdoors for even short distances.		
People make excuses not to do it.		
People need to be persuaded to do it.		

An examination question may ask you to respond to each writer's ideas and attitudes separately. For example:

1 These texts both present attitudes to walking.

▶ **What are Bill Bryson's attitudes to walking?**

▶ **What are Emily Thornwell's attitudes to walking?**

Alternatively, a question may imply that you should synthesise the information:

2 What are these writers' attitudes towards walking? How do they present these attitudes?

The question may even ask you to compare the two texts directly:

3 Compare the writers' attitudes to walking. How do they present these attitudes?

For question 3 above, you would be expected to move between the texts, cross-referencing their ideas and the techniques that the writers have used to convey these ideas.

ACTIVITY 4: HOW IDEAS ARE CONVEYED

Add a fourth column to the previous exercise. With attention to the writers' techniques, analyse *how* their ideas are conveyed.

IDEAS ABOUT WALKING	EVIDENCE FROM *A WALK IN THE WOODS*	EVIDENCE FROM *THE LADY'S GUIDE TO PERFECT GENTILITY*	HOW THE WRITERS CONVEY THEIR IDEAS
People will not walk outdoors for even short distances.	'gets in her car to go a quarter of a mile.'	'from two to four miles would … appear to be an effort far too violent.'	
People make excuses not to do it.	The gym provides 'a program' but nature is 'thoughtlessly deficient … in this regard.'	It is 'suited only to those who are compelled by necessity.'	
People need to be persuaded to do it.	'I asked her once why she didn't walk to the gym and do five minutes less on the treadmill.'	'two to four miles … is precisely such an amount of exercise as they stand most in need of.'	

 Top tips

When you move between texts, you will need the appropriate vocabulary to show that you are comparing or contrasting.

Signposting similarities
- like
- as in
- both
- also
- similarly
- likewise

Signposting differences
- by contrast
- whereas
- although
- conversely

Step 3 Challenge yourself

ACTIVITY 5: ATTITUDES TO TEENAGERS

You can now identify writers' ideas, synthesise them and assess how these are conveyed.

Read the extracts on the next page.

Compare the writers' attitudes to teenage behaviour. How do they present these attitudes?

Young people are sloppy and don't dress or talk properly

'Millions of youngsters are too sloppy and slovenly to get jobs because they lack the discipline or skills needed for work,' the chief inspector of schools, Sir Michael Wilshaw, said yesterday. 'School and college leavers are careless about time, lack a work ethic, do not dress or speak well and are lackadaisical,' he added in his scathing remarks.

'Employers think teenagers and those in their early 20s have never been taught how to behave and work or about the attitude they need to get on.'

Sir Michael, head of Ofsted, said there was no point in keeping young people in education until 18 if they did not gain qualifications or were not prepared for the demands of work.

'If they dress inappropriately, speak inappropriately and have poor social skills, they are not going to get a job' he continued.

Mail Online, November 2014

How to combine elegance, style and economy (1856)

In life, you will be placed in a variety of situations. It is important that you should have that habitual self-command that will enable you readily to accommodate yourself to the peculiarities of each; and, at least, to conceal from those around you the secret that you are not perfectly at home. Possibly this is not essential to your passing in good society, but it certainly is essential to the perfection of good manners.

Avoid every approach to a haughty and overbearing manner. It is an exhibition of pride, which is one of the most hateful of all dispositions. As you value your character and usefulness, be always courteous and affable.

These texts have been written over 150 years apart. Use this as an opportunity to illustrate that ideas have changed over time or, if you find it is the case, that similar ideas have prevailed over the years.

 Self-assessment

The following ideas are a guide to points that you may have mentioned in your answer. Note that the writers may not use the same techniques. You do not need to 'tick off' the same points in each text and could pick out any differing approaches in order to show contrasts in the writers' ideas.

- Negative language
- Use of adjectives
- Spoken comments
- A negative tone
- Repetition
- Use of fact and opinion

Now that you have completed the section, do you think your confidence has increased?

I can identify the main themes and ideas in a text.

I can read critically, drawing inferences and conclusions from a text.

I can prove my understanding through supporting my points with textual evidence.

I can compare and evaluate writers' ideas from more than one text.

Always ⇨ Usually ⇨ **Sometimes**

Improve your skills

OBJECTIVES

▶ To read and evaluate texts critically
▶ To present informed judgements of the impact of different ideas in texts
▶ To summarise and synthesise information and ideas from two texts
▶ To connect, compare and contrast writers' techniques

How confident are you in these skills already?

I can read and evaluate texts critically.

I can present thoughtful judgements on the impact of writers' ideas.

I can summarise and combine information from two texts.

I can analyse writers' techniques and connect, compare and contrast them.

Always ⇨ Usually ⇨ **Sometimes**

Now that you can identify and comment on writers' ideas, connect texts and support your conclusions, you can move on to looking more closely at the word choices and techniques that writers employ. As your texts will be from different time periods, you should be able to make interesting points about the similar or different ideas that writers hold and how these ideas are presented. This will show the examiner that you can analyse in detail.

! Top tips

Your two examination texts will be linked by a similar theme or topic. Don't panic –they won't be so dissimilar that you won't be able to make any connections.

Step 1 Work on your skills

! **Top tips**

Structuring your answer

You may wish to write about one text first, then write about the other, connecting them at the end of your response. However, remember that you have limited time in the exam. To connect them at the end, you will need to go over what you have already written, repeating some of your points. You will construct a more sophisticated, analytical answer if you move from one text to the next throughout your response.

ACTIVITY 1: EXPERIENCES OF SURGERY

The language that a writer chooses will tell you something about their opinion on the subject they are writing about.

Read the two extracts below which describe the same medical procedure.

Compare and contrast:

▶ the writers' experiences of surgery

▶ how they convey these experiences.

Extract 1

I arrived at the hospital on the day of my surgery, and was shown to a consultation room where I changed into a theatre gown which looked like it had been fashioned from a circus tent! I was then escorted to the theatre suite and handed over to the theatre nurse. She took me straight into the operating theatre and asked me to lie down on the operating table. I was pleasantly surprised to see that it had sheets and a pillow. Although the room was high-tech, it did not appear to be overly surgical – mercifully! The anaesthetist then arrived, and with a little discomfort, he inserted a needle into my arm, during which time we had a rather surreal conversation about my car (I imagine this was something of a diversionary tactic!) I was not in any pain, but I did have a fiercely dry mouth.

http://www.surreyweightlosssurgery.org.uk/our-patients-gastric-bypass-diary.html

Extract 2

I refused to be held; but when, bright through the cambric, I saw the glitter of polished steel, I closed my eyes. I would not trust to convulsive fear the sight of the terrible incision. Yet, when the dreadful steel was plunged into the skin, cutting through veins—arteries—flesh— nerves—I needed no injunctions not to restrain my cries. I began a scream that lasted unintermittingly during the whole time of the incision, and I almost marvel that it rings not in my ears still, so excruciating was the agony.

The Paris Review: Medical Literature, F. Burney, 1811

You may have identified:

	EXTRACT 1	**EXTRACT 2**
First person narrative	'I was then escorted'	'I refused to be held'
Use of positive or negative language	'I was pleasantly surprised'	'convulsive fear,' 'agony'
Detail	Gown was like 'a circus tent.'	'the glitter of polished steel'
Sentence length	Both long and short. Very clear and straightforward.	Mostly long with hyphens and commas to separate the information
Use of verbs	'inserted'	'plunged'
Use of adjectives	'high-tech'	'excruciating'
Tone	Cheerful. Jokey imagery. Exclamation marks.	Dramatic. Striking.

The two patients recount very different experiences of surgery. Given that they were written over 200 years apart, we can deduce that advancements in modern surgery account for these different experiences. Look again at the extracts. If you had not been given the dates of each text, how could you tell that the first describes a modern operation and the second, 19th century surgery?

Now add a fourth column, analysing the differences in the effect of the language choices and techniques that the writers have employed.

Step 2 Practise your skills

ACTIVITY 2: OPINIONS

Read the two extracts on the next page.

▶ What are the writers' opinions of the abilities of the people they are writing about?

▶ How do they convey these opinions?

▶ Can you make any connections, comparisons or contrasts between the writers' ideas and techniques?

You may wish to consider the use of:

▶ hyperbolic (exaggerated) language

▶ verbs

▶ adjectives

▶ modal verbs ('helping' verbs, such as can, should, will)

▶ a formal or informal tone.

 Top tips

A modal verb (also called an auxiliary verb) is used to indicate modality – that means the likelihood of something. Examples include: may/might/ must, would, will could/can, should/shall. They are sometimes called helping verbs because they have to be used with another verb in order to make sense, for example: I could go. (Here, 'could' is the modal verb, and 'go' is the main verb.) Understanding the function of modal verbs can help you to analyse a writer's ideas in depth because modal verbs can indicate certainty: I will go, or possibility: I might go.

The extract below was published two days after the death of Michael Jackson.

GENIUS OR HYPE?

Comparing Jacko to Mozart shows just how bankrupt our culture is.

'He made me believe in magic,' says P. Diddy. *'His wonderment and mystery make him a legend,'* gabbles Steven Spielberg. *'He was a genius,'* claims Justin Timberlake. Really? What, like Shakespeare and Michelangelo? With the best will in the world, I don't think anything in Michael Jackson's back catalogue can quite compare with Hamlet or the Sistine Chapel. As for those who are now comparing him to Mozart and Beethoven – on Radio 4's flagship *'Today'* programme, of all places! – the only explanation is that they have never actually listened to the great composers.

Christopher Hart. The *Daily Mail*, Saturday, 27 June 2009

The extract below is about a reader's response to the poem *'Adonaïs'* by Percy Bysshe Shelley.

I am especially curious to hear the fate of 'Adonais.' I confess I should be surprised if that poem were born to an immortality of oblivion, but it has been received upon its publication with the usual howl of ignorant derision with which critics of a certain school were wont to indulge themselves upon the appearance of a new work from Shelley's pen. It will live to take its rightful place in the foremost rank of English Elegiac Verse (a position it can scarcely fail to hold), and to be known and loved by thousands of thoughtful and appreciative readers.

Thomas Wise, 1886

Percy Bysshe Shelley.

Organising your answer

As the examination paper will not provide a table of suggestions for you to complete, you may wish to familiarise yourself with the framework below. This will encourage you to move between the texts, comparing the writers' ideas and techniques throughout your answer.

Framework for connecting texts

QUESTION:	
TEXT 1:	**TEXT 2:**
Point that I'm trying to make:	
Evidence:	Evidence:
Key words to help in my explanation:	Key words to help in my explanation:

Step 3 Challenge yourself

 ACTIVITY 3: NEWSPAPER PIECES

Read the two extracts and answer the questions that follow.

Extract 1

The painful truth about trainers: are running shoes a waste of money?

Christopher McDougal

At Stanford University, California, two sales representatives from Nike were watching the athletics' team practise. Part of their job was to gather feedback from the company's sponsored runners about which shoes they preferred.

Unfortunately, it was proving difficult that day as the runners all seemed to prefer … nothing.

'Didn't we send you enough shoes?' they asked head coach Vin Lananna. They had, he was just refusing to use them.

'I can't prove this,' the well-respected coach told them. 'But I believe that when my runners train barefoot they run faster and suffer fewer injuries.'

Nike sponsored the Stanford team as they were the best of the very best. Needless to say, the reps were a little disturbed to hear that Lananna felt the best shoes they had to offer them were not as good as no shoes at all.

When I was told this anecdote it came as no surprise. I'd spent years struggling with a variety of running-related injuries, each time trading up to more expensive shoes, which seemed to make no difference. I'd lost count of the amount of money I'd handed over at shops and sports-injury clinics – eventually ending with advice from my doctor to give it up and 'buy a bike'.

The Daily Mail, 15 April 2009

1 What is the main idea of this newspaper piece?
2 How does the writer convince you that he knows his subject?
3 From what perspective is he writing? (The perspective is the position or angle he is coming from.)
   He could be:

   ▶ subjective (personally involved with experience of the problem)

   ▶ objective (a detached, impartial writer).

4 What conclusion is reached about specialist running shoes?

Extract 2

Attire for the female cyclist – 1895

The advent of the bicycle will create an inevitable reform in female dress. It seems that, in the near future, all women, whether of high or low degree, will bestride the wheel. Once liberated from the constraints of corsets and giant skirts, there are words of wisdom to be followed.

When riding a bicycle, don't wear a man's cap, loud hued leggings, or clothes that don't fit and don't wear jewellery out on a tour. Don't wear laced boots. They are tiresome. Don't go to church in your bicycle costume. Don't wear white kid gloves. There is no need for every item of your attire to match.

New York World Magazine, 1895, anonymous writer

1 What is the main idea of this newspaper piece?
2 From what perspective is the journalist writing?

Now think about both extracts and answer the following question:

Compare and contrast the writers' opinions about sportswear.

How do they convey these opinions?

Consider:

- ▶ narrative perspective
- ▶ negative language
- ▶ adjectives
- ▶ facts
- ▶ repetition
- ▶ expert advice
- ▶ personal experience
- ▶ personal pronouns

Self-assessment

	Extract 1	Extract 2	Effects (extracts 1 and 2)
Narrative perspective	third / first	Third / could argue second, as gives instructions	1 – knowledgeable, personal 2 – preaches
Negative language	'difficult', 'disturbed', 'injuries'	'low degree', 'Don't'	1 – Warns us of danger of poor shoes 2 – Apparently instructional but seems derogatory
Adjectives	'well-respected'	'inevitable', 'liberated'	1 – Lends confidence 2 – Appears positive at first – could be method to draw reader in
Facts	'when … runners train barefoot they run faster'	First two sentences appear as fact but are opinion	1 – Expert lends trust 2 – Writer is biased
Repetition	'injuries' x 2, 'injury'	'Don't'	1 – Highlights idea of avoiding injury 2 – Preaches to reader
Expert advice	'head coach'	Writer in role as expert	1 – Lends confidence 2 – Seems pompous
Personal experience	'I'd spent years struggling …'	No experience given	1 – Personal interest in topic lends weight 2 – No credentials given – we doubt their motives
Personal pronouns	'Didn't *we* send *you* …', '*I* can't prove this …'	'every item of *your* attire'	1 – Dialogue and pronouns = lively tone 2 – Seems critical

Now that you have completed the section, do you think your confidence has increased?

I can read and evaluate texts critically.

I can present thoughtful judgements on the impact of writers' ideas.

I can summarise and combine information from two texts.

I can analyse writers' techniques and connect, compare and contrast them.

Always ⇨ Usually ⇨ Sometimes

BE EXAM READY

OBJECTIVES

▶ To interpret writers' ideas
▶ To synthesise these ideas
▶ To analyse writers' techniques and connect, compare and contrast them

How confident are you in these skills already?

I can interpret writers' ideas.

I can synthesise ideas from two texts.

I can analyse writers' techniques and make links between them.

Always ⇨ Usually ⇨ Sometimes

In this unit, you have built up your skills from identifying and interpreting the main ideas in a single text, to combining information and analysing writers' ideas and techniques in two texts. You will now combine these skills in analysis of the text below.

QUESTION 1

Read the two extracts below.

Compare and contrast the writers' opinions about exercise.

How do they convey these opinions?

DAILY EXERCISES FOR MEN FROM THE 1800S

In 1883, physical culture enthusiast William Blaikie wrote a book entitled *How to Get Strong and How to Stay So*. In it, he suggests fitness routines for men. The only equipment needed is a set of dumb-bells (weights).

Morning Strength Training

On rising, let him stand upright, brace his chest firmly out, and, breathing deeply, curl dumb-bells (each of about one-fifteenth of his own weight) fifty times without stopping. This is biceps work enough for the early morning.

Then, placing the bells on the floor at his feet, and bending his knees a little, and his arms none at all, rise to an upright position with them fifty times. The loins and back have had their turn now.

After another minute's rest, let him lift the bells fifty times as far up and out behind him as he can, keeping elbows straight, and taking care, when the bells reach the highest point behind, to hold them still there a moment. Now the under side of his arms, and about the whole of the upper back, have had their work.

Next, starting with the bells at the shoulders, push them up high over the head, and lower fifty times continuously. Now the outer part of the upper arms, the corners of the shoulders, and the waist have all had active duty.

Finally, after another minute's rest, start with the bells high over the head, and lower slowly until the arms are about the position they would be on a cross, the elbows being

98

always kept unbent, liaise the bells to height again, then lower, and so continue until he has done ten, care being taken to hold the head six or more inches back of the perpendicular. Rest half a minute after doing ten, then do ten more, and so on, until fifty have been accomplished. This last exercise is one of the best-known chest-expanders.

Now that these five sorts of work are over, few muscles above the waist have not had vigorous and ample work, the lungs themselves have had a splendid stretch, and over fifteen minutes has not been spent on the whole operation. To add a little hand and fore-arm work, catch a broomstick or stout cane at or near the middle, and, holding it at arm's-length, twist it rapidly from side to side a hundred times with one hand, and then with the other.

How to Get Strong and How to Stay So, William Blaikie, 1883

Silver Sprinters: defying-age athletes

The footballer aged 72, the marathon runner in his 70s – what's their secret?

Rebecca Armstrong finds out how these senior sportsmen keep running.

Anyone who finds doing regular exercise something of a chore could do worse than following Dickie Borthwick's example. Known as Dixie to his friends, Borthwick plays football once a week, eats porridge for energy, takes vitamins every day, and gave up smoking to improve his health. Couch potatoes should also take note that Borthwick is 72 years old and played his first match aged 12. 'I don't feel like I'm in my 60th season,' he says. 'I still feel young at heart and feel like I can go on for a few years yet.'

Borthwick isn't the only older athlete putting people half his age to shame. John Starbrook, 76, competed in his first triathlon earlier this year 'for a bit of a challenge'. This gruelling event would be enough of a challenge to most people, but Starbrook also runs two marathons a year. 'I've done about 40 marathons in total. As I do two marathons every year, I basically train all year round – it's New York in November and London in April,' he says. 'In between I've started doing triathlons for a bit of fun.'

According to NHS guidelines, everyone, regardless of age, should aim to do at least 30 minutes of moderate physical activity five times a week to improve mobility and reduce the risk of heart disease. But while it can be all too easy to find excuses to avoid starting an exercise routine, Borthwick and Starbrook prove that age shouldn't stand in the way of fitness.

So what are their secrets? Borthwick is a fan of supplements and takes vitamins, but Starbrook eats a normal diet and doesn't believe in pills of any kind. He says, 'I don't eat much rubbish food – no burgers or any of that. Just good stuff. I don't take any vitamins. I don't even like taking an aspirin.'

As we age, our bodies start to change. 'The first thing is that you get a reduction in muscle strength and an increase in body fat,' says Lorenzo Masci, a sports physician. 'The second thing is that you get a reduction in heart rate and in your body's ability to take in oxygen.' Masci also warns that older people have a reduced capacity to recover from injuries. But it is not all bad news. 'A lot of these changes can be helped by exercise,' he says. According to Help the Aged, we can't store the benefits of exercise. If you were sporty until your thirties, it won't help in your seventies. But if you had an active lifestyle like Borthwick and Starbrook, you are more likely to continue exercise as you get older.

So what tips can they offer? Starbrook says, 'Running is a natural thing to do and it's free. You've just got to put your mind to it. Don't over-train, just do enough.'

But if you're out of condition – whatever your age – it's important to start slowly. The NHS recommends that anyone who has been inactive for a long period of time should try to build up to 30 minutes a day –

which can include activities like walking or gardening – and avoid high impact exercises that involve hard jolts to the body. 'It's never too late to start exercising,' says Masci.

However, it's important to speak to your doctor before embarking on a fitness kick. 'The important thing is to do things you enjoy. People who do activities they enjoy are more likely to stick with them,' says Masci.

And just remember – it's never too late to try something new. Just ask Starbrook. 'At the moment I'm hoping to try skydiving. I've never done anything like that but I'm just going to go up, shut my eyes, and shout "Geronimo" as I jump out of the plane.'

The *Independent*, November 2007

You could organise your answer by using the following structure:

Techniques	Extract 1	Extract 2
Title		
Main ideas		
Grammar		
Structure		
Language choices		
Facts		
Expert advice		
Personal pronouns		
Dramatic punctuation		

Self-assessment

Daily exercises for men

Remember to consider ideas and perspectives as well as how these are conveyed.

What ideas do you think William Blaikie had about fitness?

- The writer implies that only men will be interested in exercising.
- The focus is on strength training and stretching the chest.
- The exercises and the way they are introduced imply that they are equally suitable to all men regardless of their size, shape, age and previous health.
- The structure of the piece is a set of imperatives (instructions). These are used to organise the information: 'On rising', 'Then', 'After', 'Next', 'Finally'.
- Grammatically the writing is in the third person (him/his) and doesn't mention any names, just uses the male pronoun. This suggests that it is something all males should do.
- Each muscle group (though they're not called that) has its 'turn'. The only equipment is dumb bells, what we call weights, and there seems to be only one size available. You have to work out what that is from your own weight (your weight divided by 15).
- Verbs are used because this is an action piece: 'curl', 'lift', 'hold'.
- Words like 'duty,' and 'work' suggest an obligation to do these exercises.
- Facts are used to make the instructions more precise: 'fifteen minutes', 'a hundred times'.
- Most of the instructions are clear and precise – 'fifty times', 'after another minute's rest', 'one-fifteenth of his own weight'.
- There is little exercise jargon. 'Biceps' are mentioned but most of the language is non-technical.
- Adjectives are used in 'vigorous', 'best-known', 'ample' and 'splendid' to convey the effectiveness of the exercises.
- Adverbs are used in 'continuously' and 'rapidly' to explain how the exercises should be done.
- One or two of the words are used quite rarely now – 'loins' for example.
- Age is not mentioned at all.

Silver sprinters

What ideas are put forward about fitness? How are these conveyed?

- Title raises the idea that the key to fitness in older age is a secret that the article will reveal.
- Idea that some people consider regular exercise a 'chore'.
- There is a 'recipe' or technique to good health that involves the right food, exercise and attitude. Borthwick 'eats porridge for energy, takes vitamins every day, and gave up smoking'. He is 'a fan of supplements and takes vitamins'. Starbrook eats healthily, with no 'rubbish food' but 'just good stuff'. Careful about what he puts in his body – 'I don't even like taking an aspirin.'
- A positive attitude is put forward – 'I still feel young at heart', 'I've started doing triathlons for a bit of fun', 'it's never too late to start exercising', 'I'm hoping to try skydiving'.
- Facts are used to give an emphasis on age and the amount of sport undertaken.
- Expert advice – NHS guidelines and a sports physician. Uses more technical health vocabulary such as 'heart rate' and 'oxygen', 'body fat', 'reduced capacity' and 'high impact' exercises.
- Journalist tries to see things from a reader's viewpoint – 'It can be all too easy to find excuses to avoid starting an exercise routine'.
- Use of questions to draw us in: 'So what are their secrets?', 'So what tips can they offer?'
- Grammar is third person narrative but there is still a conversational tone, in the use of personal pronouns 'we' and 'you'.
- Structure – begins with examples of older athletes, moves to information about how our bodies age and ends with advice.
- Words such as 'But', 'However' and 'just remember' lend an advisory tone.
- The language used is straightforward and easily understood, with some commonly used health words such as 'supplements' and 'mobility'
- The piece is entertaining and informative and aimed at a wide audience.

Comparing sample answers

Tick every point you think deserves credit.
Can you think of any advice to give the first candidate?

Sample answer 1

The writers explain that exercise is easy to do. The first writer gives us clear instructions, such as 'rise to an upright position'. The second extract doesn't tell us how to do the exercises, but says 'It's never too late to start exercising.'

The first extract is more repetitive than the second. It tells us to 'rise' and 'lift' the weights a couple of times. The second extract has more of a variety of information because it has quotes from people who exercise, quotes from a sports physician and some advice about exercising. Both extracts have facts in, like 'fifty times' and 'start slowly'. They also have different amounts of exercise times in. The writer says 'fifteen minutes' in the first but it's 'thirty minutes' in the second. The first doesn't give an age for exercising but the second is more about older people.

Sample answer 2

Both writers recommend exercise for its health benefits. The first extract takes a clear, methodical approach to exercise. The writer works his way through a variety of upper body exercises, which are explained clearly in 'stand upright' and 'lift the bells fifty times'. The writer suggests that any man can do these exercises, by using the word 'him'. Blaikie explains how many times the exercises should be done, in 'do ten more' and 'a hundred times with one hand'. The writer makes it sound as if exercise is not that hard to do, does not need that much equipment apart from the 'dumb-bells' or a 'cane' and it only takes 'fifteen minutes'.

The second extract suggests that exercise can be more difficult to get into it as there is a 'secret' to it and some people consider it a 'chore'. However, by giving examples of older people who have run marathons, competed in triathlons and play football regularly, the reader receives the idea that we can all do exercise. The second extract does not explain how to do each exercise but it still gives advice, such as 'You've just got to put your mind to it' and 'build up to thirty minutes a day'. There is more emphasis on age in the second extract and we learn that 'It's never too late to start exercising'. Both extracts use exercise related language, such as 'biceps' and 'muscle strength' but there is not much jargon and the information is quite straightforward.

Both extracts are well organised. The first goes through the instructions for each exercise, in 'After', 'Next' and 'Finally' and the second has examples of older athletes, then advice about exercising in 'just remember'.

Both extracts use third person narrative. The approach in the first extract is a little strange, as the writer says 'let him' rather than 'you' as if he is not talking to the reader, but the instructions are still clear. The second writer uses a more chatty style of writing in phrases like 'So what tips can they offer?'

Both extracts suggest that exercise is a positive activity.

Now that you have completed the section, do you think your confidence has increased?

I can interpret writers' ideas.

I can synthesise ideas from two texts.

I can analyse writers' techniques and connect, compare and contrast them.

Always ⇨ Usually ⇨ **Sometimes**

Unit 9
Comparing language

OBJECTIVES

▶ To read texts with awareness of the writer's use of language and techniques
▶ To compare the techniques used in more than one text
▶ To evaluate writers' techniques from more than one text

How confident are you in these skills already?

I can comment on a writer's language choices and techniques.

I can prove my understanding through analysis of these techniques.

I can compare and evaluate writers' techniques from more than one text.

Always   ⟹   Usually   ⟹   Sometimes

When you compare extracts in Component Two you will need to cross-reference the language and writing style of two different pieces, say what they might have in common and what any differences are. You will then be able to form a judgement on the similar or differing effects of writers' techniques.

Get going

Step 1   Work on your skills

 ## ACTIVITY 1: LETTERS

Read these letters.

Identify any words that you think help to create a certain impression of the person who wrote the letter or the people who are written about. Both texts are personal, first person narrative accounts of the writer's opinions.

Letter 1

Dear Lucy,

      I have a problem. My boyfriend's parents have invited us on holiday with them next year but I don't want to go. They're lovely but my boyfriend's sister is a smug show-off and she's never really approved of me. I can't stand the thought of spending two painful weeks with her. I don't like her and she doesn't like me. I don't see why I should spend loads of money to go on a holiday which is absolutely rubbish.

I tried to bring this up with my boyfriend but he has no patience with me when I talk about his sister. He is usually understanding but he won't listen. I don't want to hurt his parents' feelings but the thought of the holiday is depressing me enormously. I work hard all year. I don't want to spend my precious two weeks' leave with someone so irritating. I don't know what to do without creating serious family problems. Any advice?

A confused reader

Letter 2

My dear friend,

     I need scarcely tell you what you must have observed, that I always feel a pleasure in your society and am selfish enough, on the present occasion, to covet it for a month, or for a longer period should it suit your convenience. If, therefore, you are not so wedded to the attractions of a New York life, as to be unwilling to leave them for a time, and will do me the great favour of making our humble and rural retreat your temporary abode, your presence will enliven our family circle, and be a real enjoyment to me.

Your sincere friend, Marion Willis.

The Lady's Guide to Perfect Gentility, 1856

Ideas

The writer of the first letter has a family problem that we may be able to sympathise with. You might have identified phrases such as, 'he has no patience with me' and 'I don't want to hurt his parents' feelings' which encourage our sympathy for the writer's difficult position. However, other phrases, such as, 'my boyfriend's sister is a smug show-off,' and 'someone so irritating' are judgemental and may reduce our sympathy. The phrase, 'a holiday which is absolutely rubbish' may also suggest to you that the writer seems determined not to enjoy themselves. You may well have mixed feelings about the writer as a result.

The writer of the second letter seems extremely polite, shown by phrases such as, 'I always feel a pleasure in your society' and 'If (you) will do me the great favour.' The writer seems likeable.

It is also worth considering the purpose of the letters. The first writer is presenting a problem so is bound to sound less satisfied than the second who is issuing an invitation.

This is a good start to comparing writers' texts through their language choices.

You can now develop these skills by taking an even closer look at the language and techniques that the writers use.

 ACTIVITY 2: LANGUAGE TECHNIQUES

Re-read the two letters. The question given in the exam was:

Compare the way the writers present their feelings in these letters.   **[10]**

You should comment on:

▶ **what is said**

▶ **how it is said.**

You must refer to the text to support your comments.

Language techniques from each text have been identified in the table on the next page.

> Remind yourself of the main parts of speech:
> **noun** – a naming word
> **adjective** – a describing word
> **verb** – an action word
> **adverb** – tells us how an action was done

On a copy of the table, fill in the blank boxes, commenting on the effects you think the techniques have.

TECHNIQUE	LETTER 1 EXAMPLE	EFFECT	LETTER 2 EXAMPLE	EFFECT
NARRATIVE STANCE	First person narrative	Outlines a personal problem	First person narrative	Makes the invitation sincere
STRUCTURE OF THE EXTRACT	States problem. Gives opinion of family members. Appeals for advice.	The nature of the writer's problem is made clear.	Writer states opinion of friend and invites them to stay.	Flatters friend in the hope they'll accept the subsequent invitation
MOOD	'depressing me enormously'	Invites our sympathy	'be a real enjoyment to me'	
POSITIVE LANGUAGE	'They're lovely'		'pleasure in your society'	
NEGATIVE LANGUAGE	'absolutely rubbish'		'am selfish enough'	This is used in an unusual way. The writer wants the friend's company and acknowledges that this may seem 'selfish'.
PERSONAL FEELINGS	'I can't stand the thought'		Could re-use any examples in previous three boxes	The writer is very fond of the friend's company.
ADJECTIVES (DESCRIBING WORDS)	Mostly negative: 'smug', 'painful', 'rubbish', 'irritating', 'serious'	Makes clear how unhappy the writer is about the situation	'dear', 'great', 'sincere', 'humble' and 'rural retreat'	Writer compliments their friend and is modest about their home in comparison to New York.
VERBS (ACTION WORDS)	'invited' 'don't want', 'never really approved', 'can't stand'	Outlines the letter's main issue Most other verbs are negative	'tell', 'feel', 'covet', 'leave', 'making', 'enliven'	Makes the writer's purpose clear and conveys their hopes

ADVERBS (TELL US MORE ABOUT HOW AN ACTION IS DONE OR THE EXTENT OF SOMEONE'S FEELINGS)	'depressing me enormously' 'absolutely rubbish'	Makes feelings of sadness clear	'I need scarcely tell you.'	Makes friendship clear.
ABSTRACT NOUNS (FEELINGS AND QUALITIES)	'no patience'	Emphasises feelings	'pleasure', 'enjoyment'	

You will note from the first column that the writers use similar techniques.

From looking at the Effects columns you may also notice that the techniques sometimes produce similar effects, such as both letters being personal and concentrating on feelings. Other techniques produce different effects, such as the negative language of the first letter, which makes the writer's unhappiness clear, but the negative word 'selfish' in the second letter is cleverly used in a positive way as it suggests that the writer is eager to have the friend's company.

When you cross-reference writers' language and techniques in the exam, you will be able to draw out these kind of similarities and differences.

! Top tips

Useful phrases for cross-referencing texts:

Signposting similarities
- like
- as in
- both
- also
- similarly
- likewise

Signposting differences
- by contrast
- whereas
- although
- conversely

Step 2   Practise your skills

ACTIVITY 3: CONTINUE THE ANSWER

Read the beginning of this student's response to the question:

Compare the way the writers present their feelings in these letters.   **[10]**

You should comment on:

▶ **what is said**

▶ **how it is said.**

You must refer to the text to support your comments.

The student has used both the Activity 2 table and Activity 3 guidelines in order to analyse a variety of the writers' techniques. They have 4 marks so far as shown in the annotations. Continue the answer, aiming for a total of 10 marks.

Engages with question immediately (1)

'More' implies comparison. Supports with evidence from the text (1)

The first writer gets straight to the point with the opening comment, 'I have a problem.' This simple sentence immediately shows why they are writing this letter. The second writer begins with a more complicated opening, 'I need scarcely tell you what you must have observed, that I always feel a pleasure in your society.'

The reader is not immediately sure what the letter is about, although we can identify that the writer seems happy because she uses the abstract noun, 'pleasure'. This positive word contrasts with the first writer's reference to her 'problem'. We get the impression that the writers have very different feelings about the situations they are in.

Identifies technique with correct terminology (1)

Remains focused on question. Specific support in use of one word quote. Contrasts with the first writer (1)

Step 3 — Challenge yourself

ACTIVITY 4: A ROYAL WEDDING

Read the following extracts and answer the question that follows.

The following extract gives an account of the marriage of Prince William to Kate Middleton on 29 April 2011.

First the Great Unveiling ... and then a collective gasp: With a plunging neckline and lots of lace, the gown was a timeless triumph

For five months, the world had waited for this moment.

And when Kate Middleton stepped out in front of her admiring public to unveil her ivory and satin Alexander McQueen gown, there were gasps of delight around the globe. Observers felt there was a timeless quality to Kate's dress, compared to the 'of the moment' designs worn by Diana Spencer and Sarah Ferguson.

Ten minutes later they were treated to the full creation as Kate climbed from her car – bringing to an end one of the best-kept secrets in fashion history and catapulting the relatively obscure but much talked about designer Sarah Burton into the limelight.

Kate's shoes, barely seen beneath her full-

length skirts, had been hand-crafted. From fleeting glimpses, they appeared to be closed-toe court shoes with heels around two and a half inches high and a lace embroidery pattern to match the trim of the dress.
Diana's dress designer, Elizabeth Emanuel,
said: 'The whole thing worked very well. It was a very regal dress and it was perfect because she looked like Kate. It was the Kate everyone loved, looking beautiful and elegant. Absolutely stunning.'

Mail Online, May 2011 by Fay Schlesinger and Maysa Rawi

The following extract gives an account of the marriage of Queen Victoria to Prince Albert on 10 February 1840.

The morning was foggy, cold and wet; but such crowds had not assembled in St. James's Park and its approaches since the rejoicings at the visit of the Allied Sovereigns in 1814, and even the inclement weather could not damp the joy of the Queen's subjects.

The wedding was celebrated with all due magnificence in the Chapel Royal, St. James's. The altar was splendidly decorated and it was laden with gold plate. Four state chairs were set – one for the Queen, one for Prince Albert, and one each for the Queen-Dowager and the Duchess of Kent.

The first carriages that drove along the Mall conveyed the ladies and gentlemen of the royal household from Buckingham Palace to St. James's. Next came the bridegroom, whose calm grace and thoughtful dignity moved all hearts; and the men clapped their hands, and the ladies waved their handkerchiefs in loyal enthusiasm as he passed. The guests wore wedding favours of lace or silver, some of great size, and many in most exquisite taste.

From *Our Queen : a Sketch of the Life and Times of Victoria, Queen of Great Britain and Ireland,* 1883

Compare both writers' accounts of a royal wedding. [10]
You should comment on:

▶ **what is said**

▶ **how it is said.**

You must refer to the text to support your comments.

Structure

You could comment on:

▶ narrative stance

▶ the structure of the extracts

▶ mood

▶ sentence structures

▶ conjunctions to start sentences

▶ positive language

▶ adjectives

▶ verbs

▶ adverbs

▶ abstract nouns.

✓ Self-assessment

	Extract 1	Extract 2	Effect
Narrative stance	Third person narrative with use of quotes	Third person narrative – omniscient	Both give a comprehensive account but Extract 2 is more formal.
Structure of the extract	Build-up, details of the dress, a quote	Description of weather, decorations, scene	Both create a sense of anticipation, then give the reader the awaited details.
Mood	anticipation/ excitement, 'first', 'then', 'gasp'	a quiet anticipation, happiness, 'could not damp the joy', 'clapped', 'waved'	Both convey expectations but the second is more reserved in tone.
Sentence structures	Complex sentences; Parenthesis; Sentence fragment: 'Absolutely stunning'	Complex sentences. Parenthesis	Plenty of additional detail given
Conjunctions to start sentences	'And when …'	None	Extract 1 – modern grammar, although technically incorrect
Positive language	'timeless triumph,' 'beautiful'	'magnificence', 'exquisite taste'	Both convey grandeur of the occasion and public approval.
Adjectives	'regal', 'elegant', 'stunning'	'calm', 'thoughtful', 'loyal'	Extract 1 focuses on clothes; Extract 2 on royal qualities.
Verbs	'stepped', 'climbed'	'assembled', 'drove', 'clapped', 'waved'	Concentration on movements to help the reader imagine the scene
Adverbs	'barely' (suggests modesty), 'absolutely'	'splendidly'	Stress the great impression made by events and sights
Abstract nouns	'delight'	'dignity', 'enthusiasm'	Positive emotions and traits

Now that you have completed the section, do you think your confidence has increased?

I can comment on a writer's language choices and techniques.

I can prove my understanding through analysis of these techniques.

I can compare and evaluate writers' techniques from more than one text.

Always ⇨ Usually ⇨ Sometimes

Improve your skills

OBJECTIVES

▷ To analyse writers' subject specific vocabulary

▷ To offer judgements about writers' language choices for their intended audience

▷ To compare and evaluate writers' techniques

How confident are you in these skills already?

I can identify a group of words that share the same subject or theme.

I can offer judgements about a writer's language choices for their intended audience.

I can compare and evaluate these techniques in more than one text.

Always ⇨ Usually ⇨ Sometimes

You have already seen that a writer's language choices affect the way that they convey their information. In order to write about an idea, a writer will use a selection of subject specific words that will be relevant to the topic and the intended audience. In this unit, you will develop your analysis of these techniques and cross-reference how writers use these techniques in different texts.

Step 1   Work on your skills

ACTIVITY 1: BOARD GAMES

Read the following extracts.

Extract 1

See which player will first become the President of the Telegraph Company. The players move metallic messenger boy pawns around a spiralling track. Some spaces direct a piece to advance for meritorious service. Spaces reflecting misbehaviour direct a piece to go back, or sometimes to prison, which requires a return to the start upon release.

Extract 2

This new edition of the popular family edition game offers fresh questions and a quick pace. Play individually or in teams with 2,400 questions about the things you know. Having trouble with an answer? Ask a friend, and if they're right, you both get a wedge. This game is packed with laughter and learning.

Copy and complete the table below with a list of the subject specific words that the writer uses. There are examples in each column to start you off.

What kind of audience do you think the extracts were written for?

What led you to this conclusion?

SUBJECT: BOARD GAMES	
SUBJECT SPECIFIC WORDS IN EXTRACT I	**SUBJECT SPECIFIC WORDS IN EXTRACT 2**
player move	edition popular
Intended audience:	**Intended audience:**

Audience

Both extracts were written for children. They are instructions for playing board games. The first extract is taken from an 1886 board game, called The Game of the District Messenger Boy. The second is an online shop's description of Trivial Pursuit.

You could identify the audience from the words 'player', 'Having trouble with an answer?', 'Ask a friend,' and 'packed with laughter and learning' as we normally associate playing games with children. It is more difficult to judge the audience in the first extract. The word 'meritorious' and 'Telegraph Company' are not commonly used in modern English. However, the writer is using language that would suit the audience of the time.

ACTIVITY 2: SMOKING

Read the extracts and complete the activity that follows.

Reasons People Start Smoking

So why do people start smoking? Let's look at the reasons why someone might pick up that first cigarette.

While there are certainly other influences that can lead a smoker into the habit, peer pressure is one of the biggest. A large part of the reason peer pressure comes under scrutiny is that one of the groups most likely to begin smoking – young teenagers – is also one of the most susceptible to peer pressure. The awkward years between childhood and young adulthood are marked for many by frustration and insecurity. Quite often, this is the time of life when young people rely most heavily on friends of the same age for social support and affirmation.

Enter cigarettes. If a child in a social circle starts experimenting with tobacco, it's all too easy for him or her to lead peers into that first nicotine puff as well. Parents committed to raising smoke-free children have to communicate that smoking is dangerous, unhealthy and unacceptable. Even as the children grow into teenagers, those parental messages will resonate, potentially protecting the young adults from becoming addicts as they grow older.

Health Online: How Stuff Works. 'Reasons People Start Smoking' by Matt Cunningham

Men do not love tobacco by nature. This dirty product is poisonous and offensive.

It revolts the taste of all animals and produces the most spontaneous opposition and disgust in its contact with the lungs. Smoking a pipe is endured only in a way of coercing and perverting nature. Its causes for being taken up are mostly identified with the following:

1 Pretending the medicinal virtues of tobacco.

2 Idleness, with nothing to do but smoke and be stupefied.

3 A precocious and absurd aping of manhood in boys, who wish to enact the fooleries of men.

4 Mental vacancy.

5 Recklessness, never thinking properly on the subject, and so gliding imperceptibly into the habit and the slavery of the practice – ignorant of their own damage.

6 False notions of what is genteel, and a willingness to be genteel on terms remarkably cheap and low.

7 The power of habit.

8 I can quit when I will; a deceptive idea or fancy that they can do so easily; and at any time – which never comes voluntarily.

The Mysteries of Tobacco, Rev. Benjamin Lane, 1845

Read the lists of words taken from each extract in the table below.

Both writers use smoking-related vocabulary to build their arguments.

With a work partner, discuss any points of comparison between the language used.

You are not necessarily trying to spot exactly the same word in both lists, but rather note if language is used in a similar way. For example, both writers may use references to the age a person is likely to start smoking. They may also use strong words to present smoking negatively.

EXTRACT 1: 'REASONS PEOPLE START SMOKING'		EXTRACT 2: *THE MYSTERIES OF TOBACCO*	
smoking	unhealthy	tobacco	disgust
cigarette	unacceptable	endured	precocious
habit	experimenting	coercing	aping of manhood
peer pressure	insecurity	dirty	habit
tobacco	frustration	poisonous	false notions
nicotine	affirmation	offensive	recklessness
dangerous	young adulthood	opposition	deceptive

The discussion you just had forms the start of the answer to the question:

Compare how the writers convey their ideas about smoking.

By discussing particular words and noting any similarities between them, you have just compared and contrasted specific language techniques from two texts.

You may also have worked out what audience you think the texts are aimed at.

What words in Extract 1 give you the impression that it is aimed at parents with teenagers?

What words in Extract 2 give you the impression that it is aimed at those who already smoke?

You may have identified words such as, 'young teenagers,' 'peer pressure,' 'a child,' 'parents' and 'parental messages.' These words give a sense of advice being given. The question, 'So why do people start smoking?' has quite a friendly tone, as if the writer is explaining teenage behaviour to parents. In Extract 2, you may have identified, 'I can quit when I will' as if these are the direct words of a smoker. Blunt words such as, 'precocious' and 'idleness' seem to judge smokers and give the piece a harsher tone than the first.

 ## ACTIVITY 3: CONTINUE THE ANSWER

The student on the page opposite has started to write the answer to the question:

Compare how the writers convey their ideas about smoking. [10]

You could consider:

▶ the use of subject specific words

▶ how the vocabulary suits the intended audiences

▶ the tone of the extracts.

They have 4 marks so far as shown in the annotations. Using the ideas from your discussion, continue the answer, aiming for a total of 10 marks.

The phrase 'both extracts' proves that the student is comparing the texts. (1)

Identifies the message of both texts. (1)

The strong, negative language used in both texts communicates the message that smoking is bad for you. Words such as, 'unhealthy' in the first text and 'poisonous' in the second text show that smoking is dangerous.

Supports point with specific reference from both texts. (1)

Again, supports point with specific reference from both texts. (1)

Both extracts suggest an age that people might start smoking. The first writer mentions 'young teenagers' and the second explains how smokers are often boys who 'wish to enact the fooleries of men.' The writers criticise how foolish this is.

Step 2   Practise your skills

The practice activities in this unit have encouraged you to look closely at language and say what effect the writers' language choices have. This is the key to a successful, analytical answer. Avoid clichéd, general expressions which do not analyse the particular quote that you have chosen.

! Top tips

Ten phrases to avoid and how to improve them:

- makes you think (makes you think about what?)
- adds effect (what effect?)
- to give more impact *and* grabs the reader's attention (these two are too general – what particular effect is created?)
- creates a mood (what mood and *how* is it created?)
- doesn't make it too hard *and* makes it easier to read (these two make it sound like you can hardly cope)
- makes you want to read on *and* keeps you reading (select a point of interest and comment on *how* it engages you)
- is effective (*how* is the language/technique effective?)

A common error is to use the wrong verb when analysing an effect. Statements such as:

- gives a metaphor
- creates a simile
- adds a verb

don't make sense.

Replace them with:

- employs *or* uses.

A tip is to avoid any phrase that could apply to a whole range of indiscriminate effects. Instead, explain why the writer might have chosen particular words and analyse the effect that these word choices create.

ACTIVITY 4: PRECISE LANGUAGE ANALYSIS

Read the following extracts.

The Art of Dancing

Certainly, the desire to dance is founded in the nature of man. As an omelette without eggs, or a magistrate without authority would be alike ridiculous, so dancing without music would be an absurdity. Indeed, if the reader has ever chanced to pass a lighted apartment where the dancers might be seen, but from which the music could not be heard, he will admit that the evolutions of the performers were most strange.

The sound of music, to anyone susceptible to its influence, can hardly be heard without an involuntary accompaniment of the head or foot; and a quick, lively air is a natural invocation, if not an inspiration, to dance.

The Art of Dancing, E. Ferrero, 1859

Ten rules of mosh pit etiquette

In my years attending punk and metal shows, I've noticed that there are a few unwritten rules when participating in a mosh pit. Ready? When moshing, if you're not prepared for the quick-footed barrage brought on by a band's driving uptempo sections, wait for the slower, heavier sections and guitar riffs. While sporadic increases in speed and intensity will crop up if an audience knows what's coming in the song, often natural lulls occur as people catch their breath. It's best to try to pace yourself according to the flow of the pit as a whole, otherwise it's easy to lose control over your own movement.

Minneapolis City Pages online: 'The rules of the mosh pit.'

The student's answer below is a response to the question:

Compare how the writers convey their ideas about dancing.

The student has structured their answer well but uses general explanations of the quotes they have chosen. They have been awarded just 4 marks for their answer.

Rewrite the underlined sections with precise language analysis.

Both extracts are about music and dancing. The first extract says that it is in our 'nature' to dance but the second says there are 'unwritten rules.' This really makes you think about the differences.

Both writers talk about watching dancers. The first writer says dancers 'might be seen' as 'strange' and the second says 'I've noticed.' These quotes are really effective.

The words 'blendings' and 'invocation' in the first extract really grab your attention.

> **! Top tip**
>
> Refer to a writer's narrative approach as first person *narrative* or third person *narrative*, not just, 'first person'.

Step 3   Challenge yourself

ACTIVITY 5: COFFEE

Read the following extracts. The question given in the exam was:

Compare the writers' accounts of buying coffee.   **[10]**

You should comment on:

▶ **what is said**

▶ **how it is said.**

You must refer to the text to support your comments.

Extract 1

The English appear to have been the first European people who used coffee as a beverage. A Turkish merchant of London, of the name of Edwards, brought the first bag of coffee to London, and his Greek servant made the first cup of coffee in London. This was in 1652, and, of course, under the government of Cromwell. The beverage remained beyond affordability for the common man. It was really brought into fashion in France through the Turkish ambassador, who treated his fashionable guests with it at his hotel. It soon became fashionable, but from its extravagant price, its use was confined to a few of the upper classes. The poet, Alexander Pope, recalls politicians as sipping coffee 'with half shut-eyes,' having probably some noted personage of the time in view whom they desired to impress.

On the History and Migration of Cultivated Plants Producing Coffee, J. Crawfurd, 1869

Extract 2

HOW MUCH ARE WE WILLING TO PAY FOR A CUP OF COFFEE?

How much would you pay for a cup of coffee? At Starbucks you'll pay around £2.75 a cup. For most of us, this sounds quite reasonable. However, if you had asked the same question perhaps 20 years ago, when for most people coffee was a powder that came from a jar and 'flat white' described a wall and little else, the response would have been very different.

Or, indeed, if you're abroad: a cup of coffee at a London café will set you back £2.50, compared with £1.63 in Paris, £1.44 in Barcelona and just 58p in Lisbon. At £2.50, the actual coffee in your cup accounts for only a very small part of the total price.

"A single shot of espresso costs a coffee chain less than 10p per shot," says retail analyst, Jeffrey Young. "Seven to eight years ago the psychological barrier was believed to be £2 which we broke through with no problem. Consumers are now paying in excess of £3 for iced coffee beverages in some outlets."

'Coffee', December 2011, published by Raconteur Media

Language techniques from each text have been identified in the table below.

On a copy of the table, fill in the blank boxes, commenting on the effects you think the techniques have.

 Remember: not *every* technique will be in *every* text. You can identify this as a difference and comment on it.

TECHNIQUE	EXAMPLES IN EXTRACT 1	EXAMPLES IN EXTRACT 2	EFFECT OF TECHNIQUE
Subject specific words	Coffee, beverage, cup, sipping.		Extract 1 – Extract 2 –
Possible intended audience	Text is a 'history (of) producing coffee'	How much would you pay?	Extract 1 – those with a particular interest in the subject Extract 2 – wider audience
Narrative stance			Extract 1 – Extract 2 –
Positive language			Extract 1 – Extract 2 –
Negative language			Extract 1 – Extract 2 –
Any other interesting use of words			Extract 1 – Extract 2 –

Now that you have completed the section, do you think your confidence has increased?

I can identify a group of words that share the same subject or theme.

I can offer judgements about a writer's language choices for their intended audience.

I can compare and evaluate these techniques in more than one text.

Always ⇨ Usually ⇨ Sometimes

BE EXAM READY

▷ To analyse a writer's use of language and techniques
▷ To compare and evaluate writers' techniques
▷ To put these skills into practice in a timed question

How confident are you in these skills already?

I can analyse a writer's use of language and techniques.

I can compare and evaluate these techniques.

I can put these skills into practice in a timed question.

Always   ⇨   Usually   ⇨   Sometimes

In this unit, you have practised reading texts with an understanding of the writers' language and techniques. You have compared and evaluated these techniques.

QUESTION 1

Read the two extracts below and answer the following question.

Compare and contrast the writers' accounts of these extreme feats.   [10]

You should comment on:
• **what is said**
• **how it is said.**

You must refer to the text to support your comments.

Text 1

NIK WALLENDA: THE MAN CROSSING THE GRAND CANYON ON A TIGHTROPE

Nik Wallenda is a man prepared to die. On Sunday, in front of a global television audience of several million, the 34-year-old will step out on a 2 inch-thick metal wire and attempt to enter the record books as the first person to walk across the Grand Canyon. Higher than the Empire State Building, higher, certainly, than Wallenda himself has ever attempted before, the wire will be suspended a stomach-lurching 1,500ft above the Little Colorado River. Without a safety net or a harness, the only equipment Wallenda will use is a pole, which he will carry for balance.

"We've tried to prepare for the possibility that I could die," he says, with an admirable absence of drama. "My wife and kids would be looked after for the rest of their lives." But there's a difference between preparing to die and expecting to die. If anyone can

119

complete the 40-minute walk across the canyon, it's Wallenda. "I've calculated it – it would take nine seconds for me to reach the bottom. That's a lot of time to think," he says. The daredevil already holds seven world records including the longest walk over a waterfall, which he achieved when he crossed Niagara Falls, and the highest bicycle tightrope (235ft), completed live on breakfast television. Wallenda's closest call was five years ago, during his bicycle tightrope, when his back wheel began to slip. "At that point, you go back to everything you have learnt in training; what happens when this happens? How do I sort it out? Your mind reacts more quickly when you are up there, which is important," he says. He pulled it back, to the relief of all those watching, and set a new world record. "It really shook me up though," he admits. Does he ever get scared? "I don't call it fear, I call it respect," he asserts. "When I walk to the edge of a 15-storey building, my heart races, just like anyone else's. But I turn that into respect and think 'I had better train well, so that I am not just prepared. I am over-prepared.'"

The *Telegraph* Online

Text 2

AN EXCITING SCENE.
M. Blondin's Feat at Niagara Falls.

Yesterday was the day announced by Mr. Blondin for his daring attempt to cross the Niagara River, on a rope extended from bank to bank. Trained as an acrobat and tightrope walker, Mr Blondin has already undertaken numerous circus feats.

At a few minutes before 5 o'clock, the 35 year old Mr. Blondin could be seen standing on the American side, dressed in tights and covered with spangles, upon which the sun shone, making him appear as if clothed in light. He appeared scarcely the size of a year old infant at that distance, and the rope upon which he was standing a mere thread over an awful abyss.

At 5 o'clock precisely he started from the American side. Without hesitation he balanced his pole in his hands, and with a calmer and less fluttering heart than could be found in the audience, he commenced his terrible walk. The slightest misstep, the merest dizziness, the least uncertainty, would cast him at once into the perdition beneath, and the crowd held their breaths in amazement as he went on and over the frightful chasm.

On his part, however, there was not the slightest irresoluteness. Calmly he tread the rope, which scarcely trembled or swayed with his weight, and, at about 550 feet from the shore, he coolly sat down on the rope, perched nearly 200 feet above the water and waved his hands to his friends. He then laid down on the rope full length with his balance pole across his chest, with the same disregard and carelessness that a person would have reclined upon a lounge.

After some little time, Mr. Blondin rose to his feet with the same certainty that had marked all his previous operations, and continued his performance.

He came slowly up the ascent on the Canadian side, amid the crash of *Sweet Home* from the brass bands, and the cheers upon cheers that went up from thousands of throats, celebrating the success of this most wonderful of all human feats, requiring the utmost skill, expertness and clearheadedness, besides a miraculous courage and nerves of adamant.

From *The Buffalo Republic*, 1 July 1859

Self-assessment

This is not a checklist. You may have identified the following:

- There is a wide intended audience as both texts are from newspaper articles. The language is accessible.
- Both texts are structured clearly, starting with a brief introduction to the men, establishing their intended feat and giving examples of past endeavours.
- Both texts are written in third person narrative. The first includes quotation from Wallenda, lending a personal tone. The second writer is a spectator, part of a contagious atmosphere.
- Varying sentence structures make the extracts lively. There is a simple sentence, 'I am over-prepared' and complex sentences in Extract 1. There are complex sentences in Extract 2. Parenthesis lends detail. Lively, varied grammatical constructions maintain the pace and interest in both texts.
- Extract 1 includes questions from both the writer and Wallenda, appealing to the reader's curiosity.
- Words related to danger make the topic clear: 'daredevil,' 'stomach-lurching,' 'heart races' (Extract 1); 'feats', 'fluttering heart' (Extract 2).
- Emotive language: 'die', (which is mentioned several times), 'scared', 'fear', (Extract 1); 'awful', 'terrible', 'frightful' (Extract 2).

- Frequent use of adjectives (many in previous point): 'stomach-lurching' (Extract 1); 'daring', 'miraculous' (Extract 2).
- Comparatives: 'higher'; superlatives: 'longest', 'highest' (Extract 1); 'most wonderful' (Extract 2).
- Dramatic verbs: 'slip', 'react', 'pulled' (Extract 1); 'balanced', 'perched' (Extract 2). More verbs relating to the actual feat in Extract 2 as the article is an account of the endeavour. Extract 1 outlines what Wallenda intends to do.
- Adverbs lend detail to the action: 'scarcely trembled', 'coolly sat' (Extract 2)
- Abstract nouns: 'relief', 'scared', 'fear', 'respect' (Extract 1); 'amazement', 'disregard', 'carelessness' (Extract 2)
- Imagery: 'Higher than the Empire State Building' (Extract 1); 'as if clothed in light' (Extract 2)
- Pronouns: 'he appeared', 'waved his hands' – sounds casual in Extract 2. The name 'Wallenda' is used frequently in Extract 1, more than pronouns. Lends authoritative tone.
- Moments of tension and calm are juxtaposed with the wide variety of language choices.
- The writing is lively and descriptive.
- Use of fact, ages, width of wire, height – these shock and impress the reader.

Comparing sample answers

Annotate each answer with examiner's comments and decide on a mark for each. Use the self-assessment box to help you decide on a mark.

Sample answer 1

Both of these activities sound incredibly dangerous. The first man knows that he might die and the writer says he 'is a man prepared to die'. The second man balances on a tightrope across Niagara Falls which is described as 'a mere thread over an awful abyss'.

Both of the men are nervous. The first man says his 'heart races' and the second man says his heart is 'fluttering'. Dramatic words are used in both texts. In the first text, the man is 'suspended' on a tightrope and in the second, he is 'balanced' over an enormous drop. Both extracts tell us that the men are high up. He is 1,500 feet up in the first and 200 feet up in the second over a 'frightful chasm'. It sounds really frightening with words like 'stomach-lurching' and 'terrible' and 'awful'.

Sample answer 2

The writers' accounts of these feats are immediately engaging. Both writers show us the men's courage, in words such as 'daredevil' and 'daring'.

The danger that the men are facing is further emphasised in 'prepared to die', 'could die', 'preparing to die' and 'expecting to die' in the first extract and falling into 'perdition' in the second extract.

Nerves are mentioned in 'heart races' and 'fluttering heart', although the crowd seem more nervous than Blondin in the second extract. Both extracts are written in third person narrative. The first has quotes from the tightrope walker to show us how he's feeling, such as, 'It really shook me up'. The second extract is written from the point of view of a spectator so there are no direct quotes from Blondin and we don't know exactly how he feels. However, we are told that he 'walked calmly', 'waved his hands' and behaved with 'disregard and carelessness' which suggests that he isn't very nervous.

Both extracts are tense. In extract one, Wallenda tells us that 'his back wheel began to slip' when he crossed a tightrope on a bicycle. The crowd are tense in the second extract because they 'held their breaths in amazement' which makes us feel as if we are watching too. Adjectives such as 'stomach-lurching' in Extract 1 and 'daring',' 'frightful' and 'miraculous' in Extract 2 have a similar striking effect and help the reader imagine that they are watching the same scene as the writers.

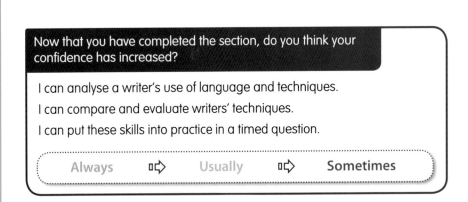

Now that you have completed the section, do you think your confidence has increased?

I can analyse a writer's use of language and techniques.

I can compare and evaluate writers' techniques.

I can put these skills into practice in a timed question.

Always ⇨ Usually ⇨ Sometimes

Unit 10
Using textual references

OBJECTIVES

▶ To be able to differentiate between different types of textual references
▶ To be precise in the use of textual references

How confident are you in these skills already?

I use information in a text to back up **explicit** and **implicit** meanings.

I select textual references precisely to support my views and opinions.

I understand the different types of textual reference and use them appropriately.

Always Usually Sometimes

'Textual references' can be in the form of a quote – words and phrases lifted directly from the text or a general reference to the events or characters' actions within the text.

All textual references should be short and precise in terms of supporting your point. If in the form of a quote, they should be individual words or short phrases (about three to five words in length).

Get going

Step 1 Work on your skills

Textual references in terms of the text's events can be useful to support your views and opinions.

You are looking to refer to things that are very much on the 'surface' of the text (in other words, what the text is about in terms of subject matter, plot and happenings). These textual references may be quite basic and help summarise what happens in a text.

explicit information – information that is stated as fact
implicit information – information that you can work out from the text

Up until now, we have been focusing on certain aspects of a text and you have already been looking for evidence to support your answers to a question.

However, as part of the critical evaluation aspect of the exam, you will be asked your own views, thoughts and ideas about a text and will need to select a range of precise textual references in order to back up your ideas. Before we look at critical evaluation in detail (in the next unit) it will be useful to explore the range of textual references that you may look for in texts similar to those you will encounter in the exam. For this purpose, we will be looking at textual references in relation to the following areas:

● events
● inference
● language
● techniques
● tone
● overview.

ACTIVITY 1: EVENTS

Read the following paragraph and think about what happens. Pick out the series of events. (It is sometimes useful to think of this as the bare minimum you would need to retell the story.)

The sirens started at one a.m. They began in Westminster and the wailing moan rippled outwards to the suburbs. Harry woke and dressed in moments, as he had learned to do in the army. He twitched the curtain open a crack. In the moonlight, shadowy figures were running across the road, making for the shelter. Huge searchlight beams stabbed the sky as far as the eye could see. He went out into the hall. The light was on and Ronnie stood there in pyjamas and dressing gown. He looked at the door of his parents' bedroom. A loud, terrified child's sobbing could be heard.

Harry felt reluctant to invade Will and Muriel's bedroom but he made himself go in. They were both in dressing gowns too. Muriel sat on the bed, nursing her sobbing daughter in her arms, making soothing noises. Harry wouldn't have thought her capable of such gentleness. Will stood looking at them uncertainly. He seemed the most vulnerable of them all. Harry felt his legs begin to tremble.

'We should go,' he said brusquely.

Muriel looked up. 'Who the bloody hell asked you?'

'Prue won't go to the shelter,' Will explained quietly.

'It's dark,' the little girl wailed. 'Please let me stay at home.'

Harry stepped forward and grasped Muriel's elbow. This was what the corporal had done on the beach at Dunkirk after the bomb fell. Muriel gave him an astonished look.

'We have to go. The bombers are coming. Will, we have to get them out.' Will took her other arm and they raised her gently. Prue had buried her face in her mother's breast, still sobbing and holding a teddy bear tightly. Its glass eyes stared up at Harry.

'All right, all right, I can walk by myself,' Muriel snapped.

They released her and they all clattered down the stairs. Ronnie switched off the light and opened the front door. The dark shape of the shelter was visible across the road. They began running but Muriel was slowed by the little girl. In the middle of the road Will turned to help her and slipped. He went down with a crash and a yell.

Winter in Madrid by CJ Sansom, Pan Macmillan, London

Retell the series of events in this text without using any of the original words. Get a learning partner to check the original and comment on how successful you've been.

What you have written will not be direct quotes, but are still textual references as they will refer to the events in the text.

This form of textual reference could be used occasionally in an exam, but may be more useful as an entry point into the text.

Step 2   Practise your skills

ACTIVITY 2: WHAT HAPPENS?

Read the following passage (about a man escaping into a waste land from unknown pursuers).

The moment that the bus moved on Mike knew he was in danger. In the dim light he saw the figures of the young men waiting under the tree. It was too late to run after the bus; it went down the dark street like an island of safety in a sea of perils. His mouth was already dry, his heart was pounding in his chest, and something within him was crying out in protest against the coming event.

His wages were in his purse; he could feel them weighing heavily against his thigh. That was what they wanted from him. Nothing else mattered to them. His wife could be made a widow, his children made fatherless. Nothing counted against that. Mercy was an unknown word to them. While he stood there uncertainly Mike heard the young men walking towards him, not only from the side where he had seen them, but from the other also. They did not speak, their intention was unspeakable. The sound of their feet came on the wind to him. They had chosen the place well, for behind him was the high wall of the convent, and the barred door that would not open before a man was dead. On the other side of the road was the waste land, full of wire and iron and the bodies of old cars. It was his only hope, and he moved towards it; as he did so he knew from the whistle that the young men were there too.

His fear was great and instant, and the smell of it went from his body to his nostrils. At that moment one of them spoke, giving directions. He felt so trapped that he was filled suddenly with strength and anger, and he ran towards the waste land swinging his heavy stick. In the darkness the figure of a man loomed up at him, and he swung the stick at him, and heard him give a cry of pain. Then he plunged blindly into the wilderness of wire and iron and the bodies of old cars. Something caught him by the leg, and he brought his stick crashing down on it, but it was not a man, only some knife-edged piece of iron. He was sobbing and out of breath, but he pushed on into the waste, while behind him they pushed on also, knocking against the old iron bodies and kicking against tins and buckets.

He fell into a tangle of wire; it was barbed, and tore at his clothes and flesh. Then it held him, so that it seemed to him that death must be near, and having no other hope, he cried out, 'Help me, help me!' in what should have been a great voice but was voiceless and gasping. He tore at the wire, and it tore at him too, ripping his face and his hands. Then suddenly Mike was free. He saw the bus returning, and in its headlights he could see the shape of a man close to him.

What happens in this section of the text? Make at least **five** textual references to what happens in the events of the text.

! Top tips

Don't see the text as one big event. Make sure you separate it into distinct stages.

narrative – refers to the story or plot

! Top tips

Sentence starters that may be useful in the exam when introducing your textual evidence:

- Events of the text start with …
- The next important thing that happens is …
- What happens next is …
- In terms of the events of the text …
- The text's **narrative** includes …

Step 3   Challenge yourself

Having got a good grasp of textual references in terms of surface events, it is now also worth considering how some textual references back up the things you have inferred (worked out) about the text.

It is vital that these textual references are used as support for things that you think are implied in the text. Use them as quotes to prove your point.

inference – using the clues in the text to work out something that the writer doesn't directly tell you

ACTIVITY 3: INFERENCE

Read the paragraph below:

I left for school that morning with my football things because I was in the team for the big one, the match against our local rivals, St Bede's High School. Dad had promised to come and watch and he always kept his promises. He'd never missed a game. But as we ran onto the pitch he wasn't among the group of parents on the halfway line. I kept looking beyond the pitch during the warm-

up, searching for a man in a car, in a taxi, on a bike, racing towards us, but there was nothing. I was gutted. It wasn't the same if Dad wasn't there for the kick off. It was all her fault.

She comes along and suddenly he's too busy with her, he's got no time for me. Still, he'd come in the end. I knew Dad.

From this passage we can work out that the main character looks up to his father and is very disappointed to be let down by him. This is an example of **inference**. What textual references can you find that will support this implicit information?

Put them in a table using the example below as a guide.

TEXTUAL REFERENCE	INFERENCE
'[Dad] always kept his promises'	The main character has faith in his father.

So far, we have looked at 20th century fiction prose texts. As you know, you will also encounter 21st century non-fiction texts like the one on the opposite page. The principles remain the same.

 Top tips

Useful connectives for textual references and inferences include: implies, infers, suggests, hints. Can you think of any more?

ACTIVITY 4: TEXTUAL REFERENCE

Read the following text.

At the Shamwari Reserve in South Africa, rescued animals recover from ill-treatment in zoos and circuses, and humans are quite well treated too.

'Get here before sunset.' The warning loomed in my mind as we raced the fading light across the rugged landscape towards Shamwari Reserve. As we reached the dirt road at the entrance, the sky darkened and a sleek, tawny-and-white animal I'd never seen before skittered across our path. We stopped to let her pass undisturbed, but she stopped and stared at us, her liquid eyes glowing in the dark. This animal, an oryx, makes a life for itself in the harshest conditions – a reminder of why we'd gone there.

Find a textual reference to support the inference:

TEXTUAL REFERENCE	INFERENCE
	People at the Shamwari reserve are kind.
	The environment is quite undeveloped.
	The writer is from a different environment.

Obviously you will not have the time to draw a table in the exam! Turn your findings into a paragraph by linking the reference and the inference. For example:

The text states that the animals are 'rescued'. This implies that the people at the reserve are kind and are trying to battle cruelty. Also ...

Now that you have completed the section, do you think your confidence has increased?

I use information in a text to back up explicit and implicit meanings.

I select textual references precisely to support my views and opinions.

I understand the different types of textual reference and use them appropriately.

Always ⇨ Usually ⇨ Sometimes

Improve your skills

OBJECTIVES

▶ To further develop the ability to differentiate between different types of textual references

▶ To consider textual references in terms of vocabulary and writers' techniques

▶ To consider textual references in terms of gaining an overview of a text

Textual references about events and inference are important but will only get you so far.

If the question includes the word 'how' you also need to make reference to language devices and vocabulary used by the writer.

This will show your understanding of the text and demonstrate that you are aware of the writer's intentions.

How confident are you in these skills already?

I understand and use textual references in terms of vocabulary and writers' techniques.

I use textual references precisely to present an overview of a text.

I fully understand the difference between all types of textual reference and use them accordingly.

Always ⇨ Usually ⇨ Sometimes

Step 1 Work on your skills

ACTIVITY 1: VOCABULARY

Let's look at another example. Read the passage carefully.

Recently married, Mary arrives at the remote farm where she will live and work with her new husband. She has not been here before.

The car stopped at last and she got out and watched Richard drive it away round the house to the back. It was suddenly very <u>dark</u> and she <u>shivered</u> a little. Listening in the complete silence, little noises rose from the bush, as if colonies of <u>strange</u> creatures had become still and watchful at their coming and were now going about their own business. The house looked shut and dark, as she approached it. Then a strange bird called, a wild nocturnal sound, and she ran, suddenly terrified, as if a <u>hostile</u> breath had blown upon her from another world. And as she stumbled in her high heels over the uneven ground, there was a stir and cackle of geese. The homely sound comforted her and she stopped and put out her hand to touch the leaves of a plant standing in a tin. Her fingers were fragrant with the familiar scent of geraniums. Then a square of light appeared in the blank wall of the house and she saw Richard's tall shape stooping inside. She went up the steps to the door and entered a room lit by a single candle. Richard had vanished again and in the dim light the room seemed tiny, tiny and very low. The roof was corrugated iron and there was a strong, musty smell, almost animal-like. Richard came back holding an old cocoa tin and began to fill the hanging lamp with paraffin, which dripped greasily down and pattered on the floor. The strong smell sickened her. The light flared up and now she could see the skins of animals on the brick floor: some kind of wildcat and a fawn coloured skin of some antelope. This tiny, stuffy room, the bare brick floor, the greasy lamp, were not what she had imagined. She sat down, bewildered by the strangeness of it all.

From The Grass is Singing by Doris Lessing

The writer makes the farm seem very unappealing to Mary and the reader.

How does the writer achieve this?

You should comment on:

▶ **what is said**

▶ **how it is said.**

You must refer to the text to support your comments.

Think about choosing textual evidence in terms of vocabulary to support this idea. Some of the words that you may want to pick out have already been underlined – see if you agree with these and then add to them by tracking through the passage and selecting other individual words.

When you have done this, think carefully about all the underlined words. What could you say to explain why you chose each word? For example:

The word 'dark' makes the farm sound mysterious and unwelcoming. The lack of light suggests little warmth or welcome.

The adjective 'strange' to refer to the creatures emphasises how weird an experience this is in Mary's eyes. It emphasises that this is a rather scary place.

Complete the task in this way.

 **Top tips**

It is advisable to have a firm grasp of the **word classes** (for example, whether the word is a noun, verb, adjective, adverb, pronoun). You can sometimes use them to add confidence to your response, as in the example here. Be warned though: you will not gain much from them without exploring the effect of the word itself and don't mix them up. If in doubt leave them out!

Step 2 Practise your skills

Another good way to explore this is to try using appropriate words yourself (this will also help with the writing section of the examination).

 ACTIVITY 2: CREATING AN ATMOSPHERE

The following excerpt is a description of a busy bus.

Think carefully about the best word to fill each of the gaps in order to create a claustrophobic, stifling atmosphere.

Compare your words with a learning partner and discuss whose are best and why.

The bus filled quickly with a _____ of people, _____ and _____ for a seat. It was soon _____ with people. Those _____ individuals who had managed a coveted chair were not to be easily shifted! Many of them looked _____ ahead, as if willing the crowd around away. One man – smug in his _____ comfort – had the trace of a _____ satisfied smile on his face.

Think about what you did here. Basically, in the reading section's 'How…' questions, you are doing this in reverse!

Step 3   Challenge yourself

ACTIVITY 3: TECHNIQUE

Now you need to look at the techniques used by the author to create particular effects.

Look at the following 19th century description of a storm at sea. It comes from *The Bible in Spain*, a travel account by George Borrow, published in 1842.

associated with the Devil?

plosive alliteration

onomatopoeia

exaggeration?

By about eight o'clock at night the wind had increased to a **hurricane**, the thunder rolled frightfully, and the only light which we had to guide us on our way was the **red forked** lightning, which burst at times from the bosom of the **big black** clouds which lowered over our heads. We were exerting ourselves to the utmost to weather the cape, which we could descry by the lightning, its brow being frequently brilliantly lighted up by the **flashes** which quivered around it, when suddenly, with a great **crash**, the engine broke, and the paddles, on which depended our lives, ceased to play.

The captain and the whole crew made the greatest exertions to repair the engine, and when they found their labour in vain, endeavoured, by hoisting the sails, and by practising all possible manoeuvres, to preserve the ship from impending destruction; but all was of no avail, we were hard on a lee shore, to which the howling tempest was impelling us. About this time I was standing near the helm, and I asked the steersman if there was any hope of saving the vessel, or our lives. He replied, 'Sir, it is a bad affair, no boat could live for a minute in this sea – none of us will see the morning.'

I kept my station, though almost drowned with water, immense waves continually breaking over our windward side and flooding the ship. The water casks broke from their lashings, and one of them struck me down, and crushed the foot of the unfortunate man at the helm, whose place was instantly taken by the captain. We were now close to the rocks, when a horrid convulsion of the elements took place. The lightning enveloped us, the thunders were louder than the roar of a million cannon, the dregs of the ocean seemed to be cast up, and in the midst of all this turmoil, the wind, without the slightest intimation, VEERED RIGHT ABOUT, and pushed us from the horrible coast faster than it had previously driven us towards it.

How do you react to George Borrow's experiences at sea?

You should comment on:

▶ **what is said**

▶ **how it is said.**

cape – land that juts out into the sea

You must refer to the text to support your comments.

This is a rich passage for examining the vocabulary choices of the writer. However, in addition to vocabulary, you can also refer to the techniques used in the writing. You will see four techniques already highlighted. Track through the text to see if you can pick out any others. Annotate a copy of the text in a similar way to the examples given.

As with word classes, while it is good to recognise techniques, it is more important to discuss their effects – you will not gain much credit for spotting a language device. If you don't have anything meaningful to say about it, leave it out!

Develop each annotation by saying what it adds to the effect on the reader.

You will find the following examples in the text provided. You may, of course, have your own ideas!

▶ Associated imagery – makes you think of something else (often as a simile or metaphor)

▶ Alliteration – repeated sounds

▶ Plosives – a consonant that is produced by stopping the airflow followed by a sudden release of air (for example, b, p)

▶ Complex sentence – extra information in a sentence

▶ Action verbs – give a sense of movement

▶ Onomatopoeia – sound words

▶ Speech – reported words spoken by a person or character

The **tone** of a piece of writing will be influenced by the purpose and audience of a text. For example, an information sheet for adults may have a serious tone whereas a magazine article for young people may have a more informal, humorous tone.

ACTIVITY 4: TONE

Textual references can also link to the **tone** of the text. This can be harder to pin down in a single reference, but it is worth considering.

Read the following extract from *Notes from a Small Island* by Bill Bryson. It describes Bryson's first day in Britain, where he has come as a young American. Having got off the ferry in the middle of the night, he has nowhere to stay and has to sleep rough in Dover.

Further along Marine Parade stood a shelter, open to the elements but roofed, and I decided that this was as good as I was going to get. With my backpack for a pillow, I lay down and drew my jacket tight around me. The bench was slatted and hard and studded with big roundheaded bolts that made reclining in comfort an impossibility – doubtless their

131

intention. I lay for a long time listening to the sea washing over the shingle below, and eventually dropped off to a long, cold night of mumbled dreams … I awoke with a gasp about three, stiff all over and quivering from cold. The fog had gone. The air was now still and clear, and the sky was bright with stars. A beacon from the lighthouse at the far end of the breakwater swept endlessly over the sea. It was all most fetching, but I was far too cold to appreciate it. I dug shiveringly through my backpack and extracted every potentially warming item I could find: a flannel shirt, two sweaters, an extra pair of jeans. I used some woollen socks as mittens and put a pair of flannel boxer shorts on my head as a kind of desperate headwarmer, then sank heavily back onto the bench and waited patiently for death's sweet kiss. Instead, I fell asleep.

I was awakened again by an abrupt bellow of foghorn, which nearly knocked me from my narrow perch, and sat up feeling wretched but fractionally less cold … I took off my sock mittens and looked at my watch. It was 5.55 a.m. I looked at the receding ferry and wondered where anybody would be going at that hour. Where would I go at that hour? I picked up my backpack and shuffled off down the prom, to get some circulation going.

… I came across an old guy walking a little dog. The dog was frantically trying to pee on every vertical surface and in consequence wasn't so much walking as being dragged along on three legs.

The man nodded a good-morning as I drew level. 'Might turn out nice,' he announced, gazing hopefully at a sky that looked like a pile of wet towels. I asked him if there was a restaurant anywhere that might be open. He knew of a place not far away and directed me to it. 'Best transport caff in Kent,' he said.

'Transport calf?' I repeated uncertainly, and retreated a couple of paces as I'd noticed his dog was straining desperately to moisten my leg.

'Very popular with the lorry drivers. They always know the best places, don't they?' He smiled amiably, then lowered his voice a fraction and leaned towards me as if about to share a confidence. 'You might want to take them pants off your head before you go in.'

I clutched my head 'Oh!' and removed the forgotten boxer shorts with a blush. I tried to think of a succinct explanation, but the man was scanning the sky again.

The text is quite humorous in many ways. Select some textual references that you think highlight the humour. Try to add some explanation as to why they might be considered amusing to the reader.

REFERENCE	HUMOROUS BECAUSE ...
The shelter was 'as good as I was going to get'.	It is not very good at all!

 Use your work to answer the following question:

How does Bryson show what he thinks of his first experience of Britain?

You should comment on:

▶ **what is said** ▶ **how it is said.**

You must refer to the text to support your comments.

 ## ACTIVITY 5: OVERVIEW

An overview is not just about summing up a passage or text. It entails discussing a text from a wider angle.

You could consider:

▶ the issues that the text explores
▶ the effects of events on different people in the text
▶ the effects over the passage of time
▶ comparing places and/or situations
▶ the **prejudices, bias** and **morals of society** at the time the text was set or written.

> **prejudice** – having a preformed idea about a person, place or event without good reason or evidence
> **bias** – putting forward an unbalanced point of view about something
> **morals of society** – the widely held views and opinions of the majority of people in a country at a given time

Read carefully the excerpt from the passage below. It is set in America's Midwest during the years following the Great Depression. Claudia, a black American, looks back at her childhood and remembers a time when she was ill.

Our house is old, cold, and green. At night a kerosene lamp lights one large room. The others are braced in darkness, peopled by roaches and mice. Adults do not talk to us – they give us directions. They issue orders without providing information. When we trip and fall down they glance at us; if we cut or bruise ourselves, they ask us are we crazy. When we catch colds, they shake their heads in disgust at our lack of consideration. How, they ask us, do you expect anybody to get anything done if you all are sick? We cannot answer them. Our illness is treated with contempt, foul Black Draught, and **castor oil** that blunts our minds.

When, on a day after a trip to collect coal, I cough once, loudly, through bronchial tubes already packed tight with phlegm, my mother frowns. 'Great Jesus. Get on in that bed. How many times do I have to tell you to wear something on your head? You must be the biggest fool in this town. Frieda? Get some rags and stuff that window.' Frieda restuffs the window. I trudge off to bed, full of guilt and self-pity. I lie down in my underwear, the metal in the black **garters** hurts my legs, but I do not take them off, because it is too cold to lie stockingless. It takes a long time for my body to heat its place in the bed. Once I have generated a silhouette of warmth, I dare not move, for there is a cold place one-half inch in any direction. No one speaks to me or asks how I feel. In an hour or two my mother comes. Her hands are large and rough, and when she rubs the Vicks salve on my chest, I am rigid with pain. She takes two fingers' full of it at a time, and massages my chest until I am faint. Just when I think I will tip over into a scream, she scoops out a little of the salve on her forefinger and puts it in my mouth, telling me to swallow. A hot flannel is wrapped about my neck and chest. I am covered up with heavy quilts and ordered to sweat, which I do, promptly.

Later I throw up, and my mother says, 'What did you puke on the bed clothes for? Don't you have sense enough to hold your head out the bed? Now, look what you did. You think I got time for nothing but washing up your puke?'

The puke swaddles down the pillow onto the sheet – green-gray, with flecks of orange. It moves like the insides of an uncooked egg. Stubbornly clinging to its own mass, refusing to break up and be removed. How, I wonder, can it be so neat and nasty at the same time?

My mother's voice drones on. She is not talking to me. She is talking to the puke, but she is calling it my name: Claudia. She wipes it up as best she can and puts a scratchy towel over the large wet place. I lie down again. The rags have fallen from the window crack, and the air is cold. I dare not call her back and am reluctant to leave my warmth. My mother's anger humiliates me; her words chafe my cheeks, and I am crying. I do not know that she is not angry at me, but at my sickness. I believe she despises my weakness for letting the sickness 'take holt.' By and by I will not get sick; I will refuse to. But for now I am crying. I know I am making more snot, but I can't stop.

My sister comes in. Her eyes are full of sorrow. She sings to me: 'When the deep purple falls over sleepy garden walls, someone thinks of me …' I doze, thinking of plums, walls, and 'someone.'

But was it really like that? As painful as I remember? Only mildly. Or rather, it was a productive and fructifying pain. Love, thick and dark as Alaga syrup, eased up into that cracked window. I could smell it – taste it – sweet, musty, with an edge of wintergreen in its base – everywhere in that house.

> **castor oil** – unpleasant tasting medicine
> **garters** – bands worn around the top of the leg to hold stockings up

It stuck, along with my tongue, to the frosted windowpanes. It coated my chest, along with the salve, and when the flannel came undone in my sleep, the clear, sharp curves of air outlined its presence on my throat. And in the night, when my coughing was dry and tough, feet padded into the room, hands repinned the flannel, readjusted the quilt, and rested a moment on my forehead. So when I think of autumn, I think of somebody with hands who does not want me to die.

From *The Bluest Eye* by Toni Morrison

How does Claudia's family react to her illness?

You should comment on:

▶ **what is said**

▶ **how it is said.**

You must refer to the text to support your comments.

In the text above, textual references in terms of overview can be found, referring to:

▶ wider issues that the text explores, for example:
What was the situation for ordinary black people in America at that time?

▶ the effects on a character over the passage of time, for example:
What was the overall effect of the incident on Claudia's later life?

▶ the effects of events on different people, for example:
What was the overall effect of the illness on: Claudia, her mother, her sister?

▶ different points of view, for example:
What are the differences in the views held by Claudia's mother and sister?

This is not an exhaustive checklist, but may give you an insight into what the examiner is looking for in terms of the elusive 'overview'.

 ACTIVITY 6: IDENTIFY THE CATEGORY

Look at the following extracts from students' examination answers in the table on the next page. Each extract relates to a text that you have looked at in this unit. Even though the extracts are out of context, you should be able to identify the category in which each extract fits.

Match each extract to one of the following categories and give a reason for the match:

▶ events

▶ inference

▶ language

▶ technique

▶ tone

▶ overview.

EXTRACT	CATEGORY AND REASON FOR MATCH
The use of the onomatopoeic word 'howling' makes the storm seem alive. It not only gives me a sense of the noise the wind was making, but gives me the idea that the storm was like an animal, preparing to attack.	
Bill Bryson has a very uncomfortable night in a shelter on the sea front. This is clear through the bolts making comfort an 'impossibility'. This makes it clear that he is in for a hard, uncomfortable night.	
It appears that the man is used to meeting all sorts of people. This impression is created because he carries on talking about the weather and doesn't seem bothered by the underpants on Bryson's head.	
It is obvious that ordinary black families were very poor. The passage states that a single lamp 'lights one large room'. This gives a sense of the poverty at the time.	
A sense of danger is built up through a series of happenings in the narrative – first Mike spots his attackers, then he runs into the waste land. When he gets here, however, there are a series of other difficulties that he has to face.	
The article is factual and informative. This is built up through a series of personal observations and facts about the reserve.	

Now you have completed the section, do you think your confidence has increased?

I feel confident in using textual references in terms of vocabulary and writers' techniques.

I can use textual references precisely to present an overview of a text.

I fully understand the difference between all types of textual reference and use them accordingly.

Always ⇨ Usually ⇨ Sometimes

Next steps...

By now, you have a good understanding of the areas of textual reference that you can draw on to back up your opinions. The next step is to use your knowledge as part of a wider evaluation of a text.

This can be done by exploring the next section, which looks at critical evaluation.

BE EXAM READY

▶ To practise using the full range of textual references in an exam context
▶ To feel confident about writing under timed conditions

How confident are you in these skills already?

I can make a range of textual references to answer this type of exam question.

I can use a mark scheme to assess my textual references.

I can use a mark scheme to assess other students' use of textual references and suggest improvements.

Always ⇨ Usually ⇨ Sometimes

You have already practised recognising and selecting a range of textual references. Now you will have the chance to look at sample answers to exam questions, mark your own responses and write under timed conditions. The text is a little shorter than you will find in the exam, so practise answering the question in 10 minutes rather than the 15 minutes (approximately) you would normally have.

QUESTION 1

Read the following excerpt from *Life of Pi* by Yann Martel. Pi Patel, a 16-year-old Indian boy, describes being on board a ship, carrying humans and animals, that sinks when crossing the Pacific Ocean.

The ship shook and there was that sound, the monstrous metallic burp. What was it? Was it the collective scream of humans and animals protesting their oncoming death? Was it the ship itself giving up the ghost? I fell over. I got to my feet. I looked overboard again. The sea was rising. The waves were getting closer. We were sinking fast. …
I ran for the stairs to the bridge. Up there was where the officers were, the only people on the ship who spoke English, the masters of our destiny here, the ones who would right this wrong. They would explain everything. They would take care of my family and me. I climbed to the middle bridge. There was no one on the starboard side. I ran to the port side. I saw three men, crewmembers. I fell. I got up. They were looking overboard. I shouted. They turned.

They looked at me and at each other. They spoke a few words. They came towards me quickly. I felt gratitude and relief welling up in me. I said, 'Thank God I've found you. What is happening? I am very scared. There is water at the bottom of the ship. I am worried about my family. I can't get to the level where our cabins are. Is this normal? Do you think –' One of the men interrupted me by thrusting a life jacket into my arms and shouting something in Chinese. I noticed an orange whistle dangling from the life jacket. The men were nodding vigorously at me. When they took hold of me and lifted me in their strong arms, I thought nothing of it. I thought they were helping me. I was so full of trust in them that I felt grateful as they carried me in the air. Only when they threw me overboard did I have doubts.

What do you think and feel about this section of the story?
You should comment on:
- **what is said**
- **how it is said.**
You must refer to the text to support your comments.

✔ Self-assessment

Your teacher may provide you with a detailed mark scheme to review your answer. In the meantime, use the following prompts as a guide to check your progress or give you ideas of the sort of thing to write. As ever, this is not a checklist – you will have your own ideas!

- Have you discussed the events of the text? For example:
  The ship shook and Pi 'fell over'.
- Have you linked this textual reference to your personal opinion (perhaps an emotional response) that shows understanding of the events? For example:
  I thought the text was exciting, wondering if Pi would survive.
- Have you picked out specific words and commented on their effect? For example:
  The adjective 'monstrous' describes the unknown sounds being made as the ship is sinking. This makes me as the reader feel like Pi is battling an unknown horrible creature.

- Have you discussed the text's effects, supported by well-selected textual references? For example:
  The writer builds suspense through a series of questions being used, ('What was it?') which adds to the confused atmosphere.
- Have you mentioned the tone of the text? For example:
  Although the situation is very serious, there is a wry humour in the text, as seen in 'Only when they threw me overboard did I have my doubts'.
- Have you discussed the overall effect of the text? For example:
  The tone is one of growing danger. The tension builds through a series of events which highlights the growing danger to Pi.
- Have you made accurate and perceptive comments? For example:
  Martel makes us feel sorry for Pi as he is treated quite roughly by the crewmembers. They speak different languages, which adds to the confusion. There is a clash of ages, authority and culture between the boy and the crewmembers.

! Top tips

To save time, textual references can be embedded in the sentence you are writing. Quoting within the sentence will add emphasis and can be a useful aid to speeding you up. If you find this difficult, putting a reference in brackets is another useful trick.

Comparing sample answers

Assess the four sample answers to suggest what the student did well and what they might need to do to improve.

Answer 1

The noun 'sinking' is used which is bad. There are lots of adjectives and onomatopoeia. Pi says, 'I climbed to the middle bridge. There was no one on the starboard side. I ran to the port side. I saw three men, crewmembers. I fell. I got up. They were looking overboard. I shouted. They turned. They looked at me and at each other.' This is bad. Also, we don't know what happens to him.

 Top tips

This candidate makes a number of classic mistakes including:

- using the wrong word class
- a lack of explanation to address the question
- mentioning techniques without expanding
- textual references that are too long.

Answer 2

I think the story is a good one. It makes me feel that Pi must be scared and frightened at being on a sinking ship. He feels alone and that makes me wonder what it would be like. I thought it would be okay when he met the crewmembers but all they do is throw him over the side! Lots of words such as 'monstrous' and 'shook' make me think that this is a serious situation.

Answer 3

This section of the story is effective as it builds the tension of Pi being alone on a sinking ship. The vocabulary used is startling – the writer throws in words such as 'monstrous', 'screams', 'ghosts' and 'death' to make us in no doubt that the situation is a matter of life and death. Onomatopoeia is used effectively as well as questions which draw the reader in and add to the confusion that we know Pi must be feeling. As Pi explores the ailing ship, he can't find any other person and this gives me a nightmarish quality – like when you are looking for help but can't find it. When Pi does meet the men, they don't listen to him and Pi is just confused by what they do.

Overall, the text is effective at portraying an awful situation.

Answer 4

The narrative is very effective in portraying Pi's confusion and distress at being onboard a sinking ship.

The use of words such as 'monstrous' and 'screams' have an unsettling, ominous quality which builds the feeling that this is a doomed ship. Other examples, such as 'death' and 'ghost' add to this in obvious ways. In addition, the use of lots of questions such as, 'what was it?' build on each other, and add to the sense of Pi's confusion.

The confusion is compounded by the use of short sentences, such as, 'I fell over. I got to my feet.' This emphasises the erratic nature of the situation. The first person narrative really makes me empathise with Pi's situation and imagine it happening to me.

There is a cultural sense that no one cares about Pi and his family. The officers are described as 'masters of our destiny' – they are almost like gods. Pi has complete faith in them as he is matter of fact when he says 'they would take care of my family and me.'

The sense of isolation is increased by 'there was no one on the starboard side'. This gives the feeling that Pi is alone and helpless.

An attitude of confusion prevails. 'I shouted' gives a sense of noise – that Pi has to shout to be heard.

Pi seems quite naïve – he feels 'relief and gratitude', but we know all is not well. He talks incessantly which gives us the sense that he is relieved and frightened, and all his fears come tumbling out.

The interruption comes and the actions of the men sound panicky and rough – 'thrust' and 'nodded vigorously' add to this.

Finally, there is a wry humour, that Pi only doubts the men when they 'threw him overboard'. He seems accepting of the situation and this adds to the black humour.

Now you have completed the section, do you think your confidence has increased?

I feel confident in using textual references in terms of vocabulary and writers' techniques.

I can use textual references precisely to present an overview of a text.

I fully understand the difference between all types of textual reference and use them accordingly.

Always   ⇨   Usually   ⇨   Sometimes

Unit 11
Evaluating critically

OBJECTIVES

▶ To develop a clear understanding of what it means to 'evaluate critically'
▶ To think about a clear approach to questions that demand critical evaluation skills

---

How confident are you in these skills already?

I understand what it means to critically evaluate.

I have a clear approach to critical evaluation questions.

I can use textual references to support my critical evaluation.

Always ➡ Usually ➡ Sometimes

Get going

Step 1 — Work on your skills

What does it mean to evaluate critically? Well, you will have to give your opinion and views on a text – what you think and feel. You will already have done some of this, but in a more focused way (for example, your views on a character or place). This time, you will have to consider the whole text or a section of the text.

The best way to explore this is to have a look at what a question might look like.

> **Critical evaluation** involves giving your opinion about a text. It often means considering a statement about a text and deciding if that statement is true, or to what extent you agree with it. Don't forget that 'evaluating' involves judging the quality or worth of something.

ACTIVITY 1: RELATIONSHIP ADVICE

Look at the following text. It is taken from a relationship advice manual, *How to be Happy Though Married*, written in 1849 by Reverend Edward John Hardy.

Men are often as easily caught as birds, but as difficult to keep. If the wife cannot make her home bright and happy, so that it shall be the cleanest, sweetest, cheerfullest place that her husband can find refuge in—a retreat from the toils and troubles of the outer world—then God help the poor man, for he is virtually homeless!

In the home, more than anywhere else, order is Heaven's first law. It is the duty of a wife to sweetly order her cage so that it may be clean, neat, and free from muddle. Method is the oil that makes the wheels of the domestic machine run easily. The mistress of a home who desires order, and the tranquillity that comes of order, must insist on the application of method to every branch and department of the household work. She must rise and breakfast early and give her orders early. Doing much before twelve o'clock gives her a command of the day. But a cage-making wife is much more than a good cook and housekeeper. Indeed it is possible for a wife to be too careful and cumbered about these things. When such is the case she becomes miserable and grumbles at a little dust or disorder which the ordinary mortal does not see, just as a fine musician is pained and made miserable at a slight discord that is not noticed by less-trained ears. Probably her husband wishes his house were less perfectly kept, but more peaceful. A woman should know when to change her rôle of housewife for that of the loving friend and companion of her husband. She should be able and willing to intelligently discuss with him the particular political or social problem that is to him of vital interest.

Women's lives are often very dull; but it would help to make them otherwise if wives would sometimes think over, during the hours when parted from their husbands, a few little winning ways as surprises for them on their return, either in the way of conversation, or of some small change of dress, or any way their ingenuity would have suggested in courting days. How little the lives of men and women would be dull, if they thought of and acted towards each other after marriage as they did before it! Certainly, it does a wife good to go out of her cage occasionally for amusement, although her deepest, truest happiness may be found at home.

What do you think and feel about Rev. Edward John Hardy's views on relationships and running a home? [10]

You should comment on:

► **what is said**

► **how it is said.**

You must refer to the text to support your comments.

In the last unit, we looked at one approach to making textual references. These references are vital to show that you have understood the texts you have read and also to support your critical evaluation. You should provide a wide range of evidence based on what you judge to be the most important factors and justify how you have made your choice.

The following questions are based on the categories covered in the previous unit. They may serve as a useful toolkit to help you explore the text. You can also now layer on your opinion – what you think and feel about each element. In other words, start to critically evaluate! Look at how the questions have changed. What has been added?

► What is the text about and what do you think about this?

► What can you infer from the text and what do you feel about these inferences?

► What is your opinion about the language used?

► What do you think about the techniques the writer uses?

► What is the tone of the text?

► What is your overview of the text?

Look at the table. In the middle column are some textual references that you may have picked. Add your thoughts and feelings about each point to a copy of the table.

	TEXTUAL REFERENCE	MY VIEWS (THOUGHTS AND FEELINGS)
Main points/content	The text says that it is essential to have a well maintained, looked after home.	
Inference	It implies that it is a wife's duty to keep house and look after her husband.	
Language	'Cage' is used as an extended metaphor for the home.	
Technique	Superlatives ('cleanest, sweetest') are used to infer that a woman's home should be the best possible.	
Tone	The writer uses an imperative tone.	
Overview	Hardy expresses a view that is very much rooted in the 19th century values and views of a woman's role to keep house, look after her husband and adapt seamlessly to his needs and wishes.	

Build on this by thinking of two other references you could add to the middle column.

Then give your opinion about each of these.

Step 2 Practise your skills

ACTIVITY 2: SENTENCE STARTERS

You are not going to have the time to draw and fill in tables in the exam! However, it is critical that you understand the approaches to take. Use the work so far to attempt to write an answer to the question in Activity 1 in clear paragraphs.

Here are some sentence starters that you may want to use:

▶ The text says that it is essential to have a well-maintained, looked after home. I think . . .

▶ It implies that it is a wife's duty to keep house and look after her husband . . .

▶ 'Cage' is used as an extended metaphor which suggests . . .

▶ The writer uses an imperative tone, which comes across as . . .

▶ Hardy expresses a view that to us in the 21st century seems . . .

Step 3 Challenge yourself

ACTIVITY 3: HOW A LADY SHOULD CONDUCT HERSELF

Read this passage from *The Ladies' Book of Etiquette* by Florence Hartley (written in 1860). In this section, Hartley discusses how a lady should conduct herself when walking in the street.

Conduct in the street

A lady's conduct is never so entirely at the mercy of critics, because never so public, as when she is in the street. Her dress, carriage, walk, will all be exposed to notice; every passer-by will look at her, if it is only for one glance; every unlady-like action will be marked; and in no position will a dignified, lady-like deportment be more certain to command respect.

First, your dress. Not that scarlet shawl, with a green dress, I beg, and—oh! spare my nerves!—you are not so insane as to put on a blue bonnet. That's right. If you wish to wear the green dress, don a black shawl, and—that white bonnet will do very well. One rule you must lay down with regard to a walking dress. It must never be conspicuous. Let the material be rich, if you will; the set of each garment faultless; have collar and sleeves snowy white, and wear neatly-fitting, whole, clean gloves and boots. Every detail may be scrupulously attended to, but let the whole effect be quiet and modest. Wear a little of one bright color, if you will, but not more than one.

Wear no jewelry in the street excepting your watch and brooch. Jewelry is only suited for full evening dress, when all the other details unite to set it off. If it is real, it is too valuable to risk losing in the street, and if it is not real, no lady should wear it. Mock jewelry is utterly detestable.

What are you doing? Why did you not dress before you came out? It is a mark of ill-breeding to draw your gloves on in the street. Now your bonnet-strings, and now—your collar! Pray arrange your dress before you leave the house! Nothing looks worse than to see a lady fussing over her dress in the street. Take a few moments more in your dressing-room, and so arrange your dress that you will not need to think of it again whilst you are out.

Do not walk so fast! you are not chasing anybody! Walk slowly, gracefully!

Oh, do not drag one foot after the other as if you were fast asleep—set down the foot lightly, but at the same time firmly; now, carry your head up, not so; you hang it down as if you feared to look any one in the face! Nay, that is the other extreme! Now you look like a drill-major, on parade! So! that is the medium. Erect, yet, at the same time, easy and elegant.

Now, my friend, do not swing your arms. You don't know what to do with them? Your parasol takes one hand; hold your dress up a little with the other. Not so! No lady should raise her dress above the ankle.

Loud talking and laughing in the street are excessively vulgar. Not only this, but they expose a lady to the most severe misconstruction. Let your conduct be modest and quiet.

What do you think and feel about Florence Hartley's views on how women should behave in public? **[10]**

You should comment on:

▶ what is said

▶ how it is said.

You must refer to the text to support your comments.

Now you have completed the section, do you think your confidence has increased?

I understand what it means to critically evaluate.

I have a clear approach to critical evaluation questions.

I can use textual references to support my critical evaluation.

Always ⇨ Usually ⇨ Sometimes

! **Top tips**

- Use your toolbox of approaches to help you if necessary.
- Track through the text and find evidence to support your views.
- Add in your opinion.

Improve your skills

OBJECTIVES

▶ To explore critical evaluation in terms of bias
▶ To consider unsupported statements
▶ To explore approaches to questions that ask you to consider a statement about a text

How confident are you in these skills already?

I can recognise bias and unsupported statements.

I can explore other people's opinions about a text with confidence.

I can recognise and answer questions that lead in with a statement about the text.

Always ⇨ Usually ⇨ Sometimes

As well as critically evaluating what is in the text in terms of content, language, techniques and so on, you may also need to consider things that are not directly found in the text itself. This may sound a little strange but, when you think about it, any writer is influenced by the time they live in and other pressures and ideas they have. This is known as **bias** and you may need to explore this in your critical evaluation of a text. As a way of thinking about this, consider the following bullet points. They will help you to consider any biases held by the writer about the topic.

- An opinion of the writer, backed up with evidence
- An opinion of the writer, *not* backed up with relevant evidence
- The views and attitudes of society at the time the text was written or set

Step 1   Work on your skills

📄 ACTIVITY 1: LOOKING FOR BIAS

Look for bias in the text that follows, a newspaper article, taken from an 1888 edition of the *London Times*.

ANOTHER WHITECHAPEL MURDER

Another murder of the foulest kind was committed in the neighbourhood of Whitechapel in the early hours of yesterday morning, but by whom and with what motive is at present a complete mystery.

At a quarter to 4 o'clock Police constable Neill, 97J, when in Buck's Row, Whitechapel, came upon the body of a woman lying on a part of the footway, and on stooping to raise her up in the belief that she was drunk he discovered that her throat was cut almost from ear to ear. She was dead but still warm. He procured assistance and at once sent to the station and for a doctor. He inspected the body at the place where it was found and pronounced the woman dead. He made a hasty examination and then discovered that, besides the gash across the throat, the woman had terrible wounds in the abdomen.

After the body was removed to the mortuary of the parish, in Old Montague Street, Whitechapel, steps were taken to secure, if possible, identification, but at first with little prospect of success. The clothing was of a common description, but the skirt of one petticoat and the band of another article bore the stencil stamp of Lambeth Workhouse. As the news of the murder spread, however, first one woman and then another came forward to view the body, and at length it was found that a woman answering the description of the murdered woman had lodged in a common lodging-house, 18, Thrawl-street, Spitalfields.

Women from that place were fetched and they identified the deceased as 'Polly,' who had shared a room with three other women in the place on the usual terms of such houses – nightly payment of 4d. each, each woman having a separate bed. It was gathered that the deceased had led the life of an 'unfortunate' while lodging in the house, which was only for about three weeks past. Nothing more was known of her by them but that when she presented herself for her lodging on Thursday night she was turned away by the deputy because she had not the money.

🔍 Read through these examples from the text and then look for further examples.

▶ A statement by the writer, backed up with evidence:

The dead woman was named Polly and shared a room with three other women at the lodging house. (Women's evidence.)

▶ A statement by the writer, not backed up with relevant evidence:

This was a murder of the 'foulest kind'.

▶ The views and attitudes of society at the time the text was written or set:

At the time, the poor were looked down upon and treated as criminals.

 Use this work to answer the following question:

'The newspaper article does not show much sympathy for the victim.' Do you agree?

Step 2 Practise your skills

So far in this unit, we have looked only at 19th century non-fiction texts. However, it is important to remember that the same skills need to be applied to 20th century prose fiction texts and 21st century non-fiction texts too.

You may wonder how you can do this for an extract from a piece of fiction, but the ideas remain the same. In fiction, the writer may show his/her biases through the actions of the characters and the events of the story, instead of being more direct as in non-fiction.

 ACTIVITY 2: YOUR THOUGHTS AND FEELINGS

Read the following text excerpt:

Then a squad car pulled up and a short cop got out. He looked real hard at me, then at Manny.

'What are you two doing?'

'He's practising shots. I'm watching. Ain't it obvious?' I said with my smart self.

The cop just stood there and finally turned to the other one who was just getting out of the car.

'Who unlocked the park gate?' the big one snarled.

'It's always unlocked,' I said. Then we three just stood there watching Manny go at it.

'Is that true?' the big guy asked, tilting his hat back with the thumb the way tough guys do in the movies. 'Hey you,' he said, walking over to Manny. 'I'm talking to you.' He finally grabbed the ball to get Manny's attention. But that didn't work. Manny just stood there with his arms out waiting for the pass. He wasn't paying no attention to the cop. So, quite naturally, when the cop slapped his head it was a surprise.

'Gimme the ball, man.' Manny's face was all tightened up and ready to pop.

'Did you hear what I said, black boy?'

Now, when somebody says that word like that, I gets warm. And crazy or no crazy, Manny became like my brother at that moment and the cop became the enemy.

'You better give him back his ball,' I said. 'Manny don't take no mess from no cops. He ain't bothering nobody. He's gonna be Mister Basketball when he grows up. Just trying to get a little practice in.'

'Look here, sister, we'll run you in too,' the short cop said.

'I sure can't be your sister seeing as how I'm a black girl and you're a white cop. Boy, I sure will be glad when you run me in so I can tell everybody about that. You're just picking on us because we're black, mister.'

The big guy screwed his mouth up and let out one of them hard-day sighs. 'The park's closed, little girl, so why don't you and your boyfriend go on home.'

That really got me. The 'little girl' was bad enough but that 'boyfriend' was too much.

From *The Hammer Man* by Toni Cade Bambara

Consider the biases of the writer. Here are some prompts to help you:

▶ What is the writer's opinion of these policemen? What backs this up?

▶ What is the writer's opinion of the girl narrating the story? What backs this up?

▶ What are the views and attitudes of society at the time the text was written or set?

Now consider a typical exam-style question:

What are your thoughts and feelings as you read this text?

You could now think of your thoughts and feelings on each of the bullet points.

As this question puts the emphasis on **your** thoughts and feelings, it may also be worth considering the following:

▶ Biases held by you about the topic

▶ Your own thoughts and feelings

▶ The views/attitudes of society today

▶ Knowledge of other texts/references of the time

However, be sure to keep your answer firmly focused on the text itself.

Step 3 Challenge yourself

As part of critical evaluation, you may also be given a statement and asked if you agree or disagree with it.

For example the question to accompany the next text reads:

'In this article, the writer portrays a negative view about long distance sailing.'

To what extent do you agree with this view?

You should look for points that support the statement and points that contradict it. These will cover exactly the same things that have already been looked at in this unit and the previous one. You can draw an overall conclusion about the statement based on an evaluation of the text in terms of content, inference, language, literary devices, bias and so on.

ACTIVITY 3: LONG-DISTANCE SAILING

Read the following internet article about modern-day sailing.

The not-so-beautiful briny sea

By Louise Brooks

Reports are emerging of five British yachtsmen being held for a week in Iran after getting lost on the water. Disney may have popularised the image of the beautiful briny sea, but in these troubled times, perhaps sailing isn't the relaxing pastime many believe it to be...

Appealing or appalling?

'Humans have been sailing the seas and oceans for fun for over a century,' says Ross Southard of Sailing Monthly magazine. 'Changes in technology and superb levels of communications have meant more people than ever taking it up as a hobby.'

For lots of ordinary people, long-distance sailing is a way of getting away from their daily worries and woes. It offers the lure of the unknown and an exciting escapade away from ordinary life.

However, in a small number of cases, the dream becomes a nightmare.

Last Wednesday, after being locked up for a week, Iran finally released a five-man sailing team who unwittingly strayed into Iranian waters while sailing to Dubai. Elsewhere, talks are frantically taking place in an attempt to secure the release of a British couple who were kidnapped by Somali pirates last October.

Seemingly, 21st century sailors have more to worry about than high winds and a diet of food rations!

Safe passage?

British people have long been accustomed to the Foreign Office advising holidaymakers of troubled countries to avoid, but few people realise that officials also offer a list of maritime 'no go' areas. For example, there is a stretch of water in the Arabian Sea known as 'Pirate Alley' because boats are so likely to be attacked.

However, avoiding this stretch of water also means avoiding the Suez Canal, a shortcut between the Mediterranean and Indian Oceans. The alternative is to navigate round the Southern tip of Africa - the infamous

Cape of Good Hope – a route notorious for its danger to sailing vessels.

'You'd have to be barking mad to attempt it!' says Southard. 'Although, the Suez route is also often problematic due to violent headwinds and ruinous reefs.'

Made it through Suez? Now contend with the increasingly complex political tensions of the Middle East...

So why bother?

With all this making it sound like more hassle than it's worth, why do ordinary Britons risk everything to sail rather than take the presumably faster, cheaper and simpler option of flying?

David Ormrod, 76, of Cornwall, says, 'Nothing will put me off. The sense of freedom and being in control you get from being on the open waters is priceless. You forget all your worries and get away from all your problems.'

His wife, Margaret, joins in: 'The world is getting more dangerous, whatever way you travel. Nothing would put us off going. What's the alternative? Stay in your house forever? You could die falling down the stairs!'

The couple know what they are talking about. They have made dozens of sea journeys since they retired and have even been held up by armed pirates whilst sailing around the world. David finishes by saying, 'It's all part of the experience! When you dock at port you are respected by the locals. You are also part of a wonderful community of sailors all over the world. That's priceless.'

'In this article, the writer portrays a negative view about long-distance sailing.'

To what extent do you agree with this view? **[10]**

You should comment on:

▶ **what is said**

▶ **how it is said.**

You must refer to the text to support your comments.

Use everything we have looked at so far to help you answer the question. Note that this style of question presents a statement and asks how far you agree. You are able to build a case for and against, using the approaches taken. You may want to use the following table to help you.

	NEGATIVE VIEW OF SAILING	**POSITIVE VIEW OF SAILING**
Content (main points)		
Inferences		
Language		
Techniques		
Bias		

Add at least two points to each section of the table. Then, try writing up your points into a paragraph. End with a conclusion – overall, do you agree with the statement that it portrays a negative view of sailing? Remember, you have three choices – yes, no or partly!

OBJECTIVES

▶ To adopt a confident approach to answering exam questions that assess critical evaluation

▶ To feel confident about writing under timed conditions

▶ To apply the mark scheme with confidence

How confident are you in these skills already?

I can recognise questions that require critical evaluation.

I can answer these questions under timed conditions.

I can assess my own response to critical evaluation.

I can assess others' responses to critical evaluation.

Always ⇨ Usually ⇨ Sometimes

We have worked through many of the possible approaches to critical evaluation. You are now ready to try an exam-style question under timed conditions. Give yourself 15 minutes to answer each question.

QUESTION 1

The following extract is from a 19th century travel book, *Wild Wales*. Its author, George Borrow, recounted his travels around Wales. In this extract, he writes about visiting Neath Abbey, a ruin not far from Swansea. This would be one of two texts in the exam. Your teacher may provide you with the partner text.

Wild Wales – Neath Abbey

I reached a small village half-way between Swansea and Neath, and without stopping continued my course, walking very fast. I had surmounted a hill, and had nearly descended that side of it which looked towards the east, having on my left, that is to the north, a wooded height, when an extraordinary scene presented itself to my eyes. Somewhat to the south rose immense stacks of chimneys surrounded by grimy diabolical-looking buildings, in the neighbourhood of which were huge heaps of cinders and black rubbish. From the chimneys, notwithstanding it was Sunday, smoke was proceeding in volumes, choking the atmosphere all around. From this pandemonium, at the distance of about a quarter of a mile to the south-west, upon a green meadow, stood, looking darkly grey, a ruin of vast size with window holes, towers, spires, and arches. Between it and the accursed pandemonium, lay a horrid filthy place, part of which was swamp and part pool: the pool black as soot, and the swamp of a disgusting leaden colour. Across this place of filth stretched a tramway leading seemingly from the abominable mansions to the ruin. So strange a scene I had never beheld in nature. Had it been on canvas, with the addition of a number of Diabolical figures, proceeding along the tramway, it might have stood for Sabbath in Hell—devils proceeding to afternoon worship, and would have formed a picture worthy of the powerful but insane painter, Jerome Bos.

After standing for a considerable time staring at the strange spectacle I proceeded. Presently meeting a lad, I asked him what was the name of the ruin.

'The Abbey,' he replied.

'Neath Abbey?' said I.

'Yes!'

Having often heard of this abbey, which in its day was one of the most famous in Wales, I determined to go and inspect it. It was with some difficulty that I found my way to it. It stood, as I have already observed, in a meadow, and was on almost every side surrounded by majestic hills. To give any clear description of this ruined pile would be impossible, the dilapidation is so great, dilapidation evidently less the effect of time than of awful violence, perhaps that

of gunpowder. The southern is by far the most perfect portion of the building; there you see not only walls but roofs. Fronting you full south, is a mass of masonry with two immense arches, other arches behind them: entering, you find yourself beneath a vaulted roof, and passing on you come to an oblong square which may have been a church; an iron-barred window on your right enables you to look into a mighty vault, the roof of which is supported by beautiful pillars. Then – but I forbear to say more respecting these remains, for fear of stating what is incorrect, my stay amongst them having been exceedingly short.

From *Wild Wales* by George Borrow

'In this extract, the writer George Borrow, portrays a very negative view of South Wales.'
To what extent do you agree with this view? **[10]**
You should comment on:
- **what is said**
- **how it is said.**
You must refer to the text to support your comments.

Comparing sample answers

Candidate 1

The text shows a poor place. It is very dirty and sooty. There is lots of smoke. The swamp is mentioned – this is not a nice place to be. There is loads of dirty stuff around as well as an old ruin, so what's the point, there is nothing to see or buy there.

Candidate 2

Yes, I agree with the statement as the author paints a very negative view of the place. He calls it 'horrid and filthy', a 'swamp' which sounds very much like a dirty disgusting place. There is an atmosphere of death as he describes the place as 'choking' the surrounding area and uses words like 'dirty', 'grimy' and 'black' which literally sound filthy. Borrow emphasises the size of the industry in the area – 'huge', 'immense' and 'mansion', this makes the scale of the description seem overwhelming.

The place is like Hell, with 'devils' mentioned and that it is like something that someone would make up.

The Abbey itself also sounds terrible – 'grey' and 'dilapidation' is mentioned which obviously sounds crumbling and run down. The tone of his visit at the abbey is business like, he quickly recounts the basic features – it is like he can't wait to get away!

So, yes, overall I agree with the statement.

Candidate 3

The overall effect of the passage is certainly a negative one, so in this respect I agree with the statement. The vision of 'Hell' that Borrow seems to chance upon is obviously one that he doesn't want to stay around. He describes it as a scene where 'devils … worship', and this would have been powerful imagery to use in the 19th century, when religion was so strong amongst ordinary people. Indeed, he mentions that smoke rises from the chimneys 'notwithstanding it was Sunday' and this reinforces the ungodliness of the place (the people are working on a day of rest).

In fact Borrow says it was like something from the mind of a 'powerful but insane' artist which certainly gives a negative impression.

The language used is uncompromising in its negativity. The passage is full of adjectives such as 'dirty', 'grimy' and 'black', which contrasts with the 'small village' and 'woody height' that the passage starts with. Indeed, he says it was something he 'had never beheld in nature' and this reinforces how unnatural it is. 'Abominable' and 'accursed' seem to add to the monstrous nature of the place.

The image of confusion (' pandemonium' and 'seemingly') is also strong.

The ruin itself at first seems quite negative – it is described as 'darkly grey' and a 'ruin of vast size' which makes it seem daunting. The architectural features of, 'window holes, towers, spires, and arches' sound traditionally Gothic – like a foreboding, haunted mansion popular in the fiction of the time.

Borrow seems to have to go to a great effort to see the ruin – he 'determined' to see it and 'with some difficulty' but manages it. This shows that it is not easy to get to. Again, at first the negative atmosphere comes through – he focuses on the 'dilapidation' of the place (and notes that this is manmade not just because of the building's age). However, gradually Borrow seems won over by the building – he acknowledges that there is a 'perfect portion' a 'mighty vault' with 'beautiful pillars'. This rather goes against the statement and we see some beauty in the extract.

Finally, we are left with the impression that Borrow cannot wait to get out. His stay was 'exceedingly short'.

I would say that I agree with the statement as the overall impression is one of negativity, but there are hints that the ruin has more to offer and that Borrow is impressed with the surrounding countryside. I would be interested to read what he says about other places in South Wales to see if he has a more positive view.

What advice would you give each candidate?

Now you have completed the section, do you think your confidence has increased?

I can now confidently approach exam questions that assess critical evaluation.

I feel confident about writing under timed conditions.

I understand the mark scheme and how it will be applied.

Always ⇨ Usually ⇨ Sometimes

Unit 12
Communicating clearly and effectively

OBJECTIVES

▷ To learn to present your ideas clearly and effectively
▷ To improve your technical accuracy

How confident are you in these skills already?

I can present my ideas in an organised and clear way.

I can use different types of sentences and paragraphs to organise my ideas effectively.

| Always | ◁▷ | Usually | ◁▷ | Sometimes |

It is important to remember what you will be expected to do in the exam.
Don't feel worried when you hear the words 'Assessment Objectives'! These are just the success criteria or standards that will be used to assess your work in the writing tasks in the exams. Look at the table below to help you work out what the Assessment Objectives actually mean.

Assessment Objectives – the simple truth

Assessment Objective	What it says	What it means
AO5	Communicate clearly, effectively and imaginatively.	This means you need to express your ideas and viewpoint clearly.
AO5	Selecting and adapting tone, style and register for different forms, purposes and audiences.	This means you need to select the correct format for your writing (for example, a speech, a letter, a report or an article). You need to adapt your tone/register (it will be either informal or formal) and your vocabulary according to the task and the people who will read it.
AO5	Organise information and ideas to support coherence and cohesion of texts.	This means you need to plan and organise your writing into sentences and paragraphs.
AO5	Using structural and grammatical features.	This means using techniques/devices such as linking words (connectives), etc. to join your ideas and make it easier for the reader to follow.

AO6	Use a range of vocabulary and sentence structure for clarity, purpose and effect, with accurate spelling and punctuation.	This means you need to vary the types of sentences you use (simple, compound and complex) and the length of your sentences. Make sure your punctuation (full stops, commas, colons, semi colons, speech marks and apostrophes) is correct. Make sure your spelling is accurate. Make sure you choose the most suitable words to put your point across.

Get going

Step 1 Work on your skills

 ACTIVITY 1: PARAGRAPHS

A paragraph is a series of sentences about the same topic or which follow on from each other.

You should use paragraphs to divide and organise your ideas. Paragraphs help your readers follow your train of thought.

Write four paragraphs describing what you did at the weekend.

You may want to use some of these linking words (connectives) to help you link your paragraphs or come up with some of your own:

also   too   however   anyway   besides   first of all   secondly   then   finally
lastly   so   since   to begin with   next   to sum up   in a nutshell   in the end

 ACTIVITY 2: CONNECTIVES

Write several paragraphs persuading your parents to let you do something such as go on holiday with a friend, have a party or change your name by deed poll to the name of your favourite celebrity!

You may want to use some of the connectives below to link your paragraphs and help your argument to flow smoothly.

for example   for instance   consequently   therefore   so   firstly   secondly   provided that   finally   to sum up   in a nutshell   to conclude   as a result

What persuasive devices could you use to make your argument so convincing that your parents wouldn't be able to refuse you?

Top tips

Whatever writing tasks you attempt, you need to do the following:

- Spend 5 minutes gathering your thoughts and ideas.
- Organise and sequence your ideas in the best possible order.
- Decide on your introduction and conclusion.
- Never begin writing before you have decided how to finish.

ACTIVITY 3: STARTING A NEW PARAGRAPH

Read the following reviews and decide where the new paragraphs should start. For each review, explain why you have chosen to begin a new paragraph in each case.

Review 1

Are you a thrill seeker or a fright junkie who enjoys some good old fashioned romance thrown in for good measure? If so, why not check out these classic reads that may have you jumping at shadows or simply snuggling up that little bit closer to that special someone in your life. 'Wuthering Heights' by Emily Bronte is a timeless tale of love, obsession and tragedy coupled with a sinister gothic atmosphere that will make the hairs on the back of your neck stand on end. It is an ageless tale of ghosts and the supernatural and a violent, tragic love that will haunt you. It focuses on the undying and destructive love between Cathy Earnshaw and Heathcliff, a wild and mysterious orphan boy who is taken in by the family. Without giving it away, let's just say that Heathcliff's love leads to tragic and far reaching consequences as he plots a vicious and sadistic revenge against all who crossed his path. If you're hooked by gothic and attracted by dark novels, try 'Jane Eyre' by another Bronte sister, Charlotte. Read this novel to follow the trials and obstacles faced by the young orphan Jane as she struggles to overcome the tragedy in her life until she finally gets her man! However, as Shakespeare said, the path of true love never does run smoothly…especially in literature and you guessed it, there's more suffering before the end!

Review 2

At first glance, Mauritius looks like it should be part of the Caribbean, with its immaculate, idyllic beaches and crystal blue sea. Tempted to take a plunge in these breathtaking, calm waters, home to groups of elegant dolphins, swimming playfully around the boats? Fancy a more active holiday? Then you'll have the opportunity to indulge your passion for watersports like snorkelling or for the more adventurous there is wind and kite surfing. Mauritius has a wealth of natural history. Surrounded by high mountains

and dense forest the island is home to some of the most rare and exotic animals in the world. Mauritius was discovered more than 600 years ago and since then it has absorbed the influences from so many different cultures. You can enjoy creole cooking and Grand Gaube is considered to be the culinary hot spot of the island. Also dotted around the island you can enjoy the spectacle of architectural splendour in the form of chateaux built during the time of the French occupation of the island.

ACTIVITY 4: THE BEST POSSIBLE ORDER

Using paragraphs helps you to organise your thoughts when you are writing. This is important because in order for your work to make sense your ideas need to be in the best possible order.

Write a few paragraphs about each of the following topics and organise your ideas into the best possible order.

- ▶ **My best birthday**
- ▶ **A celebrity I admire or dislike**
- ▶ **My first memories of school**
- ▶ **A time when I remember feeling nervous**

ACTIVITY 5: IN THE CORRECT ORDER

Here is a speech about the disadvantages of mobile phones. The paragraphs are well written but they are a bit jumbled and so the writer's argument doesn't sound well organised. Read the speech and decide the order in which the paragraphs should be written so that the writer's ideas flow smoothly and make sense.

Are there any clues in the use of connectives to help you make your decision?

Are there any paragraphs about similar topics that might go next to each other?

Only last week in our own high street, ladies and gentlemen, a young mother was viciously mugged in broad daylight when she used her mobile to call a taxi. Surely we cannot allow this sort of appalling crime to continue?

Furthermore, mobiles are causing chaos in schools. They disturb lessons and have actually been used by dishonest pupils to help them cheat in exams!

Teenagers are stealing and shoplifting more than ever to pay their mobile phone bills. Even the Prime Minister admitted last week that he himself was very worried about how much money his own children were wasting on 'mindlesss mobile chat'.

In conclusion, I know the listeners to this programme are more intelligent people who will be just as worried about these microwave monsters as I am. I admit they can be useful in emergencies, but how often do these really happen? Meanwhile our young people are causing serious damage to the most important and delicate part of their bodies.

We have managed perfectly well without mobile phones in the past, and I strongly believe that when the real facts about them are known, we will have to cope without them in the future because they will be banned!

Thank you for listening and goodnight.

Text messaging is also causing serious problems in schools because youngsters become so used to writing in this shorthand style that they forget how to write properly and fail their GCSEs. Do we really want a younger generation who can only scrawl in meaningless slang?

A topic or focus sentence is sometimes used at the beginning of a paragraph to outline or summarise the topic or subject. It often answers the questions who, why and how. Every word in the sentence is usually important and it is followed by ideas supporting the point that has been made.

ACTIVITY 6: TOPIC SENTENCES

Here is an example of a topic sentence and paragraph on the subject of saving energy in school/college.

Avondale School is working hard to reduce energy consumption on a daily basis. At the end of each day all computer terminals are closed down and switched off. Staff and pupils are encouraged to only turn classroom lights on when needed and to make sure that when the room is empty all lights are switched off.

As you can see the first sentence is the topic sentence and the following sentences develop and add detail to the topic sentence.

Now write the next paragraph to the example above.

Write a topic sentence and a paragraph about each of the following subjects:

- ▶ Music
- ▶ Chocolate
- ▶ Television
- ▶ Space travel

ACTIVITY 7: IDENTIFYING PARAGRAPHS

Look at this piece of writing from *Help* by Penelope Lively. Identify six paragraphs in the extract. Explain why you have made these decisions.

Henry said, 'You'll have to get some help.' He said it in a tone that meant there was to be no discussion, the matter was decided. But none the less Jenny said, 'What?' She said it not because she had not heard, but, like a child, because she did not want to hear. 'You'll have to get some help. I'm tired of this mess.' Guiltily, Jenny followed his glance across the smeared table, the children's coats tumbled behind the sofa, and the clutter of toys and newspapers in the corner. 'I'd feel awkward having someone polishing my floors and things, Henry, I honestly would.' He brushed that objection aside with a snort.

> You need to use paragraphs correctly when you are writing direct speech otherwise it is unclear who is actually speaking the words. It can all become a bit confusing for the reader. Remember to begin a new paragraph whenever a different person begins to speak.

Now read this extract from *Of Mice and Men* by John Steinbeck. Identify five paragraphs here.

How did you make these decisions?

Although there was evening brightness showing through the windows of the bunkhouse, inside it was dusk. Through the open door came the thuds and occasional clangs of a horseshoe game and now and then the sound of voices raised in approval or derision. Slim and George came into the darkening bunkhouse together. Slim sat down on a box and George took his place opposite. 'It wasn't nothing,' said Slim. 'I would have had to drown most of 'em anyways. No need to thank me about that.' George said, 'It wasn't much to you, maybe, but it was a hell of a lot to him. He'll want to sleep right out in the barn with 'em!' 'It wasn't nothing,' Slim repeated.

As you read earlier, using connectives or linking words is a helpful way of joining your ideas together and they have many uses (these words will be referred to in later units as well).

Below are some connectives that may help you in your writing.

When you want to ...	Connectives
explain a point or idea	so, because, therefore, as a result of, consequently
add a point or idea	also, moreover, in addition to, furthermore
prove a point or idea	for example, for instance, such as
compare a point or idea	in the same way, likewise, similarly
show differences/ contrasting ideas	however, on the other hand, alternately, whereas

Top tips

- Start a new paragraph when you start a new point or topic.
- In a story, start a new paragraph when a different person begins to speak.
- Start a new paragraph when you write about a different time.
- Start a new paragraph when you write about a new place.

ACTIVITY 8: CATS AND DOGS

Write about the differences between cats and dogs using only three paragraphs. You may choose to use some of the connectives from the list.

ACTIVITY 9: TEENAGERS IN THE 21st CENTURY

Using the skills you have so far learned about organising your ideas and communicating clearly, write a short article for a teenage magazine about what life in the 21st century is like for a teenager.

ACTIVITY 10: IMPROVING THE OPENING

Look at the following paragraph. Complete and improve the opening to the story using adjectives, verbs, adverbs and any other techniques you think might make it more interesting.

> The woman looked upset. She walked along the street unsteadily, thinking about what had happened to her that day. She decided not to let it bother her anymore. It wasn't worth the hassle. Perhaps she should just look for another job.

Add new paragraphs where you think necessary.

Step 2 Practise your skills

In order to be a good writer, you will need to show that you
can write different types of sentences and sentences that are of
different lengths.
Here are some different types of sentences.

 ## ACTIVITY 11: SIMPLE SENTENCES

These sentences are exactly what you think they are – simple! This is because they have a subject and one verb
(an action word) and they give one piece of information. For example:

The boy chased the ball.

Make up five simple sentences of your own.

 ## ACTIVITY 12: COMPOUND SENTENCES

Don't feel worried by this term! It is just a series of simple sentences joined together. These sentences have two
(or more) verbs and give two (or more) pieces of information. For example:

The boy chased the ball and he scored a great goal.

Make up five compound sentences of your own.

It is sometimes a good idea to use connectives like 'and', 'but' and 'then' when you write compound sentences.

 ## ACTIVITY 13: COMPLEX SENTENCES

As the name suggests, these sentences are slightly more complicated because they are a bit longer and contain
more details. Often a complex sentence will have two (or more) verbs and contain two (or more) pieces of
information. The difference is that the second part of the sentence either depends on or refers back to the first
part. For example:

The boy chased the ball until he scored a goal.

You could also turn it round and write:

Until he scored a goal, the boy chased the ball.

Make up five complex sentences of your own.

 ## ACTIVITY 14: MINOR SENTENCES

These are short, incomplete sentences because they do not have a verb. For example:

Fog everywhere.

Make up five minor sentences of your own.

ACTIVITY 15: IDENTIFYING SENTENCES

What type of sentences are these?

a   The little girl sobbed because she couldn't have any sweets.
b   She threw a tantrum.
c   She screamed like a banshee.
d   When she finally stopped crying, her mother was relieved.
e   The mother took her indoors and let her watch her favourite television programme.
f   Peace at last.

How did you decide?

ACTIVITY 16: DIFFERENT TYPES OF SENTENCES

Practise the skills you have learned by writing a series of paragraphs on the following topics using the four different types of sentences at least once.

▶ A time when you felt lonely

▶ The seaside

▶ Your favourite film

▶ A sport you enjoy playing or watching

ACTIVITY 17: EFFECTIVE SENTENCES

Look at this piece of writing by a student.

> Guilt. I never liked that feeling. The feeling that almost made you sick to the stomach. I knew I was wrong and I shouldn't be doing it, but I couldn't face what was waiting for me. I just couldn't stay and let them do that to me. Although I had to run, I wondered what would happen when they found me.

How many different types of sentences can you find here?

Which sentence do you think has the biggest effect on the reader? Explain your reason.

Now write about a page to continue the story using a range of different types of sentences.

ACTIVITY 18: IN DEFENCE OF WOLVES

Here is an extract from a speech defending wolves.

I am here tonight to change your minds about one of the most misunderstood and maligned animals in the world. Like us, this animal lives in close families and loves playing and having fun. Any idea who this creature can be? Yes, the wolf.

Evil and vicious? Not so. The wolf is a clever and loving animal, nothing like the way he is presented in Little Red Riding Hood and The Three Little Pigs. When we were little we all enjoyed such stories. Now we have grown up and we can understand the truth behind the fiction.

How many different types of sentences can you find in this piece of persuasive writing?

Now write another two or three paragraphs to continue the speech. Remember to include different types of sentences.

ACTIVITY 19: PARTS OF SPEECH

It is often a good idea to think about extending your sentences by including adjectives, adverbs and prepositions. Look at the table below that contains different parts of speech.

ARTICLE	ADJECTIVE	NOUN	VERB	ADVERB	PREPOSITION	ARTICLE	NOUN
The	purple	walrus	edged	furtively	before	a	riverbed
A	miniature	spider	raced	slowly	through	the	beach
Each	rumbling	boy	bowed	hesitantly	down	that	hilltop
An	elegant	dancer	lumbered	lazily	beside	this	cottage
That	cunning	pixie	prowled	silently	past	another	shop
This	lively	fox	stalked	hopefully	above	a	school
The	intelligent	bear	dawdled	aggressively	behind	the	valley
The	smooth	footballer	hid	loudly	beneath	a	trail

a Make some sentences out of the words, choosing one from each column – some of them probably won't really make sense.

b Write down three of your best sentences.

c Change some of the words to make your sentences make sense. For example:

This intelligent fox stalked silently beside the riverbed.

The cunning pixie prowled furtively beneath the valley.

d Write five more sentences, using some of the words above, but also your own ideas. Make sure you use all the parts of speech in the columns.

! Top tips

• Sometimes it is effective to use a very short sentence or a one-word 'sentence' after a longer one to create dramatic effect or emphasise a point or to show contrast, for example:

I think not.

• A series of short sentences can also add a dramatic effect and create tension or suspense, for example:

I came. I saw. I conquered.

Step 3 Challenge yourself

If all your sentences begin in the same way, your style will feel very predictable and boring for the reader. So, sentence variety is the key to becoming a successful writer.

There are many different ways you can begin a sentence. For example, you could use a:

- adverb (describing a verb)
- pronoun (I, you, he, she, it, we, they)
- preposition (on, behind, between, over, etc.)
- -ing word (participle)
- definite or indefinite article (the/a/an)
- adjective (describing word)
- connective (linking word)
- verb.

 ACTIVITY 20: IDENTIFYING PARTS OF SPEECH

This paragraph uses each of the examples mentioned above. Can you find them all?

I screamed and ran. The window had been broken. Behind me I heard heavy breathing. Peering over my shoulder nervously, I felt the presence of someone nearby. Cold beads of sweat began to trickle down my forehead. Slowly fear gripped my body. Although I knew I was being foolish, my hands began to tremble. To run was my only option.

 ACTIVITY 21: IMPROVING AN ARTICLE

Look at the following article written by a student giving his opinion about footballers' wages.

I think it is unfair that footballers in this country earn so much money. It is unjust and scandalous. I think there should be a law that puts a limit on how much money they can earn. I think, for example, that top footballers shouldn't be allowed to earn more than one million pounds a year. I believe that a limit like this will make the game more fair and competitive and it might stop so many foreign players invading our league! I think it will help the teams in the lower leagues attract better footballers and as a result they will have a better chance of winning matches against the top teams. I also think that by doing this it will bring football back into the real world as many ordinary people feel that players are out of touch with their fans. I believe it is wrong that we seem to be valuing footballers more than doctors and nurses because they are paid so much money.

Now, using the skills you have been practising in this unit, write the rest of the article.

 Find two things that you think the article does well.

What do you think the student could do to improve this piece of writing?

Rewrite this paragraph and think about how you can vary the way you start each sentence.

When you have done this, pick out your favourite sentence and explain your choice.

ACTIVITY 22: CONTINUING THE STORY

Here is another piece of student writing.

> A crash! A clatter! The sound of someone trying to keep their voices low. Sounds of activity awoke me from my dark but silent dreams. With my eyes wide open, my ears nailed to the floor of my room, I listened patiently, waiting for a clue as to what was going on. I had no idea what caused all the noise.

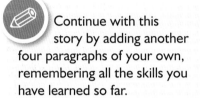

Does this paragraph sound boring and predictable? Explain your opinion.

Does the writer vary the beginning of the sentences?

Continue with this story by adding another four paragraphs of your own, remembering all the skills you have learned so far.

ACTIVITY 23: CHILDHOOD MEMORIES

Write about your childhood memories.

Remember to vary the type of sentences you use and the way you begin your sentences.

When you have finished, read through your work carefully and think about what you have written.

▶ Did you begin each sentence with a different word? If not, try to think of an alternative now.
▶ Can you find the different types of sentences you have used?
▶ Have you used paragraphs effectively?
▶ Have you varied the length of your sentences?
▶ What two things have you done well in this piece of writing?
▶ What two things do you still want to improve?

Now that you have completed this section, do you think your confidence has increased?

I can present my ideas coherently and logically.

I can use a range of sentence structures and paragraphs to organise my ideas effectively.

Always ⇨ Usually ⇨ Sometimes

Improve your skills

OBJECTIVES

▶ To make my writing more accurate technically
▶ To use apostrophes correctly
▶ To learn to proof read my work effectively

How confident are you in these skills already?

I can spell difficult words accurately.

I understand how to use an apostrophe correctly.

I know how to proof read my work.

Always ⇨ Usually ⇨ Sometimes

Step 1 Work on your skills

ACTIVITY 1: HOMOPHONES

If you are struggling to spell a word in the exam, it is a good idea to try to sound it out in your head.

However, things become a bit trickier when some words sound the same even though they are spelt differently and mean different things. These words are called homophones.

Look at the grid below and select the correct word to answer each question.

1) If I am listening to something which one is correct? here/hear	4) In my story if I am writing about something they own, which one is correct? they're/there/their	7) If I am looking out of the window at the view, which one is correct? see/sea
2) If I am thinking about walking through a forest, which one is correct? would/wood	5) If you are not sure of an answer what would you say? no/know	8) If I am asking if my answer is correct, which one is it? right/write
3) If I am describing the way that the wind is blowing which one is correct? blew/blue	6) If I am describing the way that someone eats gum which one is the correct choice? choose/chews	9) If I am describing the queen and her rule which one is correct? rain/rein/reign

Now to show you understand the difference between these homophones, write a sentence for each of the homophones you haven't already used.

Try to think of another five commonly used homophones. Then explain their different meanings.

ACTIVITY 2: FINDING MISTAKES

In this piece of writing, the student has become confused about which homophone to use.
Find the 17 mistakes and correct them.

Deer Sir,

You asked me to right a letter to ewe for homework so I have. You said I should chews what I should right. I could knot decide what two do. So I decided too tell ewe about my holiday at the seaside. I had a grate time and a lovely view of the clear blew see from my hotel. It was a long weigh from hear. I hope ewe had a good holiday to.

 ## ACTIVITY 3: IDENTIFYING MISSPELLINGS

When you are having difficulty spelling a word, write the word down in rough first. If it doesn't look right, it probably isn't, so try again.

Look at the words in the list below and decide which ones have been written correctly.

definite	definate	definit
dissappoint	disapoint	disappoint
terrifyed	terrified	terriffied
disastrus	disastrous	disasterous
argument	arguement	arguemeant

 ## ACTIVITY 4: MNEMONICS

Making up a mnemonic or a silly rule often helps you to remember and learn the spelling of a tricky word. For example:

NECESSARY – Never eat cake eat salad sandwiches and remain young.

Sometimes you can find a smaller word inside it. For example,

*ENVIRONMENT – There is always **iron** in our environment.*

Can you find a word within these tricky words to help you remember them?

▶ secretary
▶ separate
▶ soldier

▶ believe
▶ business

ACTIVITY 5: MORE MNEMONICS

Make up a mnemonic or silly rule of your own to remember how to spell the following words:

- ▶ definitely
- ▶ parliament
- ▶ embarrass

Add another three words of your own that you are not always confident about spelling correctly.

ACTIVITY 6: A PLACE YOU KNOW WELL

Write about a place you know well. It could be somewhere you have often visited, a place you go to on holiday or it could be your favourite room in your house.

Remember to divide your ideas into paragraphs. Use connectives to link up your ideas and check your spelling carefully.

Step 2 Practise your skills

Using apostrophes in the right places will also improve the accuracy of your work and help to score more marks. Remember you only need to use apostrophes for two reasons:
- when something belongs to someone (possession)
- when you shorten a word and leave letters out (omission).

ACTIVITY 7: APOSTROPHES

Here are some signs that you may come across in everyday life.

The apostrophes have not always been put in the right place, however, so rewrite the signs as you think they should be written. Be careful – some may actually be correct!

- ▶ Farm fresh carrot's and potato's for sale
- ▶ Mens' department on second floor
- ▶ Year 10 Parents Evening
- ▶ Children's Play Area at rear of pub
- ▶ Slimmer's Club. New Members' Are Welcome!
- ▶ Party Aces! Lets Plan All Your Party's
- ▶ Holiday Cottage's For Rent. Apply Within

ACTIVITY 8: MISSING APOSTROPHES

Read this paragraph and then write it out, putting in any missing apostrophes.

Toms future plans had been fully discussed by his parents and teachers but his wishes hadnt really been consulted. He wouldve preferred to grab lifes challenges and take his chances in the big, wide world rather than drift into his dads business working with his brothers in those dreary offices.

The mens opinions were clear: hed go to Oxford, to the familys traditional college, and then become his uncles assistant in the firms London branch. His female relatives had similar plans for him but they also pictured him safely married to one of the neighbours dowdy daughters. That was why when he first spotted the advert in The Independents back pages just after the womens section, his heart had missed several beats…

'Have you ever wondered whats really out there?'

Did you find the 14 missing apostrophes?

Can you explain whether the apostrophe is to show possession or omission in each case?

ACTIVITY 9: IDENTIFYING MISTAKES

Read this extract from a letter about selecting students for an outward bound trip. It was written by a student in exam conditions. There are many mistakes in spelling, punctuation and grammar.

Im writing to you today to show my feelings and thoughts on that all students should take part inn a camping and outdorr activitys every year. As I and fellow pupils' has took a query around and a very much big percentage of the school agree. The feelings and thoughts are very positive becasuse most pupils' think it would take the strass of school work to a minimum. There has been some sugestions of the class that has contributed to school life the most to be token on the activities with such contributions as award stickers, behaviour.

On a copy of the extract:

▶ circle all the spelling mistakes

▶ underline all the errors in punctuation

▶ highlight all the errors in expression.

ACTIVITY 10: IMPROVING AN ANSWER

Look at the question below and read the extract from a student response.

Your school or college magazine is publishing a series of lively articles about recent trends in music and fashion.

Write an article informing the reader about your taste in music or fashion.

Student response

> Girls, summer is upon us once more, and, for most of us that means one thing ... a new wardrobe tailored to our summer needs'. Who can survive summer without a new pair of flip-flops', open-toed sandals' or vest tops ...? Well, me for one. I don't know about you but I cant live up to this idiotic attitude that all teenage girls' are expected to fulfil. Fashion for me has always been a bit frightening. I plod along happily in my jeans and jumper until someone pulls away the earth from beneath my feet, leaving me in a desperate state of humiliation at not knowing that florescent orange, and not pink was the new black. Honestly. Are we really that fickle? Well, seemingly yes ...

 What two things do you think the student does well?

Would you like to make any corrections to this extract? If so, where do you think the errors are and why do they need to be corrected?

Now, write your own answer to this question, remembering to think about the different types of sentences you can use and making sure you have used apostrophes in the right places.

 When you have finished, check your answer carefully. Did you:

▶ divide your article into paragraphs?
▶ use different types of sentences?
▶ use sentences of different lengths to create different effects?
▶ use apostrophes correctly?
▶ work hard to spell difficult words correctly?
▶ proof read your work?

! Top tips

When you write in timed conditions you need to leave enough time to check your work very carefully for mistakes in your spelling, punctuation and grammar:

● Correct any spelling mistakes.
● Correct any mistakes in the way you use paragraphs, full stops and capital letters.
● Make sure your writing and sentences make sense.

This skill is sometimes called **proof reading**.

Step 3 Challenge yourself

ACTIVITY 11: FINDING MISTAKES

Read this letter about raising the legal driving age. It was written by a student in timed conditions.

> Dear editor, im wrighting you a letter about the age limit going up to 19 because of all the accidents they all have. Teenagers 17 to 18 should still be able to drive if they payed for there insurance they are covered about. 45% of 17 to 18 years olds drive fast and play loud music and the other 55% drive sensaball so that not fair on the people who do drive with care around the strrets. 17 to 18 years olds start getting jobs and most of them may need a car to get to work or maybe thay need to be able to drive to there jobs. You should leave the age limit as they are and as long there psying the tax and insurance there no problem. Yours senscelly.

The student has made many mistakes in spelling, punctuation, expression and paragraphing.

▶ Find as many of the mistakes as you can.

▶ Correct the mistakes.

▶ Rewrite the letter using your own ideas and the skills you have already learned in this unit.

When you have finished, check your answer carefully. Did you:

▶ divide your article into paragraphs?

▶ use different types of sentences?

▶ use sentences of different lengths to create different effects?

▶ use apostrophes correctly?

▶ work hard to spell difficult words correctly?

▶ proof read your work?

ACTIVITY 12: A FAMILY OCCASION

Write about a family occasion you remember well.

Remember to use all the skills you have been practising in this unit.

> Now that you have completed this section, do you think your confidence has increased?
>
> I can spell difficult words accurately.
>
> I understand how to use an apostrophe correctly.
>
> I know how to proof read my work.
>
> Always ⇨ Usually ⇨ Sometimes

BE EXAM READY

OBJECTIVES

▶ To use vocabulary effectively and precisely
▶ To feel confident about writing accurately

How confident are you in these skills already?

I am confident that I can use the most appropriate and effective vocabulary for writing tasks.

I am confident that I can write accurately without making careless mistakes.

Always ⇨ Usually ⇨ Sometimes

Whenever you are asked to write something it is important that the words you choose are effective and suitable. To do this well, you need to think about all the words you know and decide which word communicates exactly what you want to say. It is often a good idea to use synonyms (words with similar meanings) to stop you from repeating the same words and to make your work sound more interesting. You can use a thesaurus to help you find synonyms for different words.

QUESTION 1

Using a thesaurus, find an alternative for the following words:
a shouted   **b** old   **c** opinion   **d** nasty   **e** nice

QUESTION 2

Read this student response from a letter of complaint about a disastrous experience at a restaurant.

When we **got to** the restaurant we **got** a shock! There was no 'ample car park' so we realise we'd **got to** park our car on a narrow road outside. After we **got inside** it took us more than thirty minutes for the waiter to **get** us a table because other people had booked theirs in advance. We finally **got to** our table but after we'd ordered our meals the waiter didn't even **get** us the right food! The correct order took a further twenty minutes to **get to** us and we didn't even **get** an apology from the staff for having to wait so long. Naturally we were **getting** really annoyed but complaining to our waiter didn't **get us anywhere** as he simply ignored us! Our meal was so unsatisfactory we were glad to **get out of** there but when we **got back** to our car we were outraged; it had **got** a deep scratch all along one wing. I therefore insist on **getting** a full refund for our very disappointing meal or I will consider **getting** the police involved.

As you can see the extract sounds boring because the student has used the word 'got' too much! Replace 'got' with more appropriate and interesting words.

172

 **QUESTION 3**

Now write your own letter of complaint to the manager of a restaurant where you have experienced a disastrous meal and poor service. Think carefully about the words you choose.

Using emotive words (words that affect the way the reader feels) can add impact to your writing and make it more effective. Think carefully about the effects of the words you choose.

 QUESTION 4

Here are some synonyms for the word 'tragic':

disastrous   catastrophic   cataclysmic   devastating   terrible
dreadful   horrendous   awful   unfortunate

Each of the words generally has the same meaning but affects the reader in a slightly different way. Try to explain the difference in the meaning of each word.

 QUESTION 5

What do you think of when you read the following words?
- savagery   • aroma   • abysmal

 QUESTION 6

Write a couple of paragraphs in response to the following statement.

The youth of today are idle, loutish hooligans who waste their time hanging around street corners at night.

Remember to choose the words you use for the effect you want them to have on the reader. You can choose either to agree or disagree with the statement.

 QUESTION 7

Read the following paragraph written by a student.

People think that footballers are the role models for the teenagers of today. I think this idea is wrong because often footballers are guilty of behaving badly on the football field. Footballers clearly think that it isn't wrong to spit, argue, cheat and disrespect officials even though young children are watching them on television and they might decide to copy their footballing heroes. I think something needs to be done before youngsters lose all sense of what is right and what is wrong.

The student shows a sensible viewpoint here but the ideas sound repetitive and a bit boring because too many words are repeated.

Rewrite this paragraph by replacing the words that are frequently repeated with alternative words. It may be useful to use a thesaurus to help you with your choices.

QUESTION 8

Bearing in mind what you have learned in this section:

Write an article for your school/college magazine about whether or not you think footballers are good role models for young people.

QUESTION 9

Read the following responses about a good place to visit for a day trip. They were written by students in timed conditions. Using all the skills you have learned in this unit, try to correct as many of the mistakes in the responses as you can.

Can you explain your corrections?

Sample answer 1

Manchester is one of the finest cities in the north west of England. Not only is it an easy place to get to but the city itself is something else. It might be a very big city but if you don't fancy walking then the relatively new metro lone service is available for a small fee just look out for the yellow signs or Download the app. Another good reason to visit Manchester is that unlike other cities were all the activiys and sites are in the centre. Manchesters suburban places are just as good as the city itself. For example the newly renovated Salford Quays hosts the new home of BBC television and the world famous lowry theatre which I especially recommend around Christmas time. Carparking is no problem if you are arriving via car, if you spend £5 or more in the restaurants, shopping mall or theatre it is free all day. Fancy a change of atmosphere? Over the suspension bridge is probably the most iconic football stadium in the world, old Trafford, the home of Manchester United. Honestly, it is perfect for any type of day out whether its family related, business or a romantic break it is ideal and will provide you with your every need.

Sample answer 2

Seaside fun isn't everyones first choice but for those who want to get out the house for a family outing, go to the beach, buy a cricket set and play some games. Why stay inside watching television. Theres a wide range of fantastic little places to go all around the coast. Outstanding food and drinks in cafes yet to be bought, its allways nice and sunny so why not enjoy a nice icecream whilst catching the Rays of the sun, don't be afraid to come down and Relax the beach is open to everyone there is also a lot of activitys if you don't nececessarily want to buy anything.

QUESTION 10

Look again at the assessment criteria you read at the start of the unit.

- You need to express your ideas and opinion clearly.
- You need to plan and organise your writing into sentences and paragraphs.
- You need to vary the types of sentences you use (simple, compound and complex) and the length of your sentences.
- Your punctuation needs to be correct.
- Your spelling needs to be accurate.
- You need to choose the most suitable words to put your point across.

Thinking about these criteria, which of the sample answers do you think would score more marks?

Explain your choice.

QUESTION 11

Using all the skills you have learned from this unit, write your own response to the question:

Write a lively article for a magazine about a good place to visit for a day.

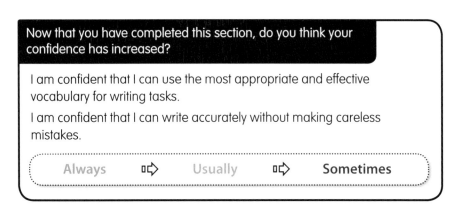

Now that you have completed this section, do you think your confidence has increased?

I am confident that I can use the most appropriate and effective vocabulary for writing tasks.

I am confident that I can write accurately without making careless mistakes.

Always ➪ Usually ➪ Sometimes

Unit 13
Communicating imaginatively

OBJECTIVES

▶ To be able to use words for effect
▶ To learn to write a successful opening for a creative prose response

How confident are you in these skills already?

I can engage the interest of a reader.

I can use a variety of techniques for effect.

I can evaluate and reassess my word choices.

Always ⇨ Usually ⇨ Sometimes

When you are asked to write a creative prose response you will need to write imaginatively and creatively. Your storyline or **plot** will need to be organised and easy to follow. You must grab the attention of your reader from the very first paragraph.

narrative – a story; an organised and coherent account of a series of connected events
plot – storyline
characterisation – the way a writer creates a picture of what a character is like. You might include details of what a character looks like, does, wears and so on.
vocabulary – the words used

Get going

Step 1 Work on your skills

 ACTIVITY 1: CREATIVE WRITING

Read the following list of statements about creative writing and decide which are true and which are false.

STATEMENT	TRUE OR FALSE?
The purpose of a **narrative** is to persuade the reader to do something.	
A narrative should be clearly and logically organised in paragraphs.	
The purpose of a narrative is to provide the reader with information.	
A narrative can be written in the first or third person.	
The purpose of a narrative is to entertain and engage the interest of the reader.	
A narrative uses subheadings.	

A successful narrative should include some direct speech.	
Nothing happens in a narrative – it only contains description.	
A successful narrative needs a strong opening and ending.	
You don't need to plan your narrative before you begin writing it.	

In order to hook the reader's attention, the opening paragraph to a story has to whet the appetite. The reader will want to continue with the story to find out the answers to the questions raised in the opening.

ACTIVITY 2: OPENINGS

Here are the opening paragraphs of some famous novels. Read the openings and consider the questions that follow.

Opening A

It was 7 minutes after midnight. The dog was lying on the grass in the middle of the lawn in front of Mrs Shear's house. Its eyes were closed. It looked as if it was running on its side, the way dogs run when they think they are chasing a cat in a dream. But the dog was not running or asleep. The dog was dead. There was a garden fork sticking out of the dog. The points of the fork must have gone all the way through the dog and into the ground because the fork had not fallen over …

From *The Curious Incident of the Dog in the Night-time* by Mark Haddon

▶ Does this opening create suspense or tension? If so, which words/phrases create this effect?

▶ Does this opening grab the reader's interest? If so, what questions would a reader want to ask?

▶ Which words do you find interesting in this opening?

Opening B

It was a bright cold day in April and the clocks were striking thirteen. Winston Smith, his chin nuzzled into his breast in an effort to escape the vile wind, slipped quickly through the glass doors of Victory Mansions, though not quickly enough to prevent a swirl of gritty dust from entering with him …

From *Nineteen Eighty-Four* by George Orwell

▶ Does the opening create suspense or tension? If so, which words/phrases create this effect?

▶ Does the opening interest the reader?

▶ Does the opening suggest anything unusual?

▶ Can you find any descriptive words/phrases here? Why do you think the writer chose to use these words?

Opening C

Far out in the unchartered backwaters of the unfashionable end of the western spiral arm of the Galaxy lies a small unregarded yellow sun. Orbiting this at a distance of roughly ninety two million miles is an utterly insignificant little blue green planet whose ape descended life forms are so amazingly primitive that they still think digital watches are a pretty neat idea …

From *The Hitchhiker's Guide to the Galaxy* by Douglas Adams

▶ Does this opening hook the reader? If so, why do you think this is?

▶ Does this opening use interesting descriptive words and detail? If so, can you find examples?

Opening D

When I wake up, the other side of the bed is cold. My fingers stretch out, seeking Prim's warmth but finding only the rough canvas cover of the mattress. She must have had bad dreams and climbed in with our mother. Of course, she did. This is the day of the reaping.

I prop myself up on one elbow. There's enough light in the bedroom to see them. My little sister, Prim, curled up on her side, cocooned in my mother's body, their cheeks pressed together. In sleep, my mother looks younger, still worn but not so beaten down. Prim's face is as fresh as a raindrop, as lovely as the primrose for which she was named …

From *The Hunger Games* by Suzanne Collins

▶ Does this opening grab the reader's attention? If so, what information would the reader want to find out?

▶ Does this opening create tension or suspense?

▶ Does this opening use a range of sentence styles? Why do you think this would be effective?

▶ Why do you think the opening is written in the present tense?

Opening E

They've gone now, and I'm alone at last. I have the whole night ahead of me, and I won't waste a single moment of it. I shan't sleep it away. I won't dream it away either. I mustn't because every moment of it will be far too precious …

From *Private Peaceful* by Michael Morpurgo

▶ Does this opening create suspense or tension? If so, can you explain why this is the case?

▶ Does this opening use a range of sentence styles? Why do you think this is? What effect does the writer want to create by doing this?

Step 2   Practise your skills

 ACTIVITY 3: TECHNIQUES TO INCLUDE

It is often a good idea to include some of the following techniques in your opening paragraph:

- ▶ direct speech
- ▶ an exclamation or question
- ▶ a description of an interesting character

- ▶ an **intriguing** statement
- ▶ an **atmospheric** scene setter
- ▶ a sound effect.

> **atmosphere** – the mood or feeling of a piece of writing
> **intriguing** – something that is fascinating or that arouses curiosity
> **adjectives** – describing words, such as, gloomy, cheerful

Read the following story openings and, using the list of techniques above, decide whether you think they are successful or not.

> The day was bitterly cold. A chill wind swirled mercilessly through the dry leaves and the skies were grey and blurred with the threat of snow.

a Can you find any interesting descriptive words (**adjectives**) here?

b What effect does the writer want to create by describing the weather in this way?

> Jane Smith. My enemy. Blond and petite with a perfect button nose and pearly white teeth which could turn on a wide smile which never quite reached her icy blue eyes. There she stood, hands on hips, in her brand new jacket and expensive boots, eyeing me coldly.

c Can you find any interesting descriptive words (adjectives) here?

d What impression of this character does the writer want to give the reader?

e What do the phrases 'turn on a wide smile which never quite reached her icy blue eyes' and 'she stood, hands on hips' tell the reader about this character?

> I was walking along the street one day when Billy Phillips asked me if I would like to join his gang.

f Can you find any interesting details in this opening?

g What would you do to improve this opening?

> Why did I do it? Why didn't I stay on the outside where I belonged?

h What does this opening tell the reader about the character of the narrator?

'I hate you! I hate you!'

I can still hear her voice now, twenty years later and the emotions of guilt and regret still overpower me just as they did then …

i What does this opening tell the reader about the character of the narrator?

j Does this opening use any other effective techniques?

k What sort of mood is created by this opening?

ACTIVITY 4: TECHNIQUES TO PRACTISE

Practise these techniques by writing an opening paragraph for each of these familiar stories.

- ▶ Red Riding Hood
- ▶ Snow White
- ▶ Jack and the Beanstalk
- ▶ Cinderella
- ▶ The Three Little Pigs

ACTIVITY 5: OPENING PARAGRAPHS

Look at the pictures below. Using the techniques you have been learning about in this section, write a successful opening paragraph for a story based on each of the pictures.

Now look back at what you have written.

Underline any interesting words that you have used.

What impression do you want to give the reader about the character/ setting you have created?

- ▶ Write down two things about your opening that you are pleased with.
- ▶ Write down one thing you would like to improve when you write an opening paragraph in future.

! Top tips

Open a sentence with a '-ing' or a '-ed' clause. For example:

Glancing furtively behind, he …
Racing ahead of the others, she …
Numbed by the recent tragic news, she …

Now practise beginning sentences in different ways by rewriting the following short paragraph. You may include more detail and description if you wish to make it more interesting.

I went out and I locked the door behind me. I ran down the street because I didn't want to miss the bus. I caught the bus, luckily, but I couldn't find a seat. I stood for the whole journey and I gazed out of the window at the gloomy, grey pavement and people trying to protect themselves against the rain. I felt glad to be inside the bus!

Step 3 Challenge yourself

In order to become a successful writer you need to be self-critical and evaluate what you write. Even the greatest writers often change their choice of words in order to maximise effect.

In the poem 'Anthem for Doomed Youth' by Wilfred Owen the poet will have changed his mind about his choice of words before he was satisfied with his final choice and the impressions he wanted to create for his readers. His original draft will have looked quite different from the final version that was published.

When you look over your work, never be afraid to make changes! Adding significant details and descriptions and/or editing unnecessary chunks that don't move your story forward may often improve the overall effect and raise your mark.

ACTIVITY 6: CREATING AN ATMOSPHERE

Look at this opening paragraph.

One day I went to the seaside at Southsea with my family. I enjoyed myself and I remember the sea was blue and the sand was golden.

This story opening is clearly undeveloped and does not grab the reader's attention.

What three things do you think the writer could do to make the paragraph more interesting to read?

Below is another version of the same paragraph.

I remember when I was younger, wearing a plain red dress and white with sun cream singing 'Walking on Sunshine' to a boy I'd only just met. I'd never been to Southsea before and I was never to go again. In a way, I consider that a good thing because my wiser eyes probably wouldn't see the shimmering golden sands and dancing blue sea that I saw through a child's eyes and fondly remember.

What details/descriptions have been included here that would interest a reader?

Think about the words the writer has used and the atmosphere that has been created.

Write your own opening to a story with the title, 'Memories of the Seaside'.

Top tips

Use repetition for effect, for example:

The streets were full … the square was overcrowded … the city was overflowing.

He inched forward nervously; he stood on the edge of the diving board; he waited.

This will create tension for the reader.

Also think about the punctuation you might use and its effect. What effect do the **ellipsis** (…) or a **semi colon** (;) have here?

ellipsis – a set of dots suggesting there is more to come

semi colon – punctuation that links clauses

ACTIVITY 7: AN EMBARRASSING MOMENT

Read this story opening which tells of an embarrassing moment.

When I was eight I had the star role in the school concert but my costume was too long and I fell over on stage in front of everyone. A boy pointed to me and laughed. Then the audience all stared at me and joined in, pointing and laughing at me. I could tell the teacher was annoyed at me.

This piece of writing can be improved to make it more entertaining to read.
Rewrite the opening by using the skills you have learned so far.
You could use direct speech, an exclamation, a sound effect, an intriguing statement.

ACTIVITY 8: WRITING OPENINGS

Look at the following titles and write your openings for each one using the techniques you have learned so far.

▶ The Rescue
▶ Write about a time when you felt proud of yourself.
▶ Stranded!

Now, read over what you have written and consider how you might improve your writing. Remember even in the exam there is nothing wrong with crossing words out to improve your writing and earn a higher mark.

Consider the following points when you try to improve your work.

WHY	HOW
To correct my mistakes	Correct spelling, punctuation, grammar errors. Check for paragraphs.
To create the best impression	Add more detail where necessary.
To achieve a higher mark	Use interesting vocab; use **similes**, **metaphors**, effective verbs, etc.

simile – a comparison of two things using like or as, for example: The rays of the sun were like piercing daggers.
metaphor – a comparison of two things without using like or as, for example: The rays of the sun were piercing daggers.

 Top tips

If you want to show the passing of time in your story it is often a good idea to use flashbacks to explain past events quickly. For example:

It had all come flooding back …
It hadn't always been like this …

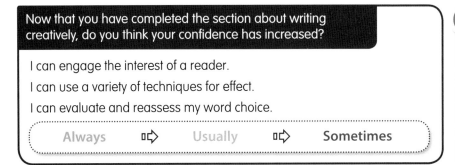

Now that you have completed the section about writing creatively, do you think your confidence has increased?

I can engage the interest of a reader.

I can use a variety of techniques for effect.

I can evaluate and reassess my word choice.

Always ⇨ Usually ⇨ Sometimes

! Top tips

Read like a writer! Be like a magpie and when you are reading collect good examples of:

- sentence structure
- words and expressions
- special effects.

Adapt them for your own stories.

Improve your skills

OBJECTIVES

▶ To organise a coherent story line
▶ To practise creating characters and setting effectively

How confident are you in these skills already?

I know how to create an effective and organised creative prose response.

I know how to create a satisfying ending to my creative prose.

I know how to create believable characters.

I know how to create a believable setting.

Always ⇨ Usually ⇨ Sometimes

! Top tips

A narrative always needs:

- an effective opening
- a strong plot, that is not too complicated
- characters and settings that the reader can imagine
- a satisfying ending.

You have already learned how to create an intriguing opening to hook the reader's attention. Now you need to make sure that the rest of your narrative is just as entertaining!

Step 1 Work on your skills

The fabulous five-part plan

The five-part plan is the most commonly used structure in story-telling. It is used in novels, plays, films and TV programmes.

1 Gripping opening
2 Introduction of a problem
3 Complication
4 Crisis or climax
5 Resolution

Use this simple but effective structure to help shape and organise your narrative plot.

It may help you to visualise the structure as a pyramid like this.

! Top tips

Use time links to gloss over unimportant sections, for example:

A few hours later... Next morning...

Use dialogue to move the plot along.

Focus on the thoughts and feelings of the characters, not just on what happens.

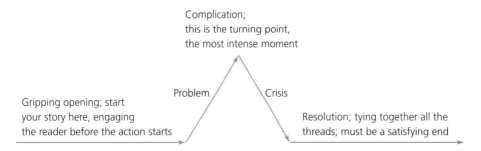

Complication;
this is the turning point,
the most intense moment

Problem / Crisis

Gripping opening; start
your story here, engaging
the reader before the action starts

Resolution; tying together all the
threads; must be a satisfying end

 ## ACTIVITY 1: FIVE-PART PLANS

Produce a five-part plan for each of the following creative story titles. You might want to think 'outside the box' for some of the titles and write down any ideas or first thoughts you may have.

a The Gift
b Write about a time when you felt you had let someone down.
c The Challenge
d Write a story that ends with this line: 'As I turned the corner and met his gaze, I knew there was no going back.'
f Write about a time when you volunteered for something.

You can write your plan as a scatter diagram, a flow chart, a timeline, a series of boxes or ideas linked by arrows. Use whatever method works for you.

Opposite is an example of how you may wish to set out your plan.

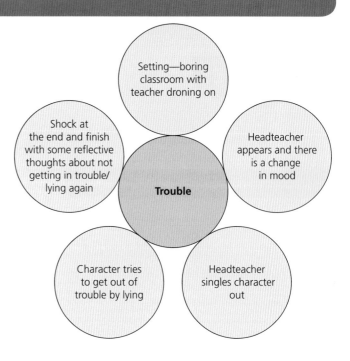

Setting—boring classroom with teacher droning on

Shock at the end and finish with some reflective thoughts about not getting in trouble/ lying again

Headteacher appears and there is a change in mood

Trouble

Character tries to get out of trouble by lying

Headteacher singles character out

 ## ACTIVITY 2: PLANNING AND WRITING A STORY

Read this opening to a story titled 'The Visitor'.

I turned my head and caught the velvet blackness of the night sky staring at me through my window. The relentless rain spat against the glass zigzagging as it wound a path down the window pane. Outside the street was empty. All I could hear was the angry rain pounding off the concrete slabs and the fierce wind bellowing an aggressive symphony in my ear.

▶ How do you think this story could develop?
▶ What could happen next?
▶ Try planning and writing the whole story.

Step 2   Practise your skills

You need to create believable characters in order to write a successful story. To do this it is a good idea to include some of these: adjectives, effective verbs and adverbs, similes and metaphors.

ACTIVITY 3: CHARACTERS

Read the description of a character from *The Hundred Thousand Kingdoms* by N. K. Jemisin.

… Face like the moon, pale and somehow wavering. I could get the gist of his features, but none of it stuck in my mind beyond an impression of astonishing beauty. His long, long hair wafted around him like black smoke, its tendrils curling and moving of their own volition. His cloak – or perhaps that was his hair too – shifted as if in an unfelt wind. The madness still lurked in his face, but it was a quieter madness now, not the rabid animal savagery of before. Something else – I could bring myself to call it humanity – stirred underneath the gleam.

On a copy of this extract, underline the adjectives and think about what they tell us about the character's personality.

What does the verb 'lurked' suggest about the character?

Sometimes you can give a reader clues about a character's personality and situation by **suggesting** it rather than **saying** it.

ACTIVITY 4: DESCRIBING A CHARACTER

Read this description of Curley's wife from *Of Mice and Men* by John Steinbeck then copy and complete the table. An example has been done for you.

Both men glanced up, for the rectangle of sunshine in the doorway was cut off. A girl was standing there looking in. She had full rouged lips and wide spaced eyes, heavily made up. Her finger nails were red. Her hair hung in little rolled clusters, like sausages. She wore a cotton house dress and red mules, on the insteps of which were little bouquets of red ostrich feathers. 'I'm looking for Curley,' she said. Her voice had a nasal, brittle quality.

DESCRIPTION	WHAT IT SUGGESTS
Rectangle of sunshine was cut off	She has an ominous, unsettling presence.

ACTIVITY 5: BODY LANGUAGE

Read this description of a character from *The Northern Lights* by Philip Pullman.

Lord Asriel was a tall man with powerful shoulders, a fierce dark face and eyes that seemed to flash and glitter with savage laughter. It was a face to be dominated by, or to fight; never a face to patronise or pity. All his movements were large and perfectly balanced, like those of a wild animal and when he appeared in a room like this, he seemed a wild animal held in a cage too small for it.

How does the writer make this character seem dangerous and threatening?

When writing about the feelings of your character try applying the same technique. Remember, don't say it … suggest it.

Look at the grid below. For each description of body language, decide what you think are the most likely feelings. An example has been completed for you.

DESCRIPTION OF BODY LANGUAGE	MOST LIKELY FEELINGS
Looking down not making eye contact	Embarrassed/shy/guilty
Eyes wide open and staring	
Folding arms and frowning	
Growing redder in the face	
Hands behind head with elbows stretched out	
Raising eyebrows and shaking head	
Shrugging shoulders	
Tapping foot or fingers	
Pointing at a person whilst talking	
Winking	

Next, look at the pictures below and write a physical description of each of the characters **suggesting** what he/she is like rather than actually stating it.

ACTIVITY 6: CHARACTERS' BEHAVIOUR

The way a character moves and behaves is also a useful way of suggesting what he or she is like without actually stating it.

Practise suggesting the personality of a character by choosing one of the characteristics and one of the activities in the table below. Mix and match them to practise developing your skills by creating different characters.

For example, describe a character who is shopping in a supermarket in a guilty way or a character who is going on a ride at a theme park in a nervous way.

CHARACTERISTIC	ACTIVITY
lazy	walking to school
terrified	dressing to go out on a date
exhausted	making a cup of tea
bored	shopping in a supermarket
delighted	doing maths homework
nervous	searching through drawers for a lost key
guilty	washing a car
suspicious	eating a burger
sneaky	trying to fix a computer
greedy	going on a ride at a theme park

ACTIVITY 7: CHARACTERS SPEAKING

Remember that the way a character speaks also suggests their personality. Instead of writing 'he said'/'she said', make sure your use of verbs is interesting and precise, for example, 'he bellowed'/'he whispered'.

How many different words can you think of for the word 'said'?

Try to make a list of at least ten alternatives and decide what the words might suggest about the way the character is feeling.

For example, the verb 'grumbled' may suggest the character is depressed, fed up or unhappy.

However, the verb 'yelled' may suggest the character is feeling scared, excited or enthusiastic.

ACTIVITY 8: AN INTIMIDATING CHARACTER

Look at this account of a menacing teacher.

The door slowly opened with a high pitched creak and my heart jumped. Everyone did the Mexican wave as he came in and it was as if we were all forced out of our seats by invisible springs. I saw two shiny black shoes appear … then I saw him. It was Mr Walters. The Head of Year. I knew why he was here.

He stood like an army general ready to bark at me for my crimes. His black malevolent eyes scanned the room threateningly, looking for the slightest of faults. I was nervous and sweating with fear as he slowly marched to the front of the room showing his gleaming white teeth. His hair was dark silver and closely shaven to his scalp and this made him appear even more threatening. The room was silent. Not a breath had been taken since he'd entered the room. 'Sit down,' he growled, as his eyes focused on me …

Do you think this student has created a believable character? Explain why/why not.

Pick out the words and descriptions that you think are effective.

Now write a couple of paragraphs describing an intimidating character. Remember to include details of the character's appearance, behaviour and movements.

Step 3   Challenge yourself

Try to apply these skills where something is suggested rather than stated, to the way you create setting and atmosphere in your creative prose response.

Consider the following points to help you in creating your setting.

- When will your story be set? Past? Present? Future?
- What time of day/night?
- Where will it be set? City/town/country? Familiar/unusual? Inside/outside? Real/imaginary?
- What atmosphere do you want to create? Frantic/loud/chaotic? Happy/excited/breathless? Frightening/sinister/eerie? Nostalgic/sentimental?

 ACTIVITY 9: CREATING ATMOSPHERE

Read this extract from *Bleak House* by Charles Dickens.

What sort of atmosphere is created by the setting? On a copy of the extract, highlight the words/phrases that have created this atmosphere.

London … Fog everywhere. Fog up the river, where it flows among green **aits** and meadows; fog down the river, where it rolls defiled among the tiers of shipping and waterside pollution of a great (and dirty city). Fog on the Essex marshes, fog on the Kentish heights. Fog creeping into the **cabooses** of **collier brigs**, fog lying out in the yards and hovering in the rigging of great ships; fog drooping on the gunwales of barges and small boats. Fog in the eyes and throats of ancient Greenwich pensioners, wheezing by the firesides of their wards; fog cruelly pinching the toes and fingers of the shivering boys. People on the bridges peeping over the parapets into a nether sky of fog, with fog all round them, as if they were up in a balloon and hanging in the misty clouds.

> **ait** – small island in a river
> **caboose** – kitchen on a ship's deck
> **collier brigs** – ships for carrying coal

Can you find:
▶ a short sentence for emphasis
▶ repetition for effect
▶ interesting and effective verbs
▶ a simile
▶ effective adjectives?

ACTIVITY 10: LANGUAGE TO CREATE ATMOSPHERE

Look at the pictures below:

What sort of atmosphere would you want to create for each of these settings?

Write a few paragraphs about each of these settings, thinking carefully about your choice of adjectives, verbs, similes and metaphors.

Now you have completed the section, do you think your confidence has increased?

I know how to create an effective and organised narrative.

I know how to create a satisfying ending to my narrative.

I know how to create believable and realistic characters.

I know how to create a believable and realistic setting.

Always   ⇨   Usually   ⇨   Sometimes

OBJECTIVES

▶ To feel confident about writing a creative response within a set time
▶ To feel confident about how to improve my writing

How confident are you in these skills already?

I am confident about choosing my title wisely.

I feel confident about planning and structuring my narrative.

I feel confident about writing at length.

I feel confident about writing in exam conditions.

Always ⇨ Usually ⇨ **Sometimes**

In Section B of the Component One exam you will be asked to write a creative prose response. You will be given a choice of four titles and you will need to choose one of the titles as a basis for your story or personal account.

You should think carefully about each title before you make your choice because some titles may suit you more than others. There will usually be a title that you may be able to relate to personal experience, for example. Sometimes making one of the titles fit a 'real experience' can make your writing more controlled and believable. Also, you will often be given a choice where the first or last line of the story has been given to you and you have to work this into your story or personal account.

It is important that you do not write purely descriptively otherwise you will not be able to meet the assessment criteria and you will lose marks.

You will be expected to write 450–600 words.

The section is marked out of 40:

● 24 marks are awarded for how you communicate and organise your work.
● 16 marks are awarded for sentence structure, spelling and punctuation.

QUESTION 1

The dos and don'ts of narrative writing

Look at the list opposite. Which do you think you should do and which should you not do in order to succeed in your narrative writing task?

Do this in the exam?	insert tick / cross
Use paragraphs and sentences of various lengths.	
Don't bother planning before you start writing.	
Use precise adjectives and verbs.	
Relax when you finish writing the story and wait for the exam to finish.	
Include as many characters as you can.	
Choose the first title on the list without reading the whole list of choices.	
Use some dialogue to help reveal character.	
Check spelling and punctuation.	
Have a strong, intriguing opening.	
Make the story as long as possible within the time you have been given.	

 QUESTION 2

Now put your skills into practice.

Choose one of the titles from the following list:
- The Visitor
- Continue the story beginning with the following line

That was it. I was trapped …
- Write about a time when you were scared.
- Childhood memories

Write a plan for the story in 10 minutes – this is the time suggested in the exam.

Now write your story in 35 minutes – this is the time suggested in the exam.

Remember to do the following:
- Use adjectives and adverbs to create atmosphere.
- Avoid boring verbs such as 'said', 'got', 'went', 'walked'. Use more interesting, precise verbs instead.
- Set out conversation/direct speech correctly.
- Use a range of punctuation, such as exclamation marks, question marks, ellipses.
- Use some complex sentences with subordinate clauses.
- Use paragraphs.
- Keep suggesting the characters' feelings.

When you have finished, read over your work carefully.

Are you satisfied with what you have written?
- Write down two things you think you have done well.
- Write down two things you can improve upon next time. These can be your targets for the story you will write at the end of this unit.

QUESTION 3

Read the extracts below which are from creative prose responses.

Extract A

I'm such a fool, Mum. Why did I ever leave the comfort of my own home? I'm such a fool. I remember waking up to those horrible curtains you put up for me. They don't seem too bad now ...

Extract B

I got up in the morning at 7am. I went downstairs and my mum was making me a full English breakfast. I went to the living room and put my favourite programme on. It was called 'Friends'. The programme is about a group of friends.

Are these good examples of creative writing?

If so, pick out two good things about each one.

If not, write down two ways in which each one could be improved.

Comparing sample answers

Read these examples of creative writing.

Text A: A day at the seaside

'I told you, I remember! I asked you in the hall, Do you have the towels and equiptment? I carn't believe you sometimes.' Mum walked off, although she had to come back soon, she had nowere to go. Dad stormed of towards her direction. It seemed I was the only person in my family who had packed and brought my things. I was left on my own looking after my 3 year old little brother aaron and my 4 year old sister Emily. Wes sat by the side of the car for half an hour before they came back walking hand in hand smiling at each other. I walked off down to the beach, certain that I needed to get a tan before school started. We came on this family holiday every year and most of the time I could escape my 2 annoying siblings I would walk for hours along cliff tops and beachs's, most of the time I painted them, I loved painting as it calmed me down. I sat down on the sandy beach and found myself dreaming of oceans filled with fosh and dolphins and many more creatures.

Text B: A day at the seaside

I hopped and skipped along, my hand held high above my head, holding onto my Mum's fingers. The dry sand on the slipway scuffed my heels and squeezed in between my toes as we ran down onto the beach. The soft dry sand above the line of the tide was difficult to walk on and my little feet sank as I tried to move forward to keep up with everybody. Granny had but up the bright, stripey winbreaks and staked her claim on our section of the beach. Towels were laid down to create a patchwork carpet, deckchairs were erected then moved this way and that while Granny oversaw the whole operation with the skill of a military commander. Seagulls screeched overhead, an eerie, melancholy sound. And then it was time. Time for my first paddle in the sea! Holding Mum's hand tightly again we walked down towards the huge grey body of water. The wet sand was cold underfoot and as we moved closer, the noise became louder. It was like a distant train moving through a tunnel, a roaring and whooshing that was all around you, above, below.

On a copy of the responses:
- Highlight what is effective and engaging, or not.
- Highlight all the technical errors of spelling and punctuation.

If you were giving feedback to the writer of each response:
- What would you say about the way they have communicated their ideas and organised their work? Think about what they do well and what they could do to improve.
- What would you say about their use of sentence structure, spelling and punctuation? Think about what they do well and what they could do to improve.

QUESTION 4

Choose one of the following titles.
- The Hero
- Write about a time when you looked after small children.
- An experience of a lifetime
- Finish your story with this line:
  ... and that's when I realised I would have to face a furious Mr Jones.

Use 10 minutes to plan your story.

Then write your story in 35 minutes.

Remember your targets from the story you wrote at the start of this section and act upon them!

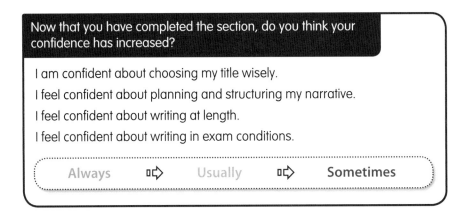

Now that you have completed the section, do you think your confidence has increased?

I am confident about choosing my title wisely.

I feel confident about planning and structuring my narrative.

I feel confident about writing at length.

I feel confident about writing in exam conditions.

Always ⇨ Usually ⇨ Sometimes

Unit 14
Style and register, purpose and audience

OBJECTIVES

▶ To use the appropriate register and style for different types of text
▶ To understand why I am writing (purpose) and who will read it (audience)

How confident are you in these skills already?

I know the reason for my writing and who will read it.

I can choose the correct layout (format) for my writing.

I can use the right level of formality in my writing.

I can select words to appeal to my audience.

Always ⇨ Usually ⇨ Sometimes

In Section B, Component Two of the exams you will be asked to write different types of **texts** and for different purposes and audiences. To write effectively you need to identify the reason for writing (purpose) and the people who will read it (audience). When you have done this, you will be able to think about the appropriate tone (**register**) and the type of words you will use (style).

Get going

Step 1 Work on your skills

Before you start a piece of writing, ask yourself the question: What am I trying to do?

It will usually be one of the following things:

● Persuade someone
● Give information
● Entertain someone
● Express an opinion
● Ask someone to take action

Sometimes you will be doing a combination of these things.

texts – different types or formats of writing, for example, reviews, articles, reports, speeches, letters
register – the tone of your writing – formal/informal; aggressive/forceful or calm/ reasonable; conversational; humorous; sarcastic and so on

ACTIVITY 1: PURPOSE

Read this list of questions and decide whether the purpose of each one is to persuade, to inform or to entertain, or a combination of these things.

a Write a report to the head teacher and governing body of your school/college giving the opinions of your year group about the growing problem of litter on the school site.
b Write an article for your school/college website about the advantages and disadvantages of using social media.
c Write a speech to be delivered to your year group about why they should elect you to the student council.
d Write a letter to your local council giving your views about the proposal to sell off the local playing fields for the purpose of building a new supermarket.
e Write a letter to your friend who has to spend the next fortnight in hospital with a broken leg.
f Write a lively review for a teenage magazine about a film or CD of your choice.

ACTIVITY 2: SUITABLE AND ACCESSIBLE LANGUAGE

Here is a paragraph from a speech delivered by a student persuading a Year 11 assembly to elect him on to the student council.

> Welcome fellow students, I am here today to talk to you about why I should be voted on to the Student Council as a representative for Year 11. I believe I would be the best person for the job because I am friendly and everyone likes me. I am a keen sportsman so I would want to develop sport and fitness levels across the year group. Also I want us to raise money for charities by holding sponsored events.

 Practise developing your ideas by adding a few more paragraphs. You may include more detail and points if you wish to make it more interesting.

A writing task will tell you the type of audience you are writing for. To produce a good answer you need to make sure that your writing and language are suitable and accessible for your audience. Ask yourself the question: Will my writing appeal to my audience?

ACTIVITY 3: AUDIENCE

Look at this list of books.

▶ *The Internet for Dummies*
▶ *A Biography of Lady Gaga*
▶ *The Official Club History of Chelsea Football Club*
▶ *Easy Meals in 30 Minutes*

Who do you think the intended audience would be for these books? What might these titles suggest about the type of audience? Use this example to help you.

An Introduction to Applied Physics — this would suggest the audience could be a science student. The title tells us it is an 'introduction' so the student probably is a beginner and needs to know the basics.

ACTIVITY 4: A TEENAGE AUDIENCE

A student has written this article about one of his favourite films for a teenage magazine.

A film I enjoyed was 'Iron Man 2'. This film was entertaining and amusing. Iron Man was slowly dying and he needed to find a cure. At the same time a man from Russia wanted revenge for the death of his friend. Also Iron Man had a fight with his friend. Then his friend stole an Iron Man suit. I liked this film because it wasn't too serious.

Do you think this article would appeal to a teenage audience? Improve this article by making it lively and interesting to read.

ACTIVITY 5: IDENTIFYING THE TYPE OF WRITING

Read this piece of writing by a student.

Do you ever wonder why the teachers hate mobiles? Because they can't use them? Or maybe they hate the way we brandish them around? Well, I'm not going to keep you guessing. Teachers, like many of our elders are not up to date with 21st century technology. So when we can text, phone, look up stuff on the internet and play games, they become jealous. Great isn't it!

I must say it is a huge blessing on our part to see people who are senior to us struggling to get to grips with these simple devices. I mean, what's so difficult about pressing a few buttons? They may have more knowledge and more experience but they can't cheat in pub quizzes by using the internet or send each other amusing pictures.

Mobile phones are the best thing since sliced bread. What is wrong with them? They are perfect! All we need now is for them to make you dinner and do your homework (just kidding, Mrs Smith) and we won't have to lift a finger ever again!

Now I would like you to decide whether they are a blessing or a curse but I hope that with my points you will say it is a blessing.

Thank you for listening.

What type of writing do you think the student was asked to produce here? How can you tell?

What do you think the student is trying to do here (purpose)?

What do you think the student's intended audience is here? How can you tell?

What sort of register or tone has the student used here? Can you find any words to prove this?

! Top tips

Try to imagine the person you are writing for. For instance, if you are asked to write for a teenage magazine, it might help you to think about a magazine that you know and have read yourself. If you are asked to write to a friend or relative, think of a real friend or family member and have them in mind as you write.

ACTIVITY 6: FAVOURITE HOBBY OR SPORT

Write an article about your favourite hobby or sport to be included in your school/college magazine.

Think about who will be reading it. Make sure that what you say and the language you use are suitable for an audience of teenagers and teachers.

ACTIVITY 7: WELCOMING YEAR 7 PUPILS

Look at this question.

Write a lively article for your school/college magazine welcoming new Year 7 pupils into the school, and giving them information and advice about their new school.

Your article should tell them what is good about the school, but also what to look out for.

Think about:

▶ what you are trying to do

▶ who is going to read the article

▶ whether your article will appeal to your audience.

Remember the skills you have learned in Unit 12 about how to use paragraphs, organise your ideas and write accurately. These skills will help you to write a successful answer here.

Now, write your article.

! Top tips

If you are writing for an audience of 11-year-olds you need to make sure that your language is suitable and that they will understand the words you use. For example:

Don't get on the wrong side of the teachers by not handing in homework on time.

is more suitable than:

Failure to submit work by the requested date will result in an unfortunate punishment. This would be very inadvisable and extremely foolhardy.

Step 2   Practise your skills

Finding the right tone and register for your responses is an important skill in becoming a successful writer.

Many tasks will expect you to write in a **formal** way, with a formal tone and using standard English.

However, some tasks will be a bit more **informal** and these are where you could be asked to write for a teenage audience. Be careful and don't become carried away! This isn't your chance to use a lot of slang and text language or abbreviations (for example, LOL). If you use slang it could make your writing sound careless and the reader might not take it seriously.

> **formal tone** – using standard English without any slang or abbreviations
> **informal tone** – using language that is more casual, familiar and sometimes colloquial

ACTIVITY 8: REGISTER

Look at this list of tasks and decide whether your register would be formal or informal.

Write a letter:

▶ of application to join the sixth form

▶ to a friend who is considering giving up his/her job to travel the world

▶ to the council about the lack of facilities for young people in your areas

▶ to a hotel manager applying for a job

▶ to your sister who has left home to study at university

▶ to your friend who is thinking of becoming a teacher.

ACTIVITY 9: RECYCLING

Read the following exam-style question carefully.

Your local council wants to encourage recycling and to reduce waste. They have suggested:

▶ **separating recyclable waste from rubbish**

▶ **charging to collect rubbish**

▶ **fining people who don't recycle**

▶ **only collecting rubbish every two weeks instead of every week.**

Write a letter to your local council giving your opinion on some or all of these suggestions.

To help you write a good answer pick out these key pieces of information you will need to focus on:

▶ your purpose

▶ your audience

▶ how your audience will affect the language and register you will use

▶ the topic you are writing about

▶ the format or layout of your response.

 Top tips

In an exam you may find it helpful to use a highlighter or underline and label these pieces of key information.

ACTIVITY 10: IMPROVING AN ANSWER

Look at this student's response to the question.

> 46 Clifford Street
>
> Newlands
>
> Sheffield
>
> SD4 7FB
>
> 20 May 2015

Dear Council,

I want to right to you about the rubbish. My household has five people in it and I'm fed up with you lot at the council telling me what I can and can't put in my bin. I think that what you want us to do is a stupid and pathetic idea. I'm busy and I dont have time to keep sorting out all my plastic bottles from my tins and my paper from my glass bottles.

What do you think were paying you to do? I'm fed up with having to put different rubbish bags out on different days! How dare you say you are going to fine me if I get the days mixed up? Perhaps you'd prefer me to dump my rubbish in the middle of the road instead? With three kids in the house it's rediculous to say that you'll only collect my rubbish every two weeks! How would you like it?

Thank you for listening to me.

FG Smith

As you can see, the answer is too informal and is not suitable for the intended audience.

▶ Pick out three examples where the student has written too informally.

▶ Find two examples where the student is rude and disrespectful.

▶ What other three pieces of advice would you give the student about how to improve this answer?

199

Rewrite the opening paragraph of the student response, remembering to use a formal register and a polite tone which is suitable for the intended audience.

Now think about other points you could include in the letter.

Put them in the order that would best suit your argument.

Use connectives between your points and think about how to organise your paragraphs.

Now write the whole letter.

smile
I
wild sa
of dazzl
no
ghost
poetry
delicious

! Top tips

Remember to show that you understand the format of the task and that you know what you are doing by using the special features of the form you have been asked to use. Always aim to set your writing out correctly.

Informal letters, as you would expect, are less formal and are usually written to someone you know well and so a more relaxed and friendly register would be appropriate.

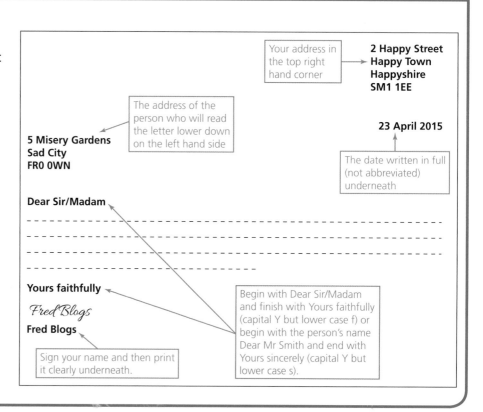

Your address in the top right hand corner → **2 Happy Street**
Happy Town
Happyshire
SM1 1EE

The address of the person who will read the letter lower down on the left hand side

5 Misery Gardens
Sad City
FR0 0WN

23 April 2015

The date written in full (not abbreviated) underneath

Dear Sir/Madam

- -
- -
- -
- -

Yours faithfully

Fred Blogs

Fred Blogs

Begin with Dear Sir/Madam and finish with Yours faithfully (capital Y but lower case f) or begin with the person's name Dear Mr Smith and end with Yours sincerely (capital Y but lower case s).

Sign your name and then print it clearly underneath.

ACTIVITY 11: DEVELOPING A LETTER

Read this informal letter carefully.

49 Albert Square,

Coronation Street

London

SE12 3TH

12 March 2015

Dear Kath,

I recently found out that you are considering moving to Spain. That would make a huge difference from the constant bad weather in the UK.

I think that moving abroad would be a great opportunity for you and your family to make a fresh start in life. I hear the food in Spain is much healthier than here.

Although I'm sure that it would be fantastic, there would be a lot of hard work finding jobs and learning the new language. What Spanish phrases can you say?

There is also that difficulty in driving on the other side of the road but I'm sure that John will have no trouble with that. I'm sure that you will make the right decision.

What are the children's views on moving to Spain? I'm sure they are very excited in going to new schools and meeting new friends.

If you do decide to go, we will be very supportive and help you in any way we can, although we will miss you all very much.

Best wishes,

Chris

Top tips

You may have noticed that an informal letter is set out differently from a formal letter and has a different set of special features. What differences did you notice? Use this table to help you identify them.

Informal letters	Formal letters
	Address of writer in top right hand corner
	Date written underneath in full (no abbreviation)
	Address of recipient underneath date on left
Begin: Dear Kath	
Informal ending: Best wishes	

The register of this letter is appropriate for the intended audience because it is entertaining and friendly and it doesn't use any slang or text language. However, the letter is a bit brief and undeveloped.

Improve and develop the letter by adding at least three or four sentences to each paragraph.

ACTIVITY 12: LETTER TO THE HEAD TEACHER/PRINCIPAL

Read the following question.

The head teacher/principal of your school/college has proposed that male and female students should play in the same sports teams.

Write a letter to him/her giving your views on this proposal.

▶ What is the question asking you to do (purpose)?

▶ Who will read your letter (audience)?

▶ What register do you think would be appropriate here (formal or informal)?

▶ What special features do you need to include for the piece of writing?

▶ How will you set out your letter?

 Now write your letter.

! Top tips

When you write a letter you may find it helps to plan your ideas using the abbreviations RDA.

Reason for the letter. This should be made clear in your opening paragraph.
Detail/development. This would be the main part of the letter where you go through all your points and arguments.
Action. This would be your final paragraph where you say what you want your letter to achieve.

? Assess yourself. Did you:

- identify the correct audience?
- use the correct letter layout?
- use the right tone throughout the whole letter?
- use paragraphs?
- organise your ideas in the best way?
- write enough?
- use different types of sentences?
- spell most words correctly?

Next steps...

1 After reflecting on your work, choose one paragraph from your letter that you think you could improve.
2 Rewrite this paragraph.

Step 3 Challenge yourself

To appeal to your intended audience you need to think about using a suitable style. You should aim to develop your vocabulary and select the words you use carefully, depending on the effect you want to create.

ACTIVITY 13: INTERESTING ADJECTIVES

Your writing will sound much more entertaining and appealing if you use interesting adjectives.

Look at this list of adjectives that can be used to liven up your writing.

Decide whether each word gives a positive or negative impression.

- mesmerising
- sophisticated
- boring
- stimulating
- moving
- exhilarating

- unconvincing
- flat
- unoriginal
- thrilling
- disappointing
- inspiring

- monotonous
- dull
- mundane
- awesome
- shocking

Make sure you look up any words you don't understand.

Now think of six adjectives of your own that you could use in your writing.

Decide whether these adjectives would create a positive or negative impression.

Make up a sentence for each adjective to practise how you would use it.

ACTIVITY 14: REVIEW

Next, read the following review of the album 'Take Me Home' by One Direction adapted from *The Guardian*.

It's not often you come across a new album that you can genuinely describe as phenomenal, but the adjective fits One Direction's 'Take Me Home'. This is remarkable stuff, not just for a runner up on the *X Factor*, but for a UK boy band. The live version of 'While We're Young' rips off the intro to The Clash's 'Should I Stay or Should I Go?' so cheekily it changes literally one note.

Elsewhere the material is of variable quality. The chorus of 'Kiss You' is hard to get out of your brain even as your brain is boggling at the thought that it took seven different writers to come up with it. 'Rock Me', however, is pretty excruciating as is perhaps inevitable from a song in which teenage boy band members try to sound nostalgic. 'Do You Remember the Sumer of '09?' they ask, making the listener want to answer with, 'Yeah, do you? You must have been about eight.' It isn't bad as albums by boy bands go nor, though, is there anything to appeal to anyone except their legions of female fans.

This review is lively and appeals to a teenage audience because the style is interesting and entertaining. It also has the special features of a review and these are listed below.

▶ Paragraphs and ideas that are organised clearly to guide the reader through the review

▶ A lively and entertaining opening sentence to grab the attention and interest of the intended audience

▶ Some details of the songs but without giving anything away

▶ Strengths of the album

▶ Weaknesses of the album

▶ Final paragraph to sum up the writer's opinion and recommendation

Can you find these features in the review?

ACTIVITY 15: REVIEW FOR YOUR SCHOOL/COLLEGE NEWSPAPER

Now look at the opening from a review of a recent television programme.

> Cleavage, firearms, swordplay, leather jerkins, grubby hostelries, chickens flapping around in streets – and more cleavage. What else, frankly, do you need to create an entertaining telly rendering of Alexandre Dumas' famous novel *The Three Musketeers*?

What makes this paragraph lively and entertaining?

This next review is also lively and appeals to the audience. How does the writer achieve this effect?

> Here we go again. Tonight's *X Factor* served up yet more arena auditions – the stage of the proceedings in which the acts who impressed the judging panel first time around are plonked into Wembley Arena to find out if they can wow a 5,000 strong crowd too.

Did you notice that questions have been used in the reviews? What, do you think, is the effect of this? Would this be a technique you could use in your own writing?

When you have finished, read through your work carefully and think about what you have written.

▶ Did you have the correct purpose, audience and register for your writing?

▶ Did you write enough?

▶ Did you begin each sentence with a different word? If not, try to think of an alternative now.

▶ What different types of sentences have you used?

▶ Have you used paragraphs effectively?

▶ Have you varied the length of your sentences?

▶ Think of two things you think you have done well in this piece of writing.

▶ What two things do you still want to improve? Make these your targets for your next piece of writing.

Now, using the skills you have learned so far, write a review for your school/college newspaper about a television programme you have watched during the last week.

Now that you have completed the section, do you think your confidence has improved?

I know the reason for my writing and who will read it.

I can choose the correct layout (format) for my writing.

I can use the right level of formality in my writing.

I can select words to appeal to my audience.

Always ⇨ Usually ⇨ Sometimes

Improve your skills

OBJECTIVES

▷ To develop a secure approach to writing in different formats

▷ To plan my points effectively

How confident are you in these skills already?

I can recognise and understand the different formats I will be expected to use.

I know the special features of different types of text.

I can organise my ideas in order to write effectively.

Always ⇨ Usually ⇨ Sometimes

Step 1 Work on your skills

Reports are formal texts that outline areas of concern, give advice and suggest possible solutions to the issue. Reports are usually written in a formal register and in an impersonal style. The purpose of a report is to pass on information, not to persuade or entertain the reader. A report is usually written for a person in authority such as a head teacher, governing body, local council or school council. Your tone should be respectful but clear and not rude or nagging.

> **! Top tips**
>
> You may find some of these connectives useful when writing your report:
>
> - firstly, then, next, secondly, thirdly, and finally
> - therefore, thus, hence, as a result of, subsequently, consequently, accordingly
> - for example, such as, it appears, for instance, is shown by, the evidence is, is indicated by, is suggested by

ACTIVITY 1: REPORT TOPICS

What sort of topics might you be asked to write a report on in relation to:

▶ school?

▶ the wider community?

Choose one topic with a school-related theme and one related to the wider community from your list in Activity 1.

Write down some ideas/points you would want to include in your report.

Put your ideas in a clear, logical order so that your points sound sensible and organised.

Write a topic sentence to begin each paragraph.

ACTIVITY 2: TRUE OR FALSE?

Read the following list of statements about report writing and decide whether they are true or false.

REPORT WRITING	TRUE OR FALSE?
Reports should be written in formal English.	
A report should be clearly organised into clear and logical paragraphs.	
The purpose of a report is to entertain the reader.	
You need to end a report with 'Yours sincerely' and a signature.	
A report should have a clear title saying who the intended audience is and the purpose.	
Your report needs to be 300–400 words in length.	
A report should be written in columns like a newspaper.	
Subheadings should be used to make the different sections clear.	
A report should have pictures to grab the attention of the reader and illustrate what you are talking about.	

Using what you have learned so far, write a list of the special features you would expect to find in a report.

ACTIVITY 3: PLANNING

Read the following exam-style question.

Write a report for your head teacher and governors on ways in which your school/college could be improved for students approaching GCSE examinations.

 For a writing task in the exam, it may help you to make a quick plan like the one below to focus on what exactly you need to do.

▶ Who is your **audience**? – head teacher/governors who are busy and well educated and already know the school well

▶ What is your **purpose**? – to make clear what is wrong with the current situation and suggest what improvements can be made to the school to help students preparing for important exams

▶ What is your **register**? – formal, polite standard English – no slang

▶ What is the **format**? – organised report with paragraphs under subheadings such as 'Revision time', 'Extra lessons'

 Planning an answer is essential if you want to write successfully.

To help you organise your ideas, jot down a heading for your report.

Write down four or five subheadings you will want to use in your report. You can use some of those suggested in the previous activity if you want to.

Write down a topic sentence to begin each paragraph under the subheadings.

What other ideas could you include in each section?

 ## ACTIVITY 4: WRITING A REPORT

Here are two different introductions to this question.

Example A

From: Year 11 Committee

To: Mr Powell, the head teacher and governing body

Purpose: To suggest ways in which Avondale School could be improved for Key Stage 4 students approaching GCSE exams.

Introduction

Year 11 School Council members were asked by the head teacher to identify the problems facing the students in school as they approach their GCSE exams and to suggest possible solutions. In my role as a member of the Year 11 council, I have consulted other Year 11 students and these are my findings.

Example B

Here is my report to the head teacher and governors about what the school needs to do to help Year 11 students as they come up to their important exams.

Which example do you think has the most appropriate introduction? Explain why.

What three things could the student do to improve Example B?

Now write your own answer to the question remembering the following features of writing an effective report.

▶ Begin with a clear title stating for whom it is written and what it is about.

▶ Include a short introduction, making clear why you are writing the report, the background to it, how you reached your conclusions and where you found your information.

▶ Using separate subheadings for each paragraph/topic is an effective way of organising your material logically and coherently. Aim for about three or four subheadings.

▶ Include a conclusion where you sum up your main points and suggest what should happen next.

▶ Use a formal register with a respectful, polite and calm tone.

Did you:

   ▶ keep your report formal?

▶ write a report that was useful to the person reading it?

▶ set out your report correctly?

▶ include enough detail?

▶ check your work carefully?

▶ check your spelling and punctuation carefully?

Based on your responses to the checklist above, what two things could you do to improve your work?

Step 2   Practise your skills

Just like the other texts you have read about, articles also have a few special features of their own. You can improve the way you write articles by using them.

Of course it's important to organise your ideas in a clear and structured way but also think about using techniques such as questions to make your audience interested in what you are writing about. Think about using exaggeration and emotive language to engage and appeal to your audience. **Irony** and **sarcasm** are sometimes used in articles as well.

irony – words or phrases that usually mean the opposite of what is said to create a humorous effect

sarcasm – words or phrases that usually mean the opposite of what is said to mock or ridicule someone

ACTIVITY 5: EFFECTIVE WORDS

A good article is carefully written, informs and appeals to its intended audience.

Read this extract from an article written by a student on the topic of his favourite band.

Whatever Happened To Rock and Roll?

Kings of Leon are three brothers and a cousin from Memphis, all with the surname Followilll and they play rock and roll like they were born doing it. Lead singer and rhythm guitarist Caleb has the smoky, leathery voice of an old bluesman, and is truly one of the most distinctive vocalists that Nashville has **ever** produced. Cousin Matthew Followill, the lead guitarist, plays reeling, glittering guitar solos that shine out from the songs like gold nuggets in the Dust Bowl.

Live, the Kings are very, very cool – Jared struts and pouts like a young Mick Jagger; Nathan drums firmly at the back; whilst Matthew and Caleb carve out the kind of guitar sounds that will be talked about for years!

The writer has chosen verbs and adjectives very carefully here to engage a teenage audience.

Pick out some of these effective words and explain why you think they are successful.

Write two or three paragraphs about your favourite singer or band that could feature in an article for a teenage magazine.

Remember to use your style and language effectively to interest your audience.

ACTIVITY 6: IDENTIFYING TECHNIQUES

Here is an extract from an article about Simon Cowell.

Simon Cowell. The human version of Marmite! You either love him or hate him. Over the years, Simon Cowell, television's very own Mr Nasty, has made hundreds, if not thousands of contestants burst into tears just by opening his mouth! The smug, super rich fan of seriously untrendy high-waisted trousers has expressed his opinions to eager contestants on some of the most popular TV programmes ever to hit our screens like *The X Factor* and *Britain's Got Talent*, so that now it's almost impossible to turn on the box without seeing his smarmy, self-satisfied grin.

The tone of this article is very sarcastic. Can you find some examples of sarcasm here?

The article uses other techniques such as:

▶ direct appeal

▶ exclamations

▶ emotive language.

Find examples of each of these techniques and think about why they make the article effective.

Can you think of anything else that makes the article successful?

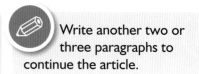 Write another two or three paragraphs to continue the article.

ACTIVITY 7: SAVING ENERGY

Now that you have learned about some of the special features of articles, read this exam-style question:

Your school/college is keen to save energy.

Write an article for the school/college magazine on this issue.

You could include:

▶ **examples of how energy is wasted at the moment**

▶ **your ideas about how the situation could be improved.**

 It will help if you plan your answer before you start writing. The following points will help you organise your ideas.

Heading/title of article

▶ Not too long

▶ Catchy – perhaps a pun or question

▶ Some indication of what the article is about

Intro/first paragraph

▶ Brief outline of topic of article

▶ Must hook the reader's attention

▶ Think about your techniques.

Main body of article

▶ Include plenty of details.

▶ Think about techniques to engage the reader.

Conclusion

▶ Brief summary of article/overview

▶ Catchy ending – this will be reader's final impression

▶ Question/pun?

▶ Relate final sentence back to heading at beginning?

When you have completed the planning stage, write your article.

 Top tips

Think carefully and identify the key words in the question.

Identify the purpose, audience, format and register for the task. Aim to write 300–400 words.

Read through your article. Did you:

▶ show clear understanding of the purpose and format

▶ show clear awareness of the reader/intended audience

▶ adapt your register to the purpose

▶ include appropriate reasons/details

▶ organise your ideas sensibly

▶ use paragraphs to show organisation

▶ vary your sentence structures

▶ use a range of punctuation mostly accurately

▶ spell most words correctly?

Do you need to make any corrections or improvements to your article? If so, then make the improvements now.

What will your target be to improve your performance next time?

Step 3 Challenge yourself

As you already know, a speech is when you address a person or group of people about a specific topic or matter. Speeches can be written to give information, to persuade or to argue a point of view.

If you are asked to write a speech it is important that you do not use any slang because your writing may not be taken seriously.

! Top tips

Remember your audience will only hear your speech once, so you need to organise your ideas into the best possible order.

Begin your speech with your strongest point but keep a good point to finish with because this will be the final impression the audience will have of you.

Your tone needs to be forceful but not rude or aggressive. Include persuasive techniques to encourage your audience to agree with you.

ACTIVITY 8: PERSUASIVE SPEECH

Read this extract from *Animal Farm* by George Orwell.

'Now, comrades, what is the nature of this life of ours? Let us face it: our lives are miserable, laborious, and short. We are born, we are given just so much food as will keep the breath in our bodies, and those of us who are capable of it are forced to work to the last atom of our strength; and the very instant that our usefulness has come to an end we are slaughtered with hideous cruelty. No animal in England knows the meaning of happiness or leisure after he is a year old. No animal in England is free. The life of an animal is misery and slavery: that is the plain truth.

'But is this simply part of the order of nature? Is it because this land of ours is so poor that it cannot afford a decent life to those who dwell upon it? No, comrades, a thousand times no!'

The writer has used several techniques to make the speech sound persuasive.

How many can you find in this speech?

Can you explain the effect they would have on an audience?

Use this example to get you started:

The writer uses emotive words such as 'comrades'. This has a persuasive effect as it makes them feel as if they are all united and standing together on the same side with one common goal.

Using some of the techniques you have found, write a short persuasive argument/speech on each of the following topics:

▶ Persuading someone you like to go out with you

▶ Persuading your parents to let you have an exotic pet

▶ Persuading someone to buy your old and damaged bike

▶ Persuading someone to buy an out-of-date train timetable

ACTIVITY 9: IMPROVING A RESPONSE

Here is the opening from a speech written by a student in response to the exam question below, complete with errors.

Your school wants to raise money for charity.

You have the chance to speak in assembly to persuade the school to support a charity of your choice.

Here are some ideas you might want to think about:

▶ **Information about the charity**

▶ **Why it is a good charity to support**

▶ **Some ideas about how to raise the money**

▶ **Why students should get involved**

Today I am going to be talking to you about the charity Help for Heroes and why I think you should support it. It is a charity all about supporting soldiers and their families.

These brave soldiers are fighting for our country risking their life for us, don't you think that deserves support? These brave people know the risks they are taking and are true heroes. I feel it is a brilliant cause. The charity also support the families of the soldiers, think how it must be for them, the constant thought of never seeing your mum, dad, brother or sister or anyone else ever again, it must be very hard for them, but they push through knowing the good that person is doing . . .

 What do you think the student could do to improve the response and thereby score a higher mark?

Make sure your advice is specific by suggesting at least one improvement in each of the following areas:

▶ Format
▶ Register
▶ Vocabulary
▶ Sentence structure
▶ Technical accuracy

 Make the improvements you have suggested and continue the response.

Now that you have completed the section, do you think your confidence has increased?

I can recognise and understand the different formats I will be expected to use.

I know the special features of different types of text.

I can organise my ideas in order to write effectively.

Always ⇨ Usually ⇨ Sometimes

OBJECTIVES

▶ To feel confident about using an appropriate register, tone and style for an intended audience
▶ To feel confident about evaluating my work to improve my performance

---

How confident are you in these skills already?

I am confident about adapting my register, purpose, style and format depending on the task.

I am confident about adapting my language for my intended audience.

I am confident that I know how to improve my writing.

Always　⫐⟩　Usually　⫐⟩　Sometimes

In Section B of the Component Two exam you will have to produce **two** transactional pieces of writing. You will not be given any choice of title and you could be offered opportunities to write for a range of audiences and purposes, adapting style to form and to real-life contexts in, for example, letters, articles, reviews, speeches etc.

You will be expected to write 300–400 words for each response and you will have approximately 30 minutes to complete each task, about 5 minutes planning, about 25 minutes writing.

Each response will be marked out of 20:
● 12 marks are awarded for how you communicate and organise your work.
● 8 marks are awarded for the way you write your sentences and how correctly you use punctuation and spell the words you use.

QUESTION 1

Read this list of exam-style questions.

1　Your school/college is planning to put on a show at the end of the year. You have been asked to give a talk encouraging students to get involved.
　　Write what you would say.

2　Some cities in Britain are proposing a congestion charge on drivers to encourage people to use public transport. This would mean drivers would have to pay every time they went into a city centre.
　　Write a letter to a newspaper giving your views on this proposal.

3 You have been asked to write a lively article for a newspaper with the title 'How to cope with teenagers'.
Write your article.

4 Your school/college is looking for ways to improve. The Head teacher/Principal has asked you to write a report suggesting how the school/college could be improved.
Write your report.

Write a plan for each of these tasks.

Take about 5 minutes for each plan.

Remember to decide on the purpose, intended audience, register and style for each task.

Write down the ideas you want to include for each task and organise them into the order that would best suit your argument.

Now write your answer in 25 minutes (the time suggested in the exam) to one of the tasks that you have planned.

QUESTION 2

When you have finished, read over your work carefully.

Are you satisfied with what you have written?

- Write down two things you think you have done well.
- Write down two things you can improve upon next time. These can be your targets for the next writing you will do.

QUESTION 3

Choose another of the tasks in question 1.

Using the plan you have already created, write your answer to the task in 25 minutes.
Aim to write 300–400 words.

Remember the targets you set yourself in question 2 and try to improve your performance in these areas.

Now that you have completed the section, do you feel your confidence has increased?

I am confident about adapting my register, purpose, style and format depending on the task.

I am confident about adapting my language for my intended audience.

I am confident that I know how to improve my writing.

Always ➪ Usually ➪ Sometimes

OBJECTIVES

▶ To understand the features of transactional and persuasive writing
▶ To write clearly and persuasively

How confident are you in these skills already?

I can choose and write in the correct format for any writing task.

I can organise my ideas in a sensible and clear way.

I can recognise and understand how to use persuasive techniques.

Always ⇨ Usually ⇨ Sometimes

Get going

Step 1 Work on your skills

The first paragraph of any writing task needs to make an impression on your intended audience. Here are some helpful techniques that you could use to improve your writing skills.

A shocking or surprising fact or statistic often grabs the reader's attention. For example:

90% of Year 11 students feel constantly stressed and exhausted because of the constant pressure of exams and the relentless workload.

A rhetorical question can be very emotive and it can force the reader to think about his/her behaviour and attitude. For example:

How many of us can honestly say that we've never done anything we're ashamed of?

A bold or challenging statement. For example:

Truancy is becoming a modern day disease in our society.

Make sure you use these techniques to back up your **own** ideas, as these are the most important part of your answer.

As you already know, texts can be written to give information to people or to persuade people to do something. For example, reports are usually written to provide the reader with information but while speeches often communicate information they also persuade people to change their opinions on a topic. Letters can often provide information and have an element of persuasion as well. As well as communicating in the correct register and style and for your intended audience, you will need to understand the special features of the different types of transactional and persuasive writing. You were introduced to these features in Unit 14.

ACTIVITY 1: DEALING WITH TEENAGE CRIME

Look at this exam-style question.

A discussion is being held in your class on the subject of how to deal with teenage crime. You have to present your views on the subject. Write what you will say.

 Write three different opening sentences that would grab the attention of your audience. Use each of the techniques suggested on page 216.
Now decide on the best sentence and write the next two or three paragraphs in your speech.

 Top tips

Avoid stating the obvious in your responses! For example, don't tell your reader what you are going to write about by saying:

In this speech I'm going to tell you about my views on how to deal with teenage crime.

Instead, aim to have more impact by writing:

The statistics for teenage crime are alarming and shockingly high.

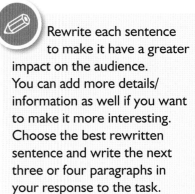

 ## ACTIVITY 2: OPENING SENTENCES

Look at these opening sentences.

Tonight I'm going to talk to you about why social media is a good thing.

This article is about how you can improve your fitness levels and live a healthier life.

I am writing to you to express how I feel about the council's decision to cut free bus passes for pensioners.

This speech is going to be about why all pupils should study a science subject until the age of 18.

Rewrite each sentence to make it have a greater impact on the audience.
You can add more details/ information as well if you want to make it more interesting.
Choose the best rewritten sentence and write the next three or four paragraphs in your response to the task.

ACTIVITY 3: ENDINGS

Now that you have practised some different ways to begin your writing, you can't forget about the ending. Remember that the final paragraph of your writing should leave a lasting impression on the reader and so, just like your beginning, your ending should have impact!

▶ You could use a question to make the reader think about what they have just been told. For example:

Surely we can no longer ignore the frightening reality of the situation?

▶ You could end with a warning, suggesting what will happen if your views are ignored. For example:

If we continue to feed our children with calorie loaded junk food, we run the risk of becoming the first generation to outlive their children.

 Using one of these techniques, write your final paragraph or conclusion for each of the topics in Activity 2.

▶ You could end on a positive, uplifting note, suggesting what will happen if your views are acted on. For example:

Our actions could result in producing a future generation who are well motivated and enthusiastic.

▶ You could end by urging your audience to take action. For example:

Don't be passive! Stand up and take control! It's up to us to protect the future of the next generation.

ACTIVITY 4: PERSUASIVE TECHNIQUES

When you are asked to write a speech or a formal letter you may often be expected to produce work that is persuasive.

Read this extract from a speech about mobile phones.

How many parents would panic if they thought deadly and invisible microwaves were passing through children's brains several times a day? Yet this is exactly what happens when youngsters chat for hours and hours on their mobile phones. Medical experts from Oxford University have suggested that there is a very serious risk of brain damage to children who use mobiles for more than half an hour every day, and they have also proven that hand held devices are no safer…in fact they may be even more dangerous! A recent survey carried out by BBC's 'Watchdog' showed that as many as 85% of children under the age of 12 have their own mobiles and use them more than an hour a day! Aren't parents concerned that their children are slowly frying their brains?

 The writer is trying to persuade the audience that mobile phones are dangerous.

Here are some of the persuasive techniques that have been used:

▶ Rhetorical questions
▶ Exclamations
▶ Ellipsis
▶ Emotive adjectives
▶ Statistics
▶ Expert opinions

Can you find examples of these persuasive techniques in the speech and explain the effect they would have on the audience? For example: *The writer uses an exclamation such as 'in fact they may be even more dangerous!' to emphasise the point and raise the emotional temperature by making the point sound more dramatic and urgent.*

Write a speech to be delivered to your English teacher, persuading him or her not to give you any homework.

Try to be entertaining and put together a persuasive argument using some of the persuasive techniques you have learned.

Spend time planning how you will begin and end your speech. Remember to organise your points into the best possible order to make your argument sound convincing.

Step 2 Practise your skills

ACTIVITY 5: MUSIC FESTIVAL

Read this exam-style question.

A local businessman has proposed holding a music festival in a nearby field.

Write a letter to your local newspaper with your views about this idea.

Here is a student response to the task.

> Dear Sir, Madame
>
> I am writing to you informing you about a music festival that is planned to go ahead in Cardiff. I am going to explain my clear opposal to this whole festival and hope you will report on it in due course.
>
> On the 21st May a local businessman, john smith applied for permission to host a music festival. Although no grant has been given yet I am already trying to enfisise my dogust and outrage to this whole idea. I believe such a festival will cause widespread disruption in my local area and will cause many people great uneeded discomfort. Here are some of the problems it may cause.
>
> Loud music will cause the eldery to be annoyed and could possible cause hearing difficultys.
>
> The festival will likely cause disruption and traffic conjestion on the roads.
>
> It may cause discomfort for ill peple in the local hospital whicj is just 300 yards from where the proposed festival will take place.
>
> As you can see this festival will affectively destroy my local area for the day and possible longer. I believe it should be immediately dismissed by the council and should be moved to a different more suitable location.
>
> What I ask from you is to report on this event if it does go ahead and also try and help me with the prevention of it by publishing an article in your newspaper showing the devasting problems it may cause unessacarilly.
>
> Yours sincerely,
>
> GD Jones

When you write a letter you can often include some persuasive techniques to make your argument sound convincing and change the viewpoint of the person who is reading your letter.

Is the task asking for a formal or informal letter to be written? Which words in the question would tell you this?

Has the letter been set out correctly? If not, how would you correct it?

Has the student used the correct tone in the letter?

Do you think the middle paragraphs have enough details to make the argument sound convincing?

Does the final paragraph clearly say what action is needed?

Can you find any spelling mistakes in the letter? If you can, try to correct them. Use a dictionary to check the trickier words.

Are there any improvements you want to make to the way the student has used paragraphs and full stops?

Now choose one paragraph from the letter and rewrite it by including more detail and more persuasive techniques. Try to make your spelling and punctuation as accurate as you can.

ACTIVITY 6: A SUCCESSFUL RESPONSE

Read this student response to the same question.

The Editor
The London Chronicle
London
W15 H89

49 Wood Court
Kingsmead
London
SW12 T68
10 June 2015

Dear Editor,

I am writing to you to show my support for Mr Smith's idea of a local outdoor music festival, a showcase of our region's prodigious talent.

As far as I'm concerned, any help we can give to the bands in our area should be welcomed with open arms. They represent our culture, and bring a vibrancy to the towns around here that attracts people from far and wide. Many people have noted how amazingly talented many bands and singers from our area are, and, I think that showing this to anyone who cares to see them in a music festival would be excellent. Why not be proud of them?

As well as being a good opportunity for bands around here, a festival of this sort could help local businesses a lot. For example, it would be a wonderful way to get people to try the amazing food from the area – what festival is complete without food stalls? It would even showcase our beautiful location – anyone who came would surely agree how stunning it is, which can only improve the tourism on which this region depends.

And for the locals? It would be great entertainment, as well as a chance to encourage people to get outdoors a little more. We have been enjoying wonderful weather recently and such an event would be a brilliant way to spend a summer's day.

Some have raised eyebrows over potential noise pollution as a result of this festival. Firstly, can music be described in any way as 'pollution'? Surely, our usual symphony of roadworks, traffic noise and groups of people who have just exited the pub is far worse? Plus, it would only be one day. Secondly, the festival will hardly be held in the middle of town, so if you don't want to hear it, you simply needn't go.

Also, there has been worry over whether such an event would attract 'the wrong sort of people'. What a ridiculous idea! Any undesirable persons would more likely be attracted to the vast array of pubs and clubs we have to amuse our bored residents. An outdoor music festival would attract people who love music, not hooligans! It would also benefit those in the hospitality industry, as most visitors will need a place to stay.

Overall, as far as I can see it, this idea is a great opportunity for our region. We would be able to showcase our amazing local talent, help tourism and trade in the area and have a great day out. I simply can't see the problem – what's not to like?

Yours sincerely,

TR Jonson

This letter is more successful than the previous response. Can you think of three reasons why this letter would get a higher mark?

The letter sounds clear and quite persuasive at times. Can you find some examples of the persuasive techniques you have learned? Try to explain the effect you think they would have on the reader.

The language used by the student in this response is interesting and sophisticated. Can you find examples of ambitious and sophisticated vocabulary?

Check the meaning of the words in the dictionary if you're not sure what they mean.

ACTIVITY 7: LETTER TO THE COUNCIL

Now read this exam-style question which tests whether you can present your point of view clearly and persuasively.

A large sum of money is to be spent on the area where you live. The council has suggested the money should be spent on one of these:

▶ **A sports centre**

▶ **An arts centre**

▶ **A science and technology centre**

The council is asking for the views of local people. Write your letter to the council, explaining your views and persuading them to adopt your ideas.

First of all, write down some ideas about what benefits and facilities each choice can bring to your area and which age group would get the most out of it.

For example, a sports centre could contain a fitness centre, a swimming pool and a sports hall.

Now do the same with the other choices.

Next, you need to think about the purpose, intended audience and register for the task.

When you have decided these things, organise your ideas into the best possible order to make your points flow smoothly. Remember that the councillor needs to be able to follow your train of thought!

Write the letter. Aim to make it 300–400 words long.

Now look over your work carefully.

> ▶ Are you satisfied with what you have written or do you think you could improve any sections of the letter?

▶ Have you used any persuasive techniques? If not, try to add a few to make your letter sound more persuasive and interesting.

▶ Have you used any connectives between paragraphs or to join your ideas? If not, think of some connectives you could use.

▶ Have you included different types of sentences? If not, try to add a few now.

▶ Do you think your vocabulary is ambitious or sophisticated? If you think the words you have chosen are a bit flat and dull, use a thesaurus to find some better alternatives.

Now rewrite two of your paragraphs by making these improvements and/or additions to your letter.

Step 3 Challenge yourself

ACTIVITY 8: SUBHEADINGS

When you write a report it is important that you communicate clearly. There is usually no need to write persuasively when you write a report.

Read this exam-style question.

The governors of your school/college are interested in the views of students. They have asked you to write a report about the possibility of having a Year 11 common room. You may like to use some of these subheadings as ideas for your writing:

▶ **The advantages of having a Year 11 common room**

▶ **Where the common room could be located**

▶ **When the students could use the common room**

▶ **Keeping order and being responsible in the room**

Do you think you need to use persuasive techniques to answer this task? Explain why or why not.

Write down some of the points you may want to include under the subheadings. Feel free to come up with subheadings of your own as well.

ACTIVITY 9: AN APPROPRIATE STYLE

Look at this student response to the question.

Report to the Governors

It would be a really good idea if we had a common room for Year 11 because we haven't got anywhere to go if it rains. You wouldn't like standing out in the rain and wind all through lunch times, would you? We wouldn't take advantage of the room. Well, some people would but the teachers would have to do duties just outside the room so they could sort it out if there was any trouble. Since we are working hard for our GCSEs we need somewhere quiet to go away from all the younger pupils. The sixth form have a common room so we should as well. Some of the things we could have in the room are computer games on laptops, a coffee and hot chocolate machine, a snooker table and a dart board. We could have it in the old geography room that is hardly ever used.

Please, please can you try to give us a common room?

Although the writer has some awareness of what to do, unfortunately the style is much too chatty and informal for the task.

Can you find examples of where the style and register are inappropriate for the task? How would you improve these phrases/sentences?

Do you think the format of the report could be improved in any way? What advice would you give the writer on ways to do this?

ACTIVITY 10: COMPLETING A REPORT

This is the opening section from a response to the same question but written by a different student.

A report to the head teacher and governors about creating a potential Year 11 common room

Introduction

Year 11 school council members were asked by the head teacher to compile a report on converting empty rooms in the main building into a Year 11 common room. As a member of the Year 11 student committee, I have conferred with other Year 11 students and these are the results of our research.

As you are aware, the school has several areas that are no longer in regular use. We are convinced that it would be sensible to use these to house the Year 11 students.

The advantages of having a Year 11 common room

Teachers often complain when they see Year 11 students loitering around the corridors during lunch and break time. A Year 11 common room could be somewhere for students to congregate,

! Top tips

The writer has used the first person plural 'we' which is appropriate because the task is to write on behalf of a group of students. This is a technique you could adopt in your own report writing.

socialise and work. It would be a haven for them and a refuge from the noise of younger students. We firmly believe that such an area could have two clear advantages for the school. Firstly, the corridors would be less crowded and it would be easier for students and lunchtime supervisors to keep control. Secondly, the students would be given an opportunity to revise and complete homework in a peaceful and controlled environment.

As you can see, this response is more successful because the student knows that he/she needs to write in a formal style and include a mixture of information and opinion or suggestions.

Using the points you came up with at the beginning of this section, write the rest of this report. Aim to write 300–400 words.

► Make sure that your tone remains polite and serious throughout the whole report.

► Remember to include a range of different types of sentences in your report.

► Organise your points clearly and sensibly and don't forgot to write a conclusion.

Now that you have completed the section, do you think your confidence has increased?

I can choose and write in the correct format for any writing task.

I can organise my ideas in a sensible and clear way.

I can recognise and understand how to use persuasive techniques.

Always   ⟹   Usually   ⟹   Sometimes

Improve your skills

OBJECTIVES

► Have a secure understanding of how to appeal to an audience

► To practise using techniques to improve transactional and persuasive writing

---

How confident are you in these skills already?

I have a clear understanding of what I need to do to make my writing interesting.

I have a clear understanding of persuasive techniques.

I have a clear understanding of when I need to use persuasive techniques.

Always   ⟹   Usually   ⟹   Sometimes

Step 1   Work on your skills

You have already learned the special features of review writing in Unit 14. Remember that when you write a review you are trying to appeal to your intended audience by making your writing sound interesting and lively. You are usually asked to give an opinion and a recommendation. You are not expected to write persuasively.

ACTIVITY 1: FILM REVIEW

Read the review of the film *The Hobbit* which appeared in the *Observer* newspaper.

THE HOBBIT: THE DESOLATION OF SMAUG

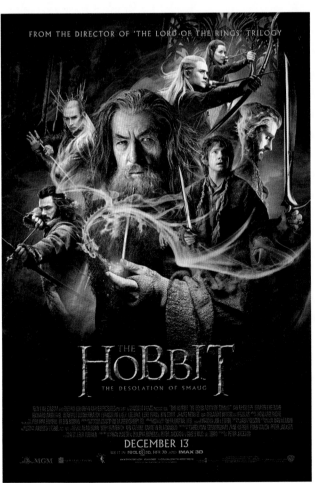

After the dawdling disappointment of 'An Unexpected Journey', Peter Jackson gets back on track with this second instalment in the adaptation of Tolkein's slim novel. With less whimsical waffle than its predecessor, 'The Desolation of Smaug' sets off at a comparatively yomping pace and proceeds to throw an endless array of spectacular sights at the audience, eager to dazzle, ready to please.

So we head through the forest of Mirkwood with its creepy pre/post Potter spiders, then on to the lost kingdom of Erebor. En route we meet an assortment of fantastical characters of all shapes and sizes, ranging from the wood elves (a surprise return by Orlando Bloom's Legolas) to the gigantic dragon Smaug voiced by Benedict Cumberbatch. At the centre of it all is Martin Freeman who is perfectly suited to the role of Bilbo Baggins.

The jury is still out on whether 'The Hobbit' really needs to be strung out over nine hours of film. For all its high tech action sequences and handsomely mounted set pieces, you get a lot of bagginess with your Baggins. The assembled masses march up hill and down dale but their ultimate goal is still a long way off. It doesn't help that the constantly sweeping visuals sometimes have the air of a supercharged computer game.

Something of a mixed bag then, with several question marks left hanging, but a definite improvement on the previous outing and hopefully a portent of better things to come in 'There and Back Again'!

What do you think is the writer's opinion of the film? How do you know? Can you find any positive or negative words?

Do you think the review is entertaining and informative? Which words or phrases make you think this?

Has the writer used different types of sentences? What types of sentences can you find?

Pick out any interesting words or techniques from the review that you think you could use in your own writing.

Top tips

Read like a writer and write like a reader!

ACTIVITY 2: WRITING A REVIEW

Look at this exam-style question.

Write a review of either a film you have recently watched or a game you have bought and played. Your review will be published in a teenage magazine called *Today's Teens*.

When you have completed your review, check over it carefully and think about whether you can improve it in any way.

▶ Pick out any words or phrases that you think would appeal to your teenage audience.

▶ Do you think you have used enough adjectives to make your review sound interesting? If not, try to add more.

▶ Have you used words that are ambitious or sophisticated? If you don't think you have, use a thesaurus to improve and extend your vocabulary.

▶ Have you varied the types of sentences that you use?

▶ Do you think your spelling is generally correct? If you are unsure about how to spell a specific word, look it up in a dictionary now and correct it.

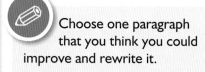

Using the skills you have picked up so far, write your review. It should be 300–400 words long.

Choose one paragraph that you think you could improve and rewrite it.

ACTIVITY 3: CATCHING THE READER'S ATTENTION

Just like a review, an article needs to be entertaining and to appeal to your intended audience.

Look at this list for some tips about how to make an article interesting.

▶ Use an effective and catchy first paragraph. You wouldn't want to read an article if the opening was boring or uninteresting and neither would your reader. Make the reader want to read the rest of your article by using effective techniques.

▶ Use questions to hook the reader's attention.

▶ Use techniques such as irony, sarcasm, exaggeration and emotive language.

Read this introduction to an article that appeared in a magazine.

Why England Should Drop Wayne Rooney

For years, the idea of England dropping Wayne Rooney has rarely been discussed – in fact it was downright laughable. Dropping England's best player over the last five years, for whom? Andy Carroll? Until now. This season, with Man United imploding, Rooney's form nowhere near his past stratospheric heights and finally the emergence of a serious challenger for England's number 9, it's no longer a question. Dropping Rooney is, amazingly, the smart move.

 This opening catches the reader's attention. Write down two ways in which you think it does this.
Do you think the writer is being a bit sarcastic here? If so, where?
Can you say anything about the different types and different lengths of sentences that the writer uses?

 ## ACTIVITY 4: THE PROBLEMS TEENAGERS FACE

Look at this exam-style question.

Write a lively article for a teenage magazine about the problems teenagers face when growing up.

 In the exam it may help you to underline the key words in the question.

Remember to think about your purpose, audience, register and style for the task.

You can use the structure below if you think it will help you to organise your ideas.

Thing of a heading or title

▶ Not too long
▶ Something catchy – perhaps a pun or question
▶ Give the reader some idea of what the article will be about.

Introduction/first paragraph

▶ Must hook the reader's attention
▶ Think about your techniques

Main part of article

▶ Include plenty of details
▶ Think about techniques to engage the reader

Conclusion

▶ Brief summary of article
▶ Catchy ending – this will be reader's final impression of what you've written
▶ Question/pun?
▶ Link the final sentence back to the heading at the beginning?

Now write your article.

 When you have finished, read through your work carefully. Make sure you haven't made mistakes with spelling, capital letters, punctuation or paragraphing

If you think you can improve your work in any way, rewrite that section.

! Top tips

Make sure your answer is long enough. You don't want to lose marks because you haven't written enough.

Step 2 Practise your skills

If you are writing an article for a travel magazine, you can use all the skills and techniques for article writing that you have been learning about and practising.

ACTIVITY 5: ARTICLES FOR A TRAVEL MAGAZINE

Look at this exam-style question.

A travel magazine has asked for articles about places that offer a good holiday either in Britain or abroad.

You could choose one of the following:

▶ **A town or city**

▶ **The countryside**

▶ **The coast**

Write the article for the magazine that describes the attractions of a place of your choice. Aim to write 300–400 words.

What do you think the purpose, audience, register and style would be for this task?

ACTIVITY 6: WORDS AND SENTENCES

Read this student response to the question.

Last summer I visited a nice coast in Spain called Costa Del Sol. In the camp there was a choice of caravan camping, tents and chalets. I went for the caravan and I wasn't disappointed because it was spacious and clean.

Along the coast the beach was excellent and I recommend it. The sand was nice and clean and white and the sea was clear blue and no pollution in it at all. The locals in Spain were really pleasant and helpful for tourists and there were many different shops along the coast. You think of a shop and it was there.

The vocabulary used here isn't very sophisticated or ambitious.

Can you improve the student's choice of words so the article is more appealing to read?

Look at the types of sentences that the student has used. Could you change them or add more variety to make the article more interesting?

ACTIVITY 7: IMPROVING A RESPONSE

Read this student response to the same question.

The city of Barcelona offers you a great family holiday. There is the home of the Barcelona football team the Nou Camp which is europes largest stadium. Also right next door is the wonderful muesium which consists of the Barcelona trophy cabinet which included the 1992 european trophy. Barcelona also have the Olympic stadium which hosts Barcelona's bitter rivals Espangol and was the venue for the 1992 olympic games. There is also a wonderful shopping option, take a trip down the world famous la Rambla and the human statues first hand. Not too far from there is wonderful Barcelona Zii which has europes only albeano gorilla. If that is not enough for you there is the nightime Barcelona fountains which has laser coloured lights along with wonderful fountains. All this has simple easy access with their fantastic underground metro system. If its just the quiet, relaxing holiday then you are never far from a beach along the costa del sol. Which can boast loverly blue seas. Go on treat yourself.

As you can see, there are several technical errors in this response. Work out where the student should have started new paragraphs.

Try to correct the student's punctuation errors.

Use a dictionary to correct the spelling mistakes.

This response is a bit 'flat' and doesn't grab the reader's interest. Why do you think this is?

What three pieces of advice would you give to help the student improve this piece of writing?

Rewrite this response by using the techniques you have been practising. You can add and make up details if you want to.

ACTIVITY 8: AN INSIDER'S VIEW

Here is an extract from a tourist guide to a city in Britain, written by a student.

If you love shopping, you'll love Liverpool, though avoid shopping on a Saturday afternoon, as it is extremely busy. Church Street contains all the usual high street names, but take a trip up the beautifully cobbled Bold Street and you'll find alternative and 'one-off' boutiques. If you've got a lot of cash to flash then visit the 'Met Quarter' where you'll find designer shops. Give Albert Docks a miss though. The old dock is a beautiful example of Cubist architecture, but I think the plan to turn it into a commercial centre seems to have been unsuccessful. Good restaurants are few and far between. If you love fast food, hotdogs and donuts, then you'll be spoilt for choice. But for sophisticated cuisine and alfresco dining, head for the other side of the river.

The response has a good sense of audience and purpose. The tone is informative and it is generally technically accurate.

Pick out some words that would appeal to a reader.

Now write your own entry about a place you know well for the tourist guide, including details the tourist board would like to see, but also providing an insider's view of any less attractive features.

229

Step 3 Challenge yourself

ACTIVITY 9: FIREWORKS

Here are some paragraphs taken from a speech to persuade people that fireworks should be banned.

Of course, not only humans are affected. Innocent animals, pets and wild creatures, are terrified by deafening bangs and crashes and some have even been injured by fires. There have been reported cases of stupid and irresponsible children actually throwing fireworks and tying them to animals' tails for fun! I am sure you agree with me that such torture is **not** fun. As caring and sensible people, you must surely agree that this **cannot** be allowed to go on.

Bonfire Night is meant to remind us about Guy Fawkes and his attempt to blow up the Houses of Parliament, but that was 400 years ago! We are living in the 21st century and we must have more important and worthwhile events to celebrate than a man being burned at the stake in 1605!

The time has come to stop this disgraceful waste of money and risk to children's safety. Remember, remember the fifth of November, ladies and gentlemen?

No! Now is the time to **forget** the past and look forward to a safer future without the danger of fireworks every year.

Little Emma Jenkins from Cardiff, aged only six, was blinded when a rocket misfired and exploded in her face, even though she was standing a 'safe' distance from it! Would you want this to happen to your child?

As you can see, these paragraphs are jumbled up and the ideas don't flow smoothly.
Arrange the paragraphs in the best order so that the speech sounds more organised.

Now improve this speech by making it longer and including points of your own. Remember to include a paragraph to introduce your speech and a concluding paragraph as well.
Use the persuasive techniques that you have learned in this unit.

When you have finished, read over your work carefully.

Underline any words that you think are emotive or ambitious and sophisticated. Do you think you need to include more? You could use a thesaurus to improve your vocabulary here.

Have you used simple, complex, compound and minor sentences? If not, try to improve your sentence structure now.

Find three things that you are pleased with.

What two things do you still need to improve upon?

ACTIVITY 10: THE SCHOOL CANTEEN

Read this extract from a speech about the need to improve facilities in a school canteen.

Have you ever attempted to eat your lunch in the school's canteen, ladies and gentlemen? If you have been brave enough to risk it, then you will know how appallingly noisy, cramped and totally unappealing the experience is.

Firstly, the building itself is ridiculously small for a school of 1600 hungry students. It is hardly surprising, therefore, that they choose to go elsewhere for their vital midday meal instead of standing for most of their precious lunch hour in an endless queue while older students push in front and grab the most edible food!

This extract has used several persuasive techniques.

Find them and explain why they are effective.

Complete the speech by writing another three paragraphs.

Now that you have completed the section, do you think your confidence has increased?

I have a clear understanding of what I need to do to make my writing interesting.

I have a clear understanding of persuasive techniques.

I have a clear understanding of when I need to use persuasive techniques.

Always   ⇨   Usually   ⇨   Sometimes

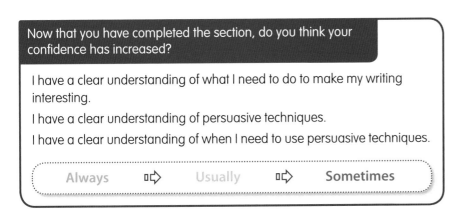

BE EXAM READY

OBJECTIVES

▶ To feel confident about writing clearly and persuasively in the exam
▶ To feel confident about improving my performance

How confident are you in these skills already?

I am confident that I will understand what is expected of me in the exam.

I am confident that my answers will be long enough.

I am confident that I can write clearly and effectively.

| Always | ⇨ | Usually | ⇨ | Sometimes |

 QUESTION 1

Read this exam-style question.

A lot of older people don't use computers or the internet either because they don't see any value in them or because they are afraid of modern technology.

You have been asked to give a talk to a group of older people to persuade them to use computers and the internet.

Identify the important words in the question.

Decide what your purpose, audience, register and style will be.

Spend 5 minutes writing a plan to help you answer this task.

 QUESTION 2

Read this extract from a student response to the task.

I understand many old people don't use computers or the internet either because they don't see any value in them or because they're afraid of modern technology. However modern technology won't bite or eat you up, so what's the point in being frightened of them? On the other hand modern technology like computers and the internet have numerous amounts of benefits out here for people to discover. You can go on Facebook or MSN for keeping in touch with distant relatives and friends. No matter where you stand, you'll find the distance is not the problem. You will still be able to have a 'hello' from them. Computers and the internet make everything closer.

Give the student three pieces of advice on how to improve this answer.

QUESTION 3

Look at this extract from another student's response to the same question.

Good afternoon ladies and gentlemen. It's a real pleasure to be here this afternoon talking to you about the wonderful world of computers and the internet.

I'm not going to give you a long list of reasons in favour of using this new technology. Instead, let me tell you about my nan, Mary ...

As you can see, this response immediately appeals to the intended audience. The tone is light, friendly and entertaining and is making use of an anecdote to get the message across.

Now write your own response to the question in approximately 25 minutes. Aim to write 300–400 words.

QUESTION 4

The following is an extract from a letter from a pensioner to your local paper.

Dear Editor,
It's time we raised the legal driving age to 19. Many accidents involve drivers aged 17 or 18. They drive too fast. They show off to their friends. They play loud music and do not concentrate.
I didn't drive until I was 25 and it didn't do me any harm.

Write to the newspaper giving your views on this subject.
Read this student response to the question.

Dear Reader,

I do not agree that the age limit for driving should be raised. I think the cause of accidents do not rely on age, but each individuals behaviour towards driving and concentrating. Not all young drivers are the same. I do agree that some do show off to their friends, but most just drive sensibly because of the fact they have places to be. Not all reckless drivers are young. A lot of older drivers do not drive sensibly either. So I don't think raising the legal age will do any good as nothing will change apart from some people will have to wait longer to get around easier. If some people agree that it should be raised then maybe you should do a survey of some sort.

The probability that you'll find a reckless driver under the age of 19 is very rare as most reckless drivers are usually under the influence of alcohol or other substances that can effect a persons driving. You are 85% more likely to be hit by a male driver over 25 than a driver under 25. So in my opinion I do not think the legal age for driving should be altered.

Thank you.

What comment would you make about this answer?
Link your comments to two things that the student does well and two things that the student needs to improve on.

QUESTION 5

Read this list of exam-style questions.

a A friend has decided to get a tattoo for his/her birthday. Write a letter to your friend giving your thoughts about his/her decision.

b Many people think that we should take holidays in Britain rather than travel abroad. Write a letter to a newspaper giving your views on this issue.

c Write a lively article for your school or college magazine with the title, 'How to Survive Your GCSE Year'.

d 'The world would be a better place without cars.' Write a speech arguing either for or against this statement.

e The governors, who are responsible for running your school, are interested in the views of students. They have asked you to write a report pointing out what you see as the strengths and weaknesses of your school. Here are some suggested subheadings for your report: facilities and equipment, buildings, range of subjects, out of school activities.

Write a plan for each of these tasks.

- Take about 5 minutes to write each plan.
- Remember to decide on the purpose, intended audience, register and style for each task.
- Write down the ideas you want to include for each task and organise them into the order that would best suit your argument.

Now write your answer to one of the tasks that you have planned. Time yourself and do this in 25 minutes (the time suggested in the exam).

When you have finished, read over your work carefully.

Are you satisfied with what you have written?

Write down two things you think you have done well.

Write down two things you can improve upon next time. These can be your targets for the next writing you will do.

QUESTION 6

Choose another of the tasks in question 5.

Using the plan you have already created, write your answer to the task in 25 minutes. Aim to write 300–400 words.

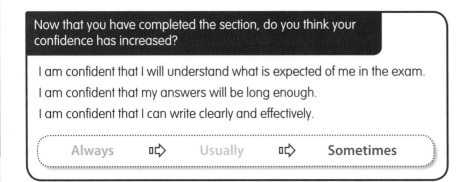

Now that you have completed the section, do you think your confidence has increased?

I am confident that I will understand what is expected of me in the exam.

I am confident that my answers will be long enough.

I am confident that I can write clearly and effectively.

Always ⇨ Usually ⇨ Sometimes